MARRIAGE AND FAMILY

A Basic Self-Instructional Guide

CONSULTING AUTHOR:

ERNEST J. GREEN

Department of Sociology
Prince George's Community College
Largo, Maryland

IN ASSOCIATION WITH

Robert F. Massey

Department of Psychology
St. Peter's College
Jersey City, New Jersey

Sharon Davis Massey

Family and Community Services
Fords, New Jersey

McGraw-Hill Book Company   New York • St. Louis • San Francisco • Auckland
Bogotá • Düsseldorf • Johannesburg • London • Madrid • Mexico • Montreal
New Delhi • Panama • Paris • São Paulo • Singapore • Sydney • Tokyo • Toronto

MARRIAGE AND FAMILY

A Basic Self-Instructional Guide

1 2 3 4 5 6 7 8 9 0   DODO   7 8 3 2 1 0 9 8 7

This is a Leogryph Book.

The series editor was Peter Salwen; the editor was Sharon Rule.
Cover and design were by Dave Epstein; the production supervisor
was Eileen Max; line drawings were done by Andrew Mudryk. It was set in
Helvetica Light by Typographic Services, Inc.
R.R. Donnelly & Sons Company was printer and binder.

Library of Congress Cataloging in Publication Data

Green, Ernest J
  Marriage and family.

  (McGraw-Hill basic self-instructional guide)
  "A Leogryph book."
  Bibliography: p.
  Includes index.
  1. Marriage. 2. Family. I. Massey, Robert F.,
joint author. II. Massey, Sharon Davis, joint author.
III. Title.
HQ734.G739   301.42   76-30848
ISBN 0-07-024261-5

p.115

CONTENTS

PREFACE

The American family has become a subject of controversy. Some investigators claim that marriage is obsolete—that "the family" is a thing of the past. To support their arguments they point to soaring divorce statistics, and to the appearance of new and varied life styles. Others point out that the family is a social institution, so it always responds to social change. They would say that the changes in style are superficial; that the family, as a way of life, is here to stay.

Ideas about the family come from many sources: from sociology, anthropology, theology, psychology, and other fields of study. Why so many? First, because the family is an essential part of life for most of us, so we give it a great deal of thought. And second, because there are many different (but valid) ways to think about such an important subject: everyone, from the Bible to Freud and beyond, has something to say about marriage and family.

This book will introduce you to most of the important modern ideas about marriage, family life, child rearing, divorce, and related topics. Our purpose has been to guide you among the main lines of thought: to help you understand the family—as a social institution, and as the background for our most important personal relationships.

■ Using This Book

You will probably find this book very different from most textbooks you have read.

This is not a "review text," nor is it a "made easy" book. It **is** a **basic text**. Every module, or short section of text, presents the main points on one or two basic topics—the basic facts and ideas you must learn to become familiar with the subject. Because you focus on the essential topics, the learning process is speeded up.

You may already be familiar with some topics, while others will be quite new to you. Some modules you will find relatively simple to understand, while others will take more time and application. You may skip some modules because they do not interest you (if you are studying independently) or because they are not part of your program (if you are enrolled in a course). However, you should be able to **master the material in every module**—learn it thoroughly—if you make the effort.

■ The Self-Instructional Features

The subtitle of this book is "A Basic Self-Instructional Guide." This emphasizes its other main feature: you should use this book **actively**—not just absorb the material in a passive way. As you finish reading each module you will come to a brief set of review questions. Use these to check yourself quickly on what you have just read. Can you answer all the questions? If not, you should run over the last few pages again, and fix the essential points more firmly in your mind. You should not leave a module until you are sure you have learned what it has to teach you.

After each chapter of the text there is a longer **review test**, containing 30 questions. Sit down with a pencil and paper, and work out the answers. Many of the questions are similar to the module review questions. Others, however, draw from several different modules in the chapter. These questions are very important, for to answer them you must use what you have learned, fitting together old pieces of information into new patterns. The last three questions of each test are short essay questions. Each one asks you to write a few sentences about what you have just learned. These questions are the most important. They ask you to **create** something—to construct an argument or summarize a group of ideas in your own words, Thus, these questions invite you to review, critically, what you have learned and how well you have learned it.

■ Reviewing The Material

At the end of the book you will find the answers to the review tests. Each of these back pages is perforated, and the part of the page containing the answers may be taken out for easy reference—**after** you have completed the review test. After each answer you will also find, printed in parentheses, one or more numbers. These refer back to the modules from which the questions are taken. If you miss any of the review questions, you should review once again the module or modules where the answers are found. And again, as with the individual modules, you should not leave a chapter until you are confident you have learned what is in it.

You will also find, at selected points throughout the book, general review tests, which cover material from several chapters of text. The general review tests are similar to the chapter reviews, with one difference: the last five questions, rather than the last three, call for essay answers. The answers to these tests are also found at the back of the book.

The general review tests can be used for periodic review of larger chunks of material. You may use them as soon as you come to them, or you may prefer to save them for review before examinations. In either case these tests are another valuable learning tool, and you should use them to check your mastery of the material.

■ Suggested Readings

Because this is a basic text, footnotes have been eliminated and technical references have been kept to a minimum. But many of you will find that your curiosity goes beyond what you can learn from this book alone. To guide you, a list of suggested readings has been provided at the end of the text. Some of these are original source materials, which can lead you to a better technical understanding. Others are more general and informal, and have been selected to enrich your "feel" for one or more topics. In each case, a short description is included in the list, to help you chose among the titles suggested. Use some of these readings to supplement your basic study, and you will soon develop a stronger, surer understanding of the subject.

■ Acknowledgments

A number of friends and associates helped us prepare this book by contributing some of the modules. To them we extend particular thanks: Maritza Campo (Module 17); Sandra Haber (Modules 8, 40, and 41); Mary Beth Horton (Modules 16, 22, 42, and 45); Ellen Mendel (Module 35); and Jacqueline Williams (Modules 48, 49, and 50). Mary Alice Costello, Barbara Demyanovich, and Ana Cecilia Navas have our thanks for typing—and retyping—the manuscript. The book was written with the editorial counsel and guidance of Peter Salwen, the series editor, and it was prepared for publication with the expert assistance of Sharon Rule.

Ernest J. Green
Robert F. Massey
Sharon Davis Massey

CHAPTER ONE
THE MEANING OF MARRIAGE

Leading thoughts:

- Each culture has its own particular concept of marriage and appropriate sex roles

- Marriage provides some social control over sexual expression and raising of children

- Couples must work to make the marriage relationship effective

- Most people today choose a marriage partner on the basis of personal compatibility

---

Marriage and Family: Theme and Variations

We are often so accustomed to living with the people around us that we are unable to describe exactly how we relate to them, nor are we aware of the alternative possibilities. Studying other cultures provides us with a different perspective. By looking at sex roles, the family structure, and norms for marriage in the other cultures, we can gain a better understanding of marriage as it exists in our own.

Marriage relationships are influenced by the way a culture defines the roles appropriate for each sex. The anthropologist Margaret Mead

has described the great variation possible in sex roles. For instance, she observed three separate cultures in New Guinea, which existed within a hundred mile radius. Each of these cultures raised its female and male children to conform to different standards.

Among the Arapesh, children of both sexes were taught to be concerned about and attentive to the needs of others. Gentleness, friendly cooperation, and peacefulness were valued in both sexes. A few men were "forced" to assume leadership roles for the good of the group. The people regarded themselves as belonging to the land, and their possessions as belonging to their children. This avoided competitiveness regarding ownership. Parents rebuked children for fighting. The future husband "grew" his prospective wife, who came as a girl to live in his parents' house, by raising special foods for her. After she reached puberty, they had little chaperonage, and eventually would go to the bush to consummate their marriage. A boy with few relatives was looked upon unfavorably as a son-in-law. So it was the boy, rather than the girl, who may have suffered disappointment because he could not marry. Among the Arapesh, both sexes seemed to have what we stereotype as a "maternal" temperament.

In contrast, both sexes among the Mundugumor acted like "super-males." They were aggressive, competitive, and possessive. Fathers and sons mistrusted each other because either might trade a daughter (sister) for a wife. Mothers disliked their daughters, who might be bartered for to replace them as wives. Sexual intercourse between young people frequently included violent, athletic foreplay involving scratching and biting. Marriage often entailed a man stealing a wife or a woman running off to a lover.

The Tchambuli reversed the sex roles we are used to. The women did the main work of fishing and trading and cooperated well with each other. The men engaged only in artistic ceremonials, and were generally distrustful and suspicious of each other. The women were considered highly sexed, and they chose their mates.

We can see from these three cultures that temperament is not fixed by biological sex. Each culture teaches its offspring the appropriate sex roles. When we see the variation in sex roles among different cultures, we understand that sex roles can change within our culture.

In the United States the **nuclear family** is the dominant family structure. Husband and wife who have chosen each other as partners live in a separate residence with their children. The increasing mobility of contemporary society often makes a larger family unit unmanageable.

In the **corporate family** the elders set the standards and control the activities of family members. Married couples and their children may live in fairly autonomous units, but more often several "families" live together. This larger family may span five or six generations. The corporate family arrangement prevailed in Confucian China. Marriages were arranged by elders, who were supposed to be wiser. A father's honor was established by his ability to marry off his daughters. The potential partners often knew of each other through kinship networks, but may not have met until the wedding day. But as time went on their respect, concern, and love for each other grew, and they enjoyed as much happiness together as couples who had chosen each other deliberately.

A third family structure is the **bilateral extended family.** In Latin Catholic Europe (Spain, Portugal, Italy, and France) families of both husbands and wives are integrated into a family circle. The nuclear units may have a good deal of autonomy, but they are consistently oriented toward the wider family—grandparents, aunts, uncles, and cousins. Most of the relating is done within the family circle, and elders strongly influence the choice of a mate. A number of American families of Latin origin retain a form of the extended family, and some non-Latins assume this structure out of economic necessity or personal choice.

A good deal of misunderstanding and controversy surrounds the black family in the United States. Most Afro-Americans are of West African origin. The West African family structures were stable, strong, and supportive of sound personal development. Forms of the extended family prevailed. Often the eldest male was head of the clan. In some places the family was **matrilineal**—the children belonged to the mother, her brother exercised paternal rights and responsibilities, and she did not belong legally to her husband. Some men took more than one wife, and cooperation among the wives distributed the work load.

In the African family, the members found respect, identity, and a place in life. The practice of slavery totally disregarded family stability and relationships. Slavery in the United States intentionally undermined black family life—no slave marriage was legal, and families were often broken up by sale of the members. The law denied almost four million people the rights to marry and raise a family. Free blacks, however, maintained family life before the Civil War.

What is generally ignored in analyzing the black family is that the black community contains members from all social classes, including upper, middle, working non-poor, working poor, and underclass. The great majority of black families enjoy marital stability comparable to a white family's. Only in the underclass is the proportion of broken families significantly greater. (Extended families are more common.) The range of customs in black families is broad. Some retain African customs, while others have totally assimilated Western European practices.

The marriage relationship, including its sexual aspect, has not always been officially limited to two people. Various societies have sanctioned men or women taking more than one spouse. **Polygamy** is a term meaning marriage customs that provide for a plurality of mates. In **polygyny,** a man has more than one wife. Jomo Kenyatta, the president of Kenya, has written a fascinating account of his people, the Gikuyu, entitled *Facing Mount Kenya.* In it, he describes how polygyny can function as an orderly, cooperative, and harmonious system, which provides for economic, sexual, and childraising interests in a socially approved way. **Polyandry** involves a wife marrying more than one husband. In Ladakh, a country surrounded by China, India and Tibet, the eldest daughter customarily married an eldest son, and up to two of his brothers if he had any. When the senior brother went away, the next brother took his place. Polyandry served to stabilize the population in this poor country.

Looking at alternative ways of learning sex roles, patterns for marriage, and methods of mate selection can give us a clearer view of our own marriage structure. It also shows us what social changes have taken place and what changes may occur in the future. Knowing the alternatives available to us enables us to make informed choices among them.

Before you go on . . . study different cultures

1. How can we learn more about alternative forms of marriage?
2. Sex roles in each culture are shaped by parents teaching children
3. In the nuclear _____ family, parents and their grown children occupy separate residences.
4. Marriage among slaves was legal in the United States. True or false?
5. What is an extended family? When nuclear is extend to aunts uncles etc. in same household
6. In traditional Oriental marriages the elders chose the spouses, who were then allowed a period of courtship. True or false?
7. Polyandry _____ is marriage between a wife and two or more husbands.

Answers:

1. We can study the structure of marriage in different cultures.

2. What children are taught.

3. Nuclear.

4. False. Slave marriages were prohibited, and black families were often deliberately broken up.

5. A nuclear family, plus a variety of grandparents, aunts and uncles, cousins or in-laws, usually occupying the same residence.

6. False. The couple usually did not meet until their wedding day.

7. Polyandry.

Marriage as an Institution 2

Marriage provides some social control over sexual expression and the raising of children. It also gives individuals a way to satisfy some of their personal needs. Marriage as an institution dictates a social pattern for stable heterosexual relationships. More than 90 percent of American men and women are married at some time during their lives.

Marriage is a contract, an agreement between the partners to assume specified responsibilities toward each other. When two persons enter into a marriage contract, they change their status. Society now regards them as a couple rather than as individuals. They respond by internalizing this definition and considering themselves a socially sanctioned pair. Over the centuries many beliefs, expectations, and accepted ways of behaving have been associated with marriage. Society expects a couple to behave in certain ways. If they do not, the marriage contract can be declared void through **annulment** or no longer operative through **divorce.** (American divorce rates have climbed dramatically in this century, and 25 percent of marriages now end in divorce.)

Society's beliefs, expectations, and preferred ways of acting are embodied in **norms**. When people follow social norms, they receive approval and acceptance. Those who violate these norms meet with disfavor and even ostracism by society. But they are not necessarily deviants. They may be setting new standards that will eventually generate social change.

Specifically, norms govern the residence, financial support, upkeep of the home, sexual activity, children, duration of the relationship, and inheritance of the married couple. The partners are expected to take part in these activities according to the social roles assigned to each. Traditionally, the husband is responsible for financial support and the wife for homemaking. However, the couple may choose to share their responsibilities differently. As we mentioned earlier, Margaret Mead has noted that different cultures require different sex roles. Among the Arapesh of New Guinea, both males and females are expected to be gentle, peaceful, and cooperative. Their neighbors, the Mundugumor, value aggressiveness, hostility, and suspiciousness in both sexes. Among the

Tchambuli, another group in the same area, the women are cooperative, carry on the business interests, and are considered highly sexed. The men, on the other hand, engage in ceremonial art, distrust each other, and wait for the women to choose them as mates. We can see from these three groups that our individual temperaments are not fixed by biological sex, but by our childhood learning of appropriate **sex roles**.

The family can take several forms. In this country the nuclear family and the extended family are most common. In a **nuclear family**, the couple and their children live in a separate residence. The nuclear family, largely self-sufficient, was especially suited to economic survival in a vast, newly explored country. Today, however, it depends for many services on a number of non-family organizations. The nuclear family in urban Scandinavia seems to be less strained, more stable, and happier than that in the United States, mainly because so many family services are provided by the government. In an **extended family** the nuclear units are only a part of the wider family—grandparents, aunts, uncles, and cousins. The extended family is common among those of Latin American descent and Afro-Americans.

We see, then, that many marriages provide a structure within which a woman and a man can live together, have sexual relations, and raise children. The institution supplies an outline of how the relationship should work. Society supports a couple in fulfilling its social expectations. Of course, not all people are the same, nor do they all want exactly the same things from marriage. Marriage is not only a social structure. It is also a dynamic, ongoing process between two individuals.

The marriage contract itself may symbolize the couple's understanding of marriage. The bride may promise to "love, honor and obey," while the groom pledges to "love, honor, and cherish." This is at least beginning on an unequal footing. By contrast, a couple may themselves compose their marriage vows, in an effort to create their own mutually acceptable style of marriage. "I promise to live with you in a relationship of love for all our days. I entrust myself to you, my body, thoughts, feelings and ideals. . . . I will devote my energies to your

well-being and to our mutual growth. I promise to join you in caring and providing for our children." These phrases are taken from the vows exchanged by the authors of this book. Many variations are possible.

The first contract reaffirms traditional sex roles and division of labor. The second expresses more an intention to be and to seek growth together on many levels. But whatever type of relationship the couple initially envision, they will have to work to make it effective. As they grow older, they may change their beliefs and expectations of marriage. Then they are faced with a challenge to grow together in new directions.

We enter marriage with beliefs and expectations about how our relationship should develop and what roles we are supposed to play. If our attitudes and anticipations mesh, and we show them by appropriate actions, we are more likely to be happy. If not, we may face disillusionment and disappointment. Being open and honest about values and expectations can clarify our ideas and give us a chance to work out our differences. Longer engagements, during which couples learn to know each other well, are associated with a lower divorce rate.

We look for satisfaction of our emotional, social, and economic needs within marriage, although we could fulfill some of these through other social channels. But sexual intercourse is usually sanctioned only within marriage. So when a marriage relationship is not progressing satisfactorily, sex often becomes the focal point of conflict. Sex is one expression in which each partner can show the care, concern, and love that mutually gratify both.

We can consider marriage from diverse viewpoints. It is an institution through which society controls its members. For individuals, marriage provides a framework of societal expectations and obligations. Marriage is also an opportunity for personal expression and interpersonal growth.

Before you go on . . .

1. Marriage as an institution provides for both __Social__ and __personnel__ _____ needs.

2. Society sets a pattern for marriage, yet marriage represents a dynamic process between the partners. True or false?

3. The beliefs, expectations, and preferred ways of behaving are known as __norms__ _____.

4. When uncommunicated expectations about marriage are not met, disillusionment and disappointment can occur. True or false?

5. The marriage __Contract__ _____ defines the couple's obligations to each other.

6. __SEX__ _____ is socially sanctioned only within marriage.

7. For most people sex can be a pleasurable relief when the rest of the marriage is not going well. True or false?

Answers:

1. Social; personal.

2. True. Society only provides an outline for their relationship.

3. Norms.

4. True. It helps greatly to discuss them openly.

5. Contract.

6. Sexual intercourse.

7. False. Sex often becomes a focal point of conflict in marriage, and most people find it difficult to be intimate with an antagonist.

Marriage as Interpersonal Fulfillment

Considerations of economic and social security still enter into the decision to marry. But today most individuals choose a partner on the basis of personal compatibility. Most of us look for a spouse who is both personally attractive and who makes us feel more worthwhile. We want to be valued intimately and for a long time, for who we are and for what we are capable of becoming. In a marriage relationship, we hope to find someone special with whom we can share our most intimate selves and who will make our routine days seem more worth living.

We all have aspects of ourselves that we would like to share or improve on with another person who is deeply interested in us. We may hope to find our greatest fulfillment with a spouse. A spouse can be one's best friend. But that friendship doesn't happen automatically, even though people may be immediately attracted to each other and feel at ease in building a relationship with a particular person. Every relationship, including marriage, demands continual effort. Perhaps one of the crucial reasons behind the breakup of so many marriages is that the partners have not concentrated on growing together in a mutually satisfying way.

Over the years our expectations for marriage have changed, as well as the way we evaluate its success. When our country was new and mostly rural, marriage was essentially an economic contract. The economy was dominated by men, who needed sons for farm work or to carry on the business. Cooking and housekeeping were reserved for females. As our society became urbanized, couples married to satisfy their physical needs and to play out their stereotyped male and female roles. Marriage was legalized cohabitation, with romance and sex added to the contract. Couples shared tasks and activities, but they avoided too much closeness and vulnerability. Intellectually and emotionally, they often went their separate ways, with separate interests.

With today's increasing emphasis on interpersonal relationships and personal growth, a third model of marriage has emerged. Here the partners focus on constructing their relationship. They not only share interests and activities, but try to form a shared identity that blends the complementary identities of each. They strive to understand each other's private worlds, and to lower the boundaries that separate them. This **relational** type of marriage requires time, effort, and the courage to endure the psychological pain such growth may bring.

Each person has unique feelings and emotional reactions to persons and situations. But not all people are aware of their feelings or able to communicate them. When we are not aware of our feelings or cannot share them with another person who really understands us, we often act in constrained ways that suppress our potential for personal growth. Or we may feel locked up within ourselves and unappreciated.

Engagement and marriage can give us a special opportunity to feel loved and respected. We can relax and become aware of our true feelings, which will lead us to our greatest personal growth. When we experience mutual trust, we can open up and disclose our most private feelings, thoughts, plans and desires. When the other person pays attention not only to our words but also to the feelings they convey, we feel really understood. To such a person we want to entrust and commit ourselves, for we no longer feel we must defend ourselves against the other's intrusion.

The process of really getting to know another does not proceed without effort. If couples expect a relationship to develop, they must want it, plan for it, and work at building it. Nor does the process always go smoothly. In different ways, each individual will resist self-disclosure, the generous giving of self, or really trying to understand and nourish the other person. But the determined couple will be patient, encouraging, and trusting with each other. They will try to be understanding when mutual growth does not progress as quickly as they want it to.

Couples who relate on a feeling level will discover new and creative aspects of themselves. We all need to be nurtured as persons. If we were well nurtured as children, we can build on our loving openness with a partner. But if we were neglected or mistreated as youngsters, even in small ways, a beloved can nourish our personal needs and lead us toward full growth. This does not mean that marrying to reform the other person brings happy results. But marrying to grow together will lead to increasing fulfillment.

Before we can commit ourselves to a spouse, we look for dependability. We also look for a sense of vitality—a life-giving ability that makes the other person dynamically attractive, and that nourishes our best qualities.

If we limit our expectations for a relationship, or if we do not communicate them, the relationship may be constricting or may not progress as happily as we hoped. By communicating our expectations and plans, we can expand our ideas and possibilities. We look for respect, but this demands mutuality and co-operation, not trying to feel or act superior. Unity comes only through cooperative communication, which reassures us and confirms us as worthwhile and valued persons. The empathetic person who touches our unique selves becomes the one whom we want to touch and be united with in physical intimacy.

Expectations about marriage have changed and continue to do so. For many people courtship is no longer a formal process, but a time of building the relationship. Couples frequently postpone having children until they have learned to know each other better. The number of children they plan to have has decreased. They can expect to live longer and to spend part of their retirement together. And more married people are becoming true partners rather than conforming to stereotyped roles. Individuals will find greater fulfillment together the more they work on the six basic "c's"—cooperation, commitment, communication, copulation, interpersonal competence, and caring.

Before you go on . . .

1. What are some of the qualities we look for in a spouse? *someone who sees me as worthwhile*

2. Marriages were once made for *Economic* or *social* reasons, but now couples are concentrating more on their *personnel relationship*

3. Love at first sight eliminates the need for working to build a relationship. True or false?

4. We all have deeply private feelings. We will benefit by being *aware* of them and *communication* them.

5. Relating on a(n) *intimate* level can lead a couple to discover new, creative, fulfilling aspects of themselves.

6. In an atmosphere of mutual trust, disclosing one's private thoughts, feelings, and plans takes place more easily. True or false?

7. Many look for a spouse to *commit* themselves to, one with *dependable* and an attractive vitality.

Answers:

1. Compatibility, being valued, someone to grow with.

2. Social; economic; relationship.

3. False. People can be easily attracted to each other, but a long-lasting, satisfying relationship requires time, effort, and involvement.

4. Aware; communicating.

5. Feeling.

6. True.

7. Commit; dependability.

THE MEANING OF MARRIAGE *Chapter Review*

1. In what type of family do only spouses and children live together?
   (a) Corporate (b) Extended; (c) Nuclear; (d) Single.

2. Because the government provides more services, the nuclear family in urban _Scandinavian_ seems happier and less strained than in the United States.

3. The personality characteristics for each sex are pretty well fixed by anatomy. True or false?

4. Looking at marriage in different cultures gives us a different (a) perspective; (b) role; (c) status; (d) race; and shows us the range of human possibilities.

5. A(n) _divorce_ declares a marriage ended whereas a(n) _annul_ states that the marriage was void and never existed.

6. As individuals redefine appropriate sex roles, couples rearrange their ways of sharing responsibilities. True or false?

7. As an institution, _marriage_ provides for a stable pattern of heterosexual relationships.

8. In what form of marriage does a wife have more than one husband?
   (a) Nuclear; (b) Polyandrous; (c) Extended; (d) Polygamous.

9. Women are universally regarded as less interested in sex than men. True or false?

10. The agreement between marriage partners to assume certain responsibilities is called the (a) role; (b) status; (c) institution; (d) contract.

11. On the average, black families enjoy as much marital stability as white families do. True or false?

12. The standards of behavior that most people follow in their behavior are called (a) roles; (b) institutions; (c) statuses; (d) norms.

13. In Confucian China priority was given to the marriages of sons. True or false?

14. Economic discrimination and the practice of selling slaves affected the black family adversely. True or false?

15. What is most often the focal point for cooperation and antagonism in marriage? (a) Recreation; (b) Leisure; (c) Sex; (d) Buying a home.

16. The _norms_ for female sexuality are emphasizing greater responsiveness and expressiveness.

17. Friendship and marrying are different and difficult to combine. True or false?

18. We find greater fulfillment when we are _aware_ of our feelings and _communicate_ them to an understanding person.

19. About _25%_ percent of marriages in the United States presently end in divorce.

20. If a couple is really in love to begin with, the marriage generally works itself out. True or false?

21. About _90%_ percent of the people in the United States marry at one time or another.

22. More couples today are becoming (a) partners; (b) roles; (c) individuals; (d) normative; rather than living out stereotyped roles.

23. The contract a married couple agrees to may symbolize their views on sex roles and the pattern of married life. True or false?

24. Couples who emphasize really sharing themselves and knowing each other are involved in a _relationship_ rather than playing out _roles_.

25. Being regarded by society as a couple rather than as individuals involves a change in (a) contract; (b) status; (c) role; (d) personality.

26. The number of divorces in the United States is about the same as at the turn of the century. True or false?

27. _Communication_ about expectations and satisfactions often prevents unwanted problems and disappointments.

28. How is appropriate sex role behavior determined among humans?

29. What do we mean when we describe marriage as an institution? _social institu- norms & expectations_

30. Do you think that marriage can be fulfilling interpersonally? Under what circumstances? _Yes if accepting & honest & willing to try_

To find the answers, look at page 187.

CHAPTER TWO

BUILDING A RELATIONSHIP

Leading thoughts:

■ In twentieth-century America, dating is the main way for young people to explore their sex roles and learn about each other

■ People should make the decision to marry only after they have considered it carefully—NOT to get away from home, or because of loneliness or social pressure

■ Before marriage, every couple should consider their readiness, and evaluate their differences and possible problems through realistic, open discussion

■ Women's roles are changing greatly in our society. This gives women greater freedom to marry—or not marry

■ For many couples, premarital intercourse is an important part of their relationship. But the partners should share the responsibility for making this choice.

Dating

Dating fills two important functions for young people in our society. It gives them the opportunity to learn behaviors which are appropriate vis-a-vis the opposite sex. And it also offers them a chance to improve their self-knowledge and interpersonal skills.

The well-known anthropologist Margaret

Mead has described these characteristics of dating: (1) The young man need not be introduced to the young woman by a member of her family. (2) There is no chaperone. (3) The dating couple have no social obligation to one another beyond the limits of the date. (4) The couple arrange their own date; their parents are not involved in the planning. (5) Some degree of sexual intimacy is expected, the level of intimacy depending on variables such as the length of time the couple have known each other, whether or not they are dating steadily or are perhaps engaged, the social class each belongs to, their ages, their educational levels, and their religious beliefs or personal values and preferences.

Dating as we know it is a twentieth-century invention. In earlier times, it was expected that a young man first make the acquaintance of a young woman's family and obtain her parents' permission to court her. Their time together was usually chaperoned, and sexual intimacies such as hand-holding and kissing were for those who were altar-bound. Modern dating evolved after the First World War with the entrance of women into the labor market, and flourished with the development of automobile, the telephone, movies, and various labor-saving devices. For the first time, men and women were in close contact during working hours and could meet one another directly without having to meet the family as well. Telephones facilitated this direct personal communication. Automobiles enabled the couple to get away from the family parlor, and the movies provided entertainment away from the home. At the same time a variety of mechanical inventions brought shorter working hours, giving both men and women more hours to spend on recreation. The popular understanding of the new science of psychoanalysis as developed by Sigmund Freud emphasized the sexual nature of all human activity and stressed the "naturalness" of sexual behavior. All of these factors led to the development of dating as we know it today.

The predominant pattern of dating is that a young man takes the initiative in asking a young woman to accompany him to an event that he has chosen to attend. However, schools and other organizations have traditionally celebrated "Sadie Hawkins Days" or other special days when girls were expected to "reverse roles," invite boys for dates, and demonstrate other forms of chivalry (i.e., open doors for boys, carry their books). Recently dating has become more of a two-way street, at least in some parts of the country, with girls sometimes taking the initiative in inviting boys. And in some places it is

becoming more common for adolescents of both sexes to go alone or with friends of the same sex to school or community events, and then to pair off for the remainder of the evening with members of the opposite sex whom they have met there (i.e., one might go to the local pizza shop with friends and then pair off for a movie date). This means that a girl need not sit at home on a Saturday night if a boy has not called in advance to invite her to go out with him.

No doubt the emphasis of the women's liberation movement on women's need for equality has influenced recent changes in dating patterns. Especially in colleges, some young men now expect that a young woman will pay her own expenses on most casual dates. A similar trend has appeared with regard to sexual matters. In the past, the boy was expected to be active both in suggesting dates and in initiating any sexual activities. The girl's role was to accept or to reject dates or sexual advances. Under these circumstances the boy's motivation was to prove that he could "make a pass," or perhaps more than a pass. The girl's motivation was to make sure she could attract dates without becoming the mere object of sexual advances. The cross-purposes of such a dating couple often led to a kind of running battle between the sexes. Dating practices seem to be changing, albeit slowly, in the direction of norms which give females equal opportunities with males and equal responsibilities.

Most adolescents begin dating at about the age of fourteen. Most persons who marry do so by their mid-twenties, although there are some variations from this dominant pattern which are related to level of education and to social class. Persons of the upper class and those with a college education (or both) tend to marry somewhat later. People of the working classes and those with only a high school education tend both to begin dating and to marry earlier.

Upper-class dating is considerably more formal and more supervised than middle- or lower-class dating. Dating is largely restricted to other upper-class youths who are well known by the family. Attendance at exclusive private schools and clubs, and sometimes the threat of disinheritance if one crosses social boundaries, encourage young people from this class to marry each other. Working-class youth tend also to date among their own group, though an attractive girl who wants to move up in society may date middle-class boys. An exceptionally talented boy may also date above his social class. Dating in the working class is often casual and is usually carried out without parental or community supervision or intervention.

While the pattern of dating may vary from place to place, Landis and Landis describe a common pattern of the stages of its development. Each stage has its unique purpose and is characterized by different behaviors. **Casual dating** is the first stage. The purpose of casual dating is to get acquainted. The second level, **steady dating,** implies that the couple have at least a short history of dating one another, like each other's company, and expect to date each other again. It does not mean that they expect to date each other exclusively. **Going steady** usually implies that a couple intend to date no one but each other and includes a broadening of the relationship, so that the partners now see more of each other and do not need the formal structure of a date for getting together. Being **engaged to be engaged** is an extreme form of going steady. This is generally seen as a trial engagement. The couple begin to discuss their

expectations of marriage and their educational and career goals. **Engagement** is a commitment to marriage and a time of preparation for it. Traditionally the male has been the initiator in dating until at least the level of steady dating is reached; thereafter the girl is expected to take an increasing share in the planning of joint activities. Generally speaking, sexual intimacies can be expected to increase with the increasing levels of seriousness of dating.

While dating helps adolescents to learn appropriate sex-role behaviors, it also gives them the opportunity to learn how they relate to a variety of other people and to become more aware of their own personalities. One changes dating partners easily, especially in the earliest stages of dating, and this provides a chance to learn new ways of relating to others if one wishes to do so.

In addition to being fun, dating at its best is an opportunity for self-assessment and for personal development. At its worst, dating is a game played by a male and a female who have different expectations and goals because they have learned the traditional "double-standard" for sexual behavior. Under the latter circumstances it is difficult to learn the cooperation, respect for one's partner and genuine intimacy which make for good marital relationships.

Before you go on . . .

1. The anthropologist _Marg. Meade_ gives a 5-stage description of dating.

2. Dating as we know it is a nineteenth-century invention. True or false?

3. Most dating begins at an average age of _14_

4. Working-class dating is much less formal than upper-class dating. True or false?

5. Steady dating is the same as going steady. True or false?

6. At its best, dating provides an opportunity for _personnel_ and _development_ .

7. In the past, sexual intimacies such as kissing were reserved for
    Engaged couples.

Answers:

1. Margaret Mead.
2. False. Dating appeared in the twentieth century.
3. Fourteen.
4. True.
5. False. Going steady implies an exclusive relationship.
6. Self-assessment, personal development.
7. Altar-bound or marriage minded.

The Decision to Marry

The decision to marry or to remain single is perhaps the most important decision each of us will make. It has far-reaching implications for almost every other aspect of our lives. And the specific person we choose as a mate will obviously affect the style of life we can expect to live. Our choice of career and our decision regarding marriage largely determine the framework within which our work, leisure activity, and family and friendship relations will be lived out.

Why marry? A careful consideration of the marriage decision might well begin with this question. Marriage is not for everyone, and it is unfortunate that some persons feel they must marry because someone expects it—society, their parents, themselves. There is no doubt that, very often, someone does expect it. Many young women, in particular, still experience considerable pressure to marry, and one-half of the female population in the United States is married by age 20. Young men are more frequently encouraged than young women to prepare for a career before they marry, but

they too are apt to encounter some nudging by the time they finish their career preparation.

Sometimes there are practical reasons for remaining single. Persons who choose to devote themselves to very demanding careers may decide that their life style does not allow adequate time for building and maintaining a marriage relationship. A dedicated scholar or performing artist may make such a decision; certain religious workers are required to. Some persons may refrain from marrying because of poor health, or because they carry genetic defects which they do not want to pass on to their children. (However, in our day this would usually have more bearing on the question of whether or not to have children than on whether or not to marry, as we shall see later on.) And anyone who wishes to is free to make the choice of remaining single, preferring a circle of friends rather than the family as a framework within which to live.

Most persons, though, decide at some point in their lives that they want to marry. Unfortunately, they often do so for poor reasons—reasons that later turn into accusations in divorce courts and sad refrains in the offices of marriage counselors.

To avoid or escape loneliness, for example, is an insufficient reason for marrying. The person who is chronically lonely probably has few friends or forms only superficial and unsatisfying relationships with others. This is a poor foundation on which to build a marriage, an intimate relationship which requires each partner to give love and care. If one partner must constantly nurture the other without receiving nurturance in return, the marriage may become too emotionally burdensome. While it is possible to learn new ways of relating through new experiences, or with the help of counseling after marriage, the learning is often painful and inevitably involves both partners. Entering marriage as a person already capable of meaningful relationships and experienced in forming them is far better than unrealistically expecting marriage itself to solve all the problems.

Marrying in order to get away from home is also a poor risk. The young person who chafes at being under the thumb of parents not infrequently finds that a hasty marriage has resulted in union with a mate who is equally domineering. For that matter, marrying to please one's parents is about as unwise as marrying to get away from them. The person who has lived for a time away from his or her parents is likely to have gained more self-knowledge and independence of judgment, and may therefore be able to make a wiser choice. Through living, working, and relating to a variety of persons outside the family setting, one can more clearly sort out one's own interests, values, and personality. Then one can select a mate who complements oneself.

Persons who marry to spite a parent or in revenge against a former lover are usually building on a shaky foundation. Here the relationship is not with the partner so much as it is against someone else. Thus there is no reason to suppose that the persons who have chosen—perhaps hastily—to spend their lives together are really suited to one another, or are prepared to undertake the task of building a positive relationship.

It is similarly risky to marry simply because friends are marrying or out of fear of losing the chance. It is true that, in our society, most men and women who marry at all are married by their mid-twenties. But this does not mean that a person who waits will permanently remain a spinster or bachelor. Some people simply prefer to delay marriage until a later age.

Some people choose a marriage partner who has characteristics that they lack and want to possess. As a main reason for marriage, this is about as sound as marrying in order to get the other's money. A shy woman who marries a gregarious, outgoing man may soon chafe at his wishing more often than she to be in the company of others. If he easily attracts attention and enjoys it, she may be jealous, fearing that he is losing his love for her. So the very trait she wished to possess by marrying this particular man may become an important factor in the destruction of their marriage. She would have done better, if her shyness troubled her, to work at overcoming it before marriage.

Marrying because of a pregnancy is risky, though it can sometimes succeed. Research findings indicate that a high percentage of marriages in which the wife was pregnant before the wedding end in divorce. Some of the factors to be weighed in considering such a marriage are: how serious the relationship is, aside from the pregnancy; how long the couple have known each other; whether either or both families offer emotional support to the marriage and, if necessary, are willing also to offer financial support for a time; and whether the couple believe themselves to be emotionally ready to accept the responsibility for raising a child at the same time they are learning to live and work together as husband and wife. In the past, the unmarried woman who became pregnant had no socially respectable choice, except a hasty marriage. Today she may legally choose abortion if this is morally acceptable to her; or she may bear the child and place it for adoption, or keep the child with far less social stigma than in the past. It is not only for her own sake that she should honestly consider these alternatives. If the parents marry primarily out of concern for the status of the expected child, with no real interest in each other, they may later blame one another, and eventually the child, for the unhappiness of their marriage. The hostile home environment which results may be a dubious favor to the child, and a high price to pay for legitimacy.

Marriage, then, is not a cure for one's personal insufficiencies. Rather than resolving the personal problems the husband and wife bring to the union, marriage may tend to magnify them. What are healthy signs in a relationship—signs which indicate that the projected marriage is likely to endure?

If the prospective bride and groom come to the marriage feeling secure and independent in themselves, if they respect and trust each other, if they share some interests and values, if they are open with each other and communicate their disagreements as well as their agreements, their marriage has a good chance of enduring. Shared interests and values, and respect for the mate as he or she is at present, provide a stable foundation for the style of life the married couple will live. Some unique interests and values, together with the self-assurance which allows each to function as a separate person within the framework of the marriage, and a commitment to open communication with each other, provide the foundation for change and growth.

Before you go on . . .

1. What are some of the negative reasons why people feel they must marry? _Social pressure, Pregnancy, fear of living_

2. One-half of the female population in the United States is married by age 20. True or false?

3. Most people decide at some point in their lives to marry. True or false?

4. People have often married to spite their _Parents_ _____ or _____. Such marriages rarely work out well.

5. When people reach their thirties, they should marry before they lose the chance. True or false?

6. _Marriage_ _____ is not a good cure for one's insufficiencies.

7. Most marriages that occur because of pregnancy end in divorce. True or false?

Answers:

1. Social pressure; parental pressure; the feeling that it is expected of them.

2. True.

3. True.

4. Parents, former lovers.

5. False. Some people are not emotionally suited to marriage.

6. Marriage.

7. True. This is a form of forced marriage.

Readiness for Marriage

6

When a young couple have passed through the various levels of dating and are seriously contemplating marriage, one or both of them may wish to assess their readiness for marriage. Is there a way to tell beforehand whether or not a specific couple is likely to have a successful marriage?

While no one can predict with certainty the success or failure of a specific marriage, studies of large numbers of successful and unsuccessful marriages have given us some general observations which may provide guidelines for assessing one's own relationship.

In general, persons who marry at a relatively later age—in their mid-twenties, for example—are more likely to have a successful marriage than are persons who marry younger. Ordinarily, the older person has more dating experience, better vocational preparation, more self-knowledge, and more maturity than the younger person (though this is, of course, not true in every case). All of these are important elements in a successful marriage.

However, much as we hate to admit it, money is a necessary part of life. Therefore vocational preparedness is an important factor to consider if one is planning to marry. Money, for most of us, is acquired through working, and the better one's preparation for working, the more likely one is to get a job and to hold onto it. In general, the more time one spends in school or otherwise preparing for one's vocation, the better salary one draws, though this is not always true. It is important that both partners discuss their expectations regarding work for themselves and for each other. Does he expect her to work to put him through school? Does she expect to prepare for and pursue a profession? If they marry now and both plan further schooling, can they meet the financial cost without one partner's having to sacrifice his or her future plans?

A couple planning to marry may not think to discuss the health and medical history of each partner. Both need to be aware of any physical limitations in either partner, so that they can plan realistically. A thorough medical examination prior to marriage is helpful in this regard. Minor physical difficulties such as an unusually rigid hymen or the presence of infection can be remedied in advance of the marriage. If more serious problems are found—a communicable disease such as tuberculosis, or hereditary defects such as the genes for sickle-cell anemia or Tay-Sachs disease—the couple may want to reconsider their alternatives (to break the engagement, to delay marriage, to marry but to remain childless, or to adopt children) with greater knowledge of what they can realistically expect. Consultation with a doctor can also remove unnecessary fears about whether or not defects in one's family are likely to recur in oneself or in one's children—will my children be asthmatic, or colorblind, or tone-deaf, because I am?

Sexual readiness is an important area of marital preparedness. Many engaged couples find it helpful to read and discuss one or more books on human sexuality. Usually the couple have already begun the kind of sexual exploration which can develop and grow into the fullest expression of their love for each other in marriage. Whether or not full sexual intercourse takes place before marriage depends today on variables such as the personal and religious values of the people involved. Perhaps more important than the relative speed with which a couple approach a full sexual expression of their love is their ability to discuss their values, their hopes and fears regarding the sexual aspect of lovemaking, and their willingness to communicate verbally about, and even while, making love physically. (To take an example which may seem absurd: if one partner is unwilling to say,

"Please move, you are cutting off the circulation in my arm," for fear of breaking the romantic spell of lovemaking, she is not experiencing the pleasure she should be, and the other partner, who wishes to be giving only pleasure, does not know he is also causing her some pain.)

The visit to the doctor, recommended above, seems a likely time to discuss alternative methods of birth control (if a couple do not wish to have children immediately and have no religious or personal objections to birth control), and to select one. For example, the woman may be measured and fitted with a diaphragm, or may elect to have an IUD (intrauterine device) inserted prior to the wedding.

Some young couples will wish to discuss the sexual and other aspects of their marriage with a priest, minister, or rabbi of their religious faith before the wedding. Many of these will require the couple to see them for at least one interview before they will assume responsibility for performing the ceremony. If the engaged couple are from differing religions, more extensive interviews and further study of the faith in which the marriage ceremony is to be held are sometimes required. Open and searching discussion of moral or religious values helps a couple to form a clearer understanding of how they relate to each other and to work toward forming the kind of deep bond which will help them when the going gets difficult. This is an important part of marital preparedness.

No two persons are alike, no matter how similar their interests or values may be. One factor that contributes greatly to our differences is the fact that each of us has a unique set of experiences which make us the person that we are. The engaged couple represent two families. And families differ in their values, ways of relating, beliefs about people, preferred forms of entertainment, and many other respects. But individuals within families also differ from one another in important ways, even though they may share many attributes.

Thorough familiarity with each other's families, together with discussion of how the partners see themselves and each other as being like and unlike those families, can lay the groundwork for building a new relationship, and eventually a new family which draws on the strengths and seeks to overcome the weaknesses in the backgrounds of both partners.

One psychologist has given us a handy rule of thumb for measuring our own relative success or failure in life. Dr. Alfred Adler said that life presents us with three main tasks: work, friendship, and establishing an enduring relationship with a person of the opposite sex. Our success in all of these is highly dependent, he believed, on our willingness to cooperate with others in achieving our goals. Perhaps one of the best predictors of whether we will have successful work, friendship, and heterosexual relationships in the future is whether we have them now. This may be helpful to bear in mind when considering marriage.

A young couple who have the emotional maturity to look objectively at all of these factors—their age, vocational aspirations and preparedness, their physical health, their religious and moral values, their family background, and personal similarities and differences—and who find that they care enough for each other to overcome any difficulties or differences they find in this appraisal are in a good position to make realistic plans for marriage. The marriage they undertake is not as likely to be torn apart as would be the marriage of a couple who knew themselves less well.

Before you go on . . .

1. Persons who marry in their mid-twenties are likely to have a successful marriage. True or false?

2. Secure employment and ~~are~~ *financial security* are important factors in determining readiness for marriage.

3. How is the health of the partner checked before marriage? *Go to doctor*

4. The ability to discuss openly one's sexual desires and fears is of utmost importance. True or false?

5. What are some alternatives to the pill? *IUD etc.*

6. Familiarity with one another's families can strengthen the new relationship considerably. True or false?

7. How can we tell whether we are likely to have successful work, friendship, and heterosexual relationships? *Adler – if we already have them*

Answers:

1. True. People are usually mature enough by their mid-twenties.

2. Money. The lack of financial security is often a cause for divorce.

3. By a medical test, which is required by law.

4. True. If they are not discussed, serious problems can develop.

5. Diaphragm, IUD.

6. True.

7. By whether we have them now.

Evaluating Differences Between Partners

7

The more **heterogamous** a marriage—the greater the differences between the husband and wife—the greater the difficulties the couple will face. Marriages in which the partners are quite different in level of education, social class or age, and the so-called "mixed marriages," where the husband and wife are from different religions or have different racial, national, or ethnic backgrounds, are usually more risky than **homogamous** marriages—those between persons from similar backgrounds. Divorce rates are higher for heterogamous marriages.

We can think in terms of bridges. It's easy to build a solid bridge across a narrow gap. But a longer bridge across a wider gap is subject to more stress. It is harder both to build and to maintain. And some gaps are simply unbridge-able. Two protestants, a Methodist and a Baptist, who are both in their mid-twenties, middle class, college-educated and of western European origin may find that their religious differences are not great enough to cause them any real difficulties. But an Irish Catholic and a Buddhist Chinese-American can expect to have severe difficulty in building and maintaining a happy marital relationship.

If a husband and wife differ widely in educational level, they are likely to prefer different friends and different entertainment. They may find it hard to discuss each other's work. Often, a couple begin their married lives with the same level of education, but at some point one falls behind the other. She may stop schooling to stay at home while the children are young. He may stop in order to support the household while she continues her education. So some couples who start out with similar interests and values may find themselves growing slowly apart as differences in education lead them to experience life differently.

Where intellectual differences exist, a particular couple may still work out a relatively successful marriage. It may be helpful if they divide their tasks according to each partner's preference and capability rather than along traditional lines. But couples who are unaware of these differences before marriage may have unrealistic expectations of each other. These will cause friction until either the expectations are changed or the marriage collapses.

If they are from different social classes a husband and wife may have different values, expectations, and goals. If a talented young person marries above his or her class, the marriage is more likely to be successful if the person who is "marrying upward" is willing to assume the values and aspirations of the higher class, or if both are willing to meet somewhere in the middle. Personal goals and expectations should be throughly explored before marriage. The couple must determine whether they can compromise and cooperate in spite of their differences.

A small age difference between husband and wife, with the husband being older, is so common in our society that it is considered the norm. An age difference of a year or so between husband and wife probably has no significance, regardless of who is older. But great age differences mean that the two persons have had quite different experiences. We change physically and emotionally as we grow older, and the world around us also changes. Our values and expectations are shaped both by our personal development and by our experience of the changing world.

It is easy to see, for example, how friction can develop between a thirty-five-year-old woman and her twenty-five-year-old husband with regard to having children. He may wish to delay any decision about having children, preferring to have a year or so first just to enjoy the relationship with his bride. She may feel an urgent need to decide about children much sooner, since she knows that pregnancy may become more risky in a few years. A very young woman and an elderly husband may have trouble finding common friends and leisure activities. We can expect their level of physical energy both in everyday living and in sexual matters to be quite different.

Religious differences can be a serious source of friction between husband and wife, especially when these differences are regarded seriously by one or both religions. The Roman Catholic Church, for example, used to forbid any religious marriage ceremony other than its own. Both husband and wife were required to sign a promise to raise any children they might have as Catholics. Pope Paul instituted a new policy in 1966, which now permits Catholics who receive special permission from their bishop to be married in a civil ceremony or in a religious ceremony of another faith. The Catholic partner is still required to promise in the presence of a priest to raise the children as Catholics, and to inform the spouse of this promise. The non-Catholic is no longer required to participate in this agreement. The Jewish community has resisted interfaith marriages more consistently than the Protestant or Catholic communities. Orthodox rabbis will not perform interfaith marriages, but some Reform and Conservative rabbis do.

The many ethnic groups that make up our society add richness and variety to our national culture. In the United States we are not simply Americans. We are Afro-Americans, Chinese-Americans, German-Americans, and Native Americans. We are British, Polish, and Scandinavian by origin. We are French and Mexican and Yugoslav. And the list goes on. We do not have a single culture, we have many. And many of us are strongly influenced by the customs and the values of the ethnic group to which we belong. Persons who marry across ethnic lines may find great differences in their ideas about things like the woman's role, the importance of religion, and how families should interact, simply because there are different norms in the "mini-cultures" to which they belong.

Ideally, marriage across racial lines should not be discussed separately from inter-ethnic marriage. But racial prejudice is so strong in our society that interracial marriages are most difficult. In many parts of the country there is open hostility to interracial couples. At one time some states prohibited interracial marriages, especially between blacks and whites. A Supreme Court Decision in 1967 made these laws invalid. With such general lack of support for interracial marriages it is small wonder that many do fail.

There are a few places, like Hyde Park in Chicago, where black-white couples can live with relatively little harassment. But in some communities they can realistically expect to be atypical, and to be shunned by some. In a cross-racial marriage it is especially important for the couple to stress the factors that support their marriage—common interests, values, and friends. If their families approve of the marriage and they can find an area to live where the neighbors are warm and welcoming, or at least not hostile, they are fortunate indeed.

In mixed marriages the problems of child-rearing may be multiplied. Which church will the children attend? What holidays will be observed? How can children be protected from the hostility of racial prejudice? These are vitally important questions. Unfortunately, in the heat of romance they may be overlooked or minimized by an engaged couple. But they may become a focal point of irritation when the couple have children.

In discussing heterogamous marriages, it is more important than ever to repeat that it is not wise to marry with the intention of changing one's mate. If he or she is going to change religion or customs, it is best to do it—or at least plan to do it—before the wedding, not after. But on the positive side we should emphasize that the problems of heterogamous marriages are not insoluble. The ability of both partners to relate well in spite of their differences may be a demonstration of the extra maturity and understanding that are needed in such marriages.

Before you go on . . .

1. When husband and wife are very similar in background, values, and interests we can describe the marriage as ___homogamous___.

2. The divorce rate for heterogamous couples is higher than the divorce rate for homogamous couples. True or false?

3. State laws forbidding interracial marriage were made void by a decision of the U.S. Supreme Court in ___1967___.

4. A Roman Catholic who marries a non-Catholic no longer has to promise to raise their children in the Catholic faith. True or false?

5. Heterogamous marriages in which the couple are from different

national, racial, or religious backgrounds are commonly referred to as _mixed_ marriages.

6. More Jews marry outside of their religion than any other religious group. True or false?

7. Orthodox rabbis will not perform interfaith marriages. True or false?

Answers:

1. Homogamous.

2. True.

3. 1967

4. False. The Catholic partner must promise to raise the children as Catholics. The non-Catholic partner is not required to make the promise.

5. Mixed.

6. False. More Catholics and Protestants marry outside of their faith.

7. True. Some Reform and Conservative rabbis will.

Changing Roles of Women

During the 1970s, we have been exposed to a great deal of media coverage on women's liberation and the women's movement. However, the women's movement is like many other social movements where rumor and hearsay often cloud basic issues. You may have opinions on the "black pride movement," "the sexual revolution," or the "student protest movement," but these opinions are often based on myths rather than fact. Similar myths and distortions often surround the issues of women's rights.

For example, some people believe that women's liberationists, who can be men too, want all women to go out to work. Similarly, many people have the impression that **feminism**, as women's liberation is sometimes called, means that house-wifery and motherhood are out-of-

date, worthless occupations. Both of these statements are myths. The problems with being a housewife are not in the job that is done, but in the status this job has in our society. For example, a study by the Chase Manhattan Bank estimated that the average housewife worked 99.6 hours per week at 12 different jobs. The housewife remains unpaid, she has no job security, no health and medical benefits, and no vacation time. And if she becomes divorced or widowed, she has no unemployment insurance.

Another platform of the women's movement is that women have options in their lives. They may choose to be housewives and mothers, but they may also choose different lifestyles. In 1970, for example, 38 percent of women were working. Many of these women were in clerical positions, yet many other women were choosing to pursue careers in law, medicine, dentistry, and engineering. Some of these women will choose to pursue their career in addition to raising a family. Some will choose to have careers instead of families. Women's liberation wants to let the woman make the choices in her life.

Women's liberation encourages women to think about their futures, so that whether you choose marriage or a career, your choice will be made with some realistic knowledge of today's world. For example, in 1971, married women formed the largest group of working women (60 percent). Since few of these women ever anticipated working once they were married, they were often ill-prepared for any particular job and were forced into lower-paying, less satisfactory occupations. In fact, statistics indicate that nine out of ten American women will be working at some point in their lives. The average woman is now 40 years old and married, and the average number of years she will spend in the workplace is 25. Other grim facts are that women with college degrees can expect to earn less than males with high school degrees, and more than $5,000 less per year than males with the same college degrees.

Some of the different possibilities open to women today can be illustrated by an investigation we conducted. Three groups of female college seniors were studied. The first group were traditional women who were mainly interested in getting married and raising a family. These women believed that careers and families were incompatible. They felt that attempting both was too difficult, and that one or the other must eventually be given up.

Another group of women really wanted both a career and a family. These women usually chose occupations such as teaching, nursing, and social work. These professions are usually considered to be more compatible than most with family life. Leaves of absence for child-rearing may be easier to get, and the hours are flexible enough to coincide with the school schedule of young children. In such occupations, the amount of work done in the home is minimal, so that there is a relatively clear distinction between work and private life. For

example, many teachers who are also mothers teach only a few days a week, spending their free days as homemakers.

Another option for some women is a professional career such as medicine or law. Here, there will probably be some conflict between career and family life, since the working hours are long and inflexible. Many women who choose professional careers have to adjust to the probability of some amount of "absent mothering" if they choose to have children. Thirty percent of the women in this group stated that they might reject the role of motherhood altogether. All of the women, because of the amount of education and time commitment required by their anticipated profession, were expecting some delay in establishing a family. With today's emphasis on women's rights, many young women are opting for a more solid identity in their lives before taking on the challenges of raising a family.

The point is not which of these choices a woman will make, but that in this decade she is able to make a choice. This freedom to choose one's own style of life is what the changing role of women is all about.

Before you go on . . .

1. The problem with being a housewife is the status of the work. True or false?

2. According to the Chase Manhattan Bank, the average housewife works _____ hours per week.

3. The women's liberation movement is against the housewife-and-mother role in our society. True or false?

4. The average woman is now _____ years old and married.

5. A college woman's annual salary is $5,000 less than her male counterpart's. True or false?

6. A woman who wants both a career and a family usually chooses _____, _____, or _____ as an occupation.

7. What is the basic issue in today's changing role of women?

Answers:

1. True. The work of the housewife is seen as having a low status.

2. 99.6, at an average of twelve different jobs.

3. False. They feel the position should be a choice, not a place.

4. Forty.

5. True. Women with college degrees earn less than men who have only a high school degree.

6. Teaching; nursing; social work.

7. The freedom to choose one's own lifestyle.

Premarital Sex: Attitudes and Trends 9

Today young people mature sexually before they are socially and economically ready for marriage. This situation can create many emotional stresses. Young adults must learn how to deal with their sexual impulses and determine what limits to set in premarital sex relationships.

Men and women face different social expectations of sexual behavior. One such difference involves the "double standard" we discussed earlier. Other questions concern who initiates physical contact during dating, who sets limits on how far to go, how to avoid exploitation in a sex relationship, and how to distinguish love from physical attraction.

Studies show that men tend to initiate lovemaking. But today more and more couples are accepting mutual responsibility for determining when to draw the line. There are still many young couples who prefer to save sexual intercourse for marriage. This can be a difficult decision to keep.

In dealing with matters of premarital sex, there is no substitute for honest communication. Once there is clear understanding of how each partner feels about the matter, there are a number of ways to keep lovemaking and physical contact within reasonable bounds during the dating period. The couple can avoid situations designed to encourage petting by dating in groups, planning after-date activities, and keeping interesting conversations going.

Young men and women may find themselves exploiting or being exploited in a premarital sex relationship. A man may seek sexual gratification by showing an emotional involvement with a woman greater than he really feels. A woman may be so interested in catching a husband that she uses the sex relationship as bait. Researchers find that women of a lower social class are more likely to accept a sex relationship with men of higher social status, perhaps as a means of improving their social position. A man tends to expect more sex from a lower-class woman than from one of his own social class or higher.

Some people believe that premarital intercourse can be a good learning experience. Whether or not this is true depends on many factors. What may be a learning experience for one individual may be a problem for another.

For the sex relationship to be successful either in or out of marriage, there must be love and respect on the part of both partners, a relaxed atmosphere free of guilt, and the recognition that such a relationship needs time to develop and grow. Some people can achieve this easily, but for others it takes much work and effort.

Immature people who are interested only in gratifying their own desires, who rebel against conventional traditions, and who exploit their relations with the opposite sex, are unlikely to make good sex partners. They may also have

difficulty being good marriage partners. The mature young person recognizes that premarital sex cannot be used as a "test" of responsiveness or desirability of a spouse. Nor can it show how much one loves or is loved. Sex is only one step in the building of sound personal and family relationships.

There is a general belief that premarital intercourse has increased in recent years. Many attempts have been made to confirm this, but since it is difficult to get accurate information, we cannot be certain exactly what the trends have been. Some of the best studies have been done by researchers who use the same procedures to sample similar groups of people at intervals of several years. Such studies were done by Christensen and Gregg in 1958 and 1968, by Bell and Chaskes in 1958 and 1968, and by Robinson, King and Blaswisk in 1965 and 1970. Every study showed a sizable increase in the percentage of females engaging in premarital intercourse. The percentage for males remained approximately the same.

The results of many other studies over the past fifty years show no reliable trends in any direction. There are many reasons for this. Behavior patterns are quite different for different segments of the population. Many subjects who answer questions about their premarital sex experience may not be wholly truthful because they feel guilty about their actions. And answers given at one time may be less reliable than answers given many years later, when the climate of opinion allows greater freedom in discussing sexual experience.

But there are good reasons to support the belief that a rise in premarital sex has occurred. Since the number of teenagers and young adults in the population has increased, the actual number of people who engage in premarital intercourse has also increased, without necessarily raising the percentage. When more people are doing something, it is easy to assume that the incidence is also increasing. There is now greater freedom to discuss sexual matters. Because they are being talked about, it seems that behavior has also changed. The widespread acceptance of many sexual practices, such as homosexuality, may result from an atmosphere in which they are freely discussed.

Sex has become Topic A in advertising,

movies, books, and songs. The result is increased awareness and conversation about sex among people of all ages. The almost epidemic rise of venereal disease, the increase in illegitimacy, and the widespread use of contraceptives are other possible indicators of an increase in premarital intercourse.

Attitudes toward premarital sex and love vary widely. In many traditional and tribal societies, eligible young women are isolated until their marriage. In Spanish-speaking countries, chaperoning is common, to prevent sex relations among young unmarried people. Anthropological studies of simple societies generally indicate a relative absence of romantic love as a requirement for marriage. However, they vary widely in permissiveness of premarital intercourse.

Our own attitudes toward love and sex come from a long historical tradition. The early Greeks made a distinction between spiritual love, called **agape,** and erotic love. The first was considered good and the other bad. The Christian tradition, through such writers as Thomas Aquinas and St. Augustine, stressed that sex should be restricted to the marriage relationship. Passion was acceptable only if its purpose was the procreation of children. In the Middle Ages, the ideal of romantic love required that unmarried women be idolized as virgin lovers. Wives were assigned a lower status and often considered lustful.

In today's world, some traditional attitudes remain and some have changed. Wives are usually seen as virtuous, while unmarried women are often regarded as sex objects. With the declining influence of religion, the increase in the number of young people, and the availability of birth control, premarital sex relationships and alternative life styles to traditional marriage have become more acceptable. Our moral code has been extended to include sex as a wholesome and natural part of a healthy life. And we still regard romantic love as the most important basis for a sound man-woman relationship.

Before you go on . . .

1. Why must young people decide what to do about premarital sex relationships?

2. There is no relationship between social class and premarital sex. True or false?

3. Name three factors that may indicate increases in premarital sex.

4. What trends are indicated in the most reliable studies of premarital sex?

5. Premarital sex is not a good test of love. True or false?

6. The Greek word for spiritual love was _____.

7. The greater acceptability of premarital sex may be based on _____, and _____.

Answers:

1. Because they mature sexually before they are ready for marriage.

2. False. Women of a lower social class are more willing to have sex with men of a higher social class.

3. Rise in venereal disease; rise in illegitimacy; increased use of contraceptives.

4. The percentage of women has increased while the percentage of men has remained about the same.

5. True. A good sex relationship may take a long time to establish, and should be based on love and consideration of the other person.

6. Agape.

7. Declining influence of religion; increase in the number of young people in the population; availability of birth control methods.

Premarital Sex: The Personal Choice

Once we have gathered our statistical data about premarital sex and interpreted it, we still have only a set of figures, which tell us about the behavior of some other people. But how do we decide what we ourselves should do?

For many it is especially difficult to decide whether or not to engage in premarital sexual intercourse. The decision (like any other) is best made by considering, first, the facts about premarital sex, and then the related issues—the meaning of the decision for the two persons involved, their motives in having sexual intercourse, and their expectations for their relationship.

The first question is, what is the meaning of sexual intercourse for the two people involved? Do they feel that it is all right to enjoy sex casually, with little thought of what it means for the future of the relationship? Traditionally, women have preferred sexual intercourse in the context of a meaningful interpersonal relationship. Intercourse before marriage was thought of as putting the cart before the horse; full sexual intimacy was acceptable only after a couple clearly had marriage in mind. Men, on the other hand, have often had two standards for deciding about premarital sex. A male felt sex was all right for him but wrong for the woman he would eventually marry. Obviously, these values put women in a double-bind: giving in to a young man's sexual overtures meant losing his respect; not giving in meant losing his interest. Unfortunately this attitude still exists, although there are some indications that it may slowly be changing.

A second issue is closely related to the first. What is the motive for the choice? Is she afraid it will be painful? Is he escaping from loneliness? Does she want to trap him into marriage? Is he (or she) out to impress someone else? Or do they both feel it is a natural outgrowth and expression of their deep caring for each other? You could probably think of other motives. The point is to assess these motives and understand them, through open discussion, if possible.

Sometimes one or both partners is unaware of the true motives or wants to conceal them. This raises a third question: is anyone being exploited in the relationship? There are many ways that men and women can seek to exert power and control over each other, and sex is often used this way. She may withhold sex, for example, or become pregnant, to force the issue of marriage. He may use a vague promise of marriage to force the issue of sex. Exploitation is more likely when there is inequality in a relationship—one person being much older, or having a higher social status or greater sexual experience.

Sometimes a couple uses premarital sex as a "test" of what sex will be like after marriage. Is this valid? It may be, if both persons feel very comfortable with the idea of sex before marriage. But dating couples often do not have the opportunity for relaxed lovemaking. The couple may feel anxious about possible interruptions or punishment. The woman might feel that her responsiveness is being judged, and feel very tense and unable to respond. In rare cases **vaginismus**, a painful spasm of the vaginal muscles, may make penetration impossible. So we see that attitudes toward premarital sex can make a crucial difference in whether the experience is pleasurable or painful.

The expectations each person has of premarital intercourse are also important. Does the woman expect her first experience to be fully satisfying? The chances are great that it will not be. Achieving full satisfaction in intercourse is something like playing a good game of tennis—it takes practice. Does she expect him to know how to give her pleasure? He may not. Women usually respond more slowly to sexual stimulation, and their sexual feelings are more influenced by feelings about the whole relationship. The man may be baffled by his partner's seeming lack of enthusiasm; he may feel she is to blame if he does not know how to please her. If expectations are unrealistically high, one or both partners may be sorely disappointed.

Both partners should share the responsibility for deciding how far they will go in sexual intimacy. Often the male expects to initiate sexual advances, and thinks the female should be the one to draw the line. This places an unfair burden on her. If she goes along with him, against her better judgment, she may become uncomfortable in the relationship. She may feel guilt or indecision, especially if she feels her

partner does not support her choice. Under these circumstances sex can become a wedge, which begins to push a couple apart. Shared decision-making indicates that a couple is willing to cooperate, rather than to compete, in the area of sex. Cooperation is important in building any friendship, and it is essential to establishing marital harmony.

The couple should also consider the effects of a possible pregnancy. In most cases the effect on the woman is greater, even when the couple has been planning on marriage. She may not be willing—or ready—to take on the roles of motherhood so soon. In this case, how does she feel about abortion? Would she carry an unplanned child to term and then offer it for adoption? It is important to consider the effect of each of these alternatives on the couple's relationship, on their families and on career plans.

Some couples decide to reserve sexual intercourse for after marriage. They may feel that marriage offers them the most favorable circumstances for developing and deepening the sexual dimension of their relationship. They may want to save something special for marriage, or provide the best environment for any child they might have. Or religious values may be involved. Sometimes a couple will wait because one or both are uncomfortable with sexual matters. Postponing intercourse is for them a way of avoiding this issue temporarily. But a person who is truly uncomfortable with the subject of sex prior to marriage cannot expect to be comfortable with it afterwards. Dating is the way most young people in our society learn about and become comfortable with themselves as sexual beings. Most couples gradually increase their level of sexual intimacy as they proceed from casual dating through engagement (with or without sexual intercourse) and marriage. A couple that plan to marry but have had no sexual interaction at all would be very unusual in our society today.

Anyone who decides to engage in sexual intercourse should know the symptoms of venereal disease. The commonest venereal diseases are syphilis and gonorrhea. Both are spread almost exclusively through sexual intercourse with an infected person. One attack does not give immunity, and a person can be reinfected over and over.

Syphilis is a disease of the nervous system. If untreated it can lead to insanity, paralysis, or blindness. The first symptom is a painless sore or **chancre,** usually in the genital area. Unfortunately, this sore disappears without treatment, and the infected person may believe he is cured. Some months later a rash develops on various parts of the body, accompanied by symptoms that resemble flu. Throughout this period, the disease is very easy to transmit. Syphilis can be detected by a simple blood test, and responds quickly to treatment with penicillin.

The symptoms of **gonorrhea** are easier to detect. They appear within a few days after infection. A man typically experiences a painful burning sensation when he urinates, accompanied by a discharge from the penis. A woman notices similar symptoms, but often to a lesser degree. Untreated, gonorrhea can lead to severe pelvic infections, heart disease, and arthritis. Most cases of gonorrhea can be cured by penicillin, although a new penicillin-resistant strain has recently been discovered.

A couple who choose to have premarital sex should be aware that unwanted pregnancy is a serious problem, and should study available methods of contraception. And a person who decides to delay sexual intercourse until after marriage may profit from considering ways to "turn off" unwanted advances. Making one's position clearly understood, and being firm about it, is the best way to avoid being pressured about sex.

Before you go on . . .

1. A woman is just as likely as a man to feel comfortable about having casual sex. True or false?

2. Exploitation of the partner is more likely when there is some form of _____ in the relationship.

3. _____ is the term for a painful contraction of the vaginal muscles, which can make penetration impossible.

4. A first sexual experience is not likely to be as satisfying as a later one. True or false?

5. Traditionally, which partner has been responsible for drawing the line on premarital sex?

6. If you are uncomfortable with the issue of sexuality, putting off intercourse until after marriage may solve the problem. True or false?

Answers:

1. False. A woman is more likely to be concerned about the nature of the whole relationship.

2. Inequality.

3. Vaginisimus.

4. True. The chances are great that the first experience will not be fully satisfying, especially for the woman.

5. The woman (female).

6. False. Delaying sex only postpones the problem until later.

BUILDING A RELATIONSHIP *Chapter Review*

1. Which of the following factors led to the development of modern dating? (a) Entrance of women into the labor market; (b) Labor saving devices; (c) The popular understanding of psychoanalysis; (d) Telephones and automobiles

2. One-half of the female population in the United States is married by age _____.

3. Statistically speaking, marriages in which the partners are from similar backgrounds have a greater chance of success than marriages where the couples are from very different backgrounds. True or false?

4. Which of the following is probably LEAST likely to lead to friction between husband and wife? (a) Religious differences; (b) A small age difference; (c) Differences in level of education; (d) Differences in social class.

5. In general, persons who marry at a relatively later age (in their mid-twenties, for example) are more likely to have a successful marriage than are persons who marry younger. True or false?

6. Dating as we know it developed in the twentieth century. True or false?

7. Dr. Alfred Adler believed that success in life is highly dependent on our ability to _____ with our friends, marriage partners, and people at work.

8. State laws forbidding interracial marriage were made void by a decision of the U.S. Supreme Court in what year? (a) 1937 (b) 1947 (c) 1957 (d) 1967

9. The Catholic Church does not accept as valid a marriage performed outside of the church or by anyone but a Catholic priest. True or false?

10. Marriages in which the couple are from different racial, national, or religious backgrounds are commonly referred to as _____ marriages.

11. Most adolescents begin dating at about age _____. (a) 10; (b) 12; (c) 14; (d) 16

12. The Jewish community has resisted interfaith marriages more consistently than the Protestant or Catholic communities. True or false?

13. Women's liberationists want all women to go out and work. True or false?

14. The average woman today can expect to spend _____ years in her place of work.

15. If the _____ standard for male and female behavior comes into play, a date can turn into more of a contest than a cooperative and pleasant experience.

16. Being a housewife has the advantage of which of the following benefits? (a) Job security; (b) Health and medical benefits; (c) Vacation time; (d) Unemployment insurance; (e) None of the above.

17. Two common types of venereal disease are _____ and _____.

18. A small age difference between the husband and wife, with the husband being _____, is considered the norm in our society.

19. Statistics indicate that _____ out of ten women in the United States will be working at some point in their lives. (a) 9; (b) 6; (c) 3; (d) 1

20. Marriages in which the woman was pregnant before the wedding often end in divorce. True or false?

21. Of all the social classes, the _____ class places the most restrictions on the dating of young people.

22. Premarital intercourse is usually a pretty good test of whether a couple would be sexually compatible after marriage. True or false?

23. In which kind of marriages are the divorce rates lower? (a) Heterogamous; (b) Homogamous; (c) Marriages where the woman is pregnant; (d) Mixed marriages.

24. Today a woman with a college degree typically earns a salary that is _____ that of a man with the same degree. (a) more than; (b) equal to; (c) less than

25. The unmarried woman who becomes pregnant today has more alternatives than she did in the past. True or false?

26. Which of the following is LEAST likely to prevent a date's sexual overtures from snowballing past a line one has set? (a) Planning the evening's activities thoroughly in advance; (b) Making one's decision known and being firm about it; (c) Cultivating the art of conversation; (d) Willingness to do whatever one's date suggests.

27. People of the working class who have only a high school education tend to date and marry _____ in comparison with people of the upper class who have a college education. (a) early; (b) about the same; (c) late

28. Briefly describe the characteristics of the social institution of dating.

29. Why is marrying to get away from home a poor risk?

30. What are some good signs in a relationship where two people are planning to marry?

To find the answers, look at page 189.

CHAPTER THREE
ADJUSTING TO MARRIAGE

Leading thoughts:

- For most couples, the wedding and the honeymoon are a time of transition, when they first really come to know one another

- Marriage usually requires the couple to adopt a team lifestyle. They now have to adjust their habits and expectations, and learn to share labor and responsibility

- Conflict is inevitable in any marriage, but working out problems together can bring new opportunities for closeness and growth

- Relations with in-laws are a source of problems in many marriages

- Money management is a cause of even more marital problems

- Couples should work out their financial arrangements together. Many different financial plans, including a number of credit arrangements, are available

The Wedding and Honeymoon

11

The actual wedding ceremony may have a religious dimension. It always has secular and personal significance. Until the present century the religious aspect was stressed. But in our century there is increasing emphasis on marriage as a binding civil contract. Most of our everyday transactions are becoming more impersonal, romantic love is increasingly stressed by the mass media, and divorce is becoming more socially tolerated. So the personal aspect of marriage is more important now than at any time in the past. The current emphasis is on finding personal satisfaction and fulfillment in marriage.

In newspapers, magazines, and on television, romantic love is idolized and marriage tends to be judged in terms of the personal satisfaction it brings to the partners. It is important that the two persons enjoy sharing their personal goals and interests, but happiness in a marriage does not happen automatically. It has to be achieved. Some have the idea that there is only one ideal partner in the world, and that when they meet there will be instant recognition. These persons might profit from considering the following story:

A young man searched far and wide for the fair maid of his dreams. He interviewed and turned down each young woman in turn until one day almost in despair he spied still another young woman and recognized her immediately as his ideal. He ran to embrace her! Imagine his surprise when she turned away from him saying, "No, I'm looking for my ideal man!"

The fruitless search for an ideal person may cause one to remain single. Even worse, the impossible ideal in the mind of one partner may cause one to withhold love from the other, because she (or he) does not measure up to the ideal. Real relationships between actual people are built, not "found." And love is something which grows over time, not something one "falls into."

Marriage laws vary from state to state. But in most states both parties must meet a minimum age requirement or have their parents' consent. Each must undergo a blood test to determine whether they are carriers of syphilis. Most states require a waiting period of several days before the marriage license is issued. Once the license is obtained, the couple must be married by an official who is authorized by the state to perform marriage ceremonies (a justice of the peace or a minister, priest, or rabbi). The ceremony must be witnessed by two persons who are of legal age. After the wedding ceremony, the two witnesses and the official who performs the ceremony must sign the license and send it to a government agency for recording and filing.

There are some exceptions to these general rules, especially where they conflict with certain religious beliefs. Quakers, for example,

are permitted to marry themselves in a religious ceremony without the assistance of a minister or other official. And some states give legal status to common-law "marriages," in which a man and woman have chosen to live together for a requisite period of time without the benefit of a wedding ceremony.

There is considerable variation in the wedding ceremony. It can range from a simple exchange of promises before a justice of the peace to the ceremonial forms used in the various religions and the personal changes a couple may make on these. But in all weddings bride and groom exchange vows, which make known their intention to love and respect one another in spite of their shortcomings, to work together toward overcoming whatever hardships they may meet in the course of a lifetime, and to assume responsibility for the welfare of any children they may have. Men used to routinely promise to "love, honor, and cherish" their wives while the women promised to "love, honor, and obey" their husbands. Some couples make these promises even today. Out of sensitivity to the changing status of women, many religious groups have rewritten their standard vows so that both bride and groom promise to "cherish" each other. Many young people today are emphasizing the personal dimensions of their marriage by writing their own marriage vows.

Certain traditions are often observed at weddings. The bride may wear "something old, something new, something borrowed, and something blue," and toss her bouquet. The person who catches it is supposedly the one who will marry next. Rice may be thrown at the newlyweds, or they may be followed by a horn-honking procession of cars. These are all remnants of ancient traditions for which the original meanings have often been forgotten. They add to the general gaiety of the celebration, but they have no legal importance.

The single most important purpose of the wedding ceremony is to establish the new (married) status of the couple in the community. The wedding ceremony serves as a kind of public announcement. For this reason elopements and secret weddings are to be discouraged. Research has shown that more elopements and secret weddings than public weddings end in failure. If one or both families are against the marriage, it is important to try to win them over first. Parental disapproval, or hiding the fact of the marriage from parents, can create unbearable tensions, which may destroy a marriage.

In addition to conferring a new legal status upon the husband and wife, marriage serves other social purposes. It helps to preserve moral standards, to protect the property rights of the spouses, and to protect them from abuse or exploitation. Its legal requirements guard against the marriage of close relatives and determine the legitimacy of children.

A honeymoon or wedding trip can provide a couple with welcome rest after the hectic last days of wedding preparation. For the couple who have saved sexual intercourse until marriage, it offers an opportunity for learning to express fully the sexual dimension of their relationship.

Traditionally the groom is expected to pay for the cost of the honeymoon, while the bride or her family pays for most of the wedding. But this varies in practice. Some couples may decide to forgo or to delay a wedding trip for economic reasons, or because their work schedules do not permit it. Honeymoons are not essential to marital success. The couple who find that a honeymoon is not feasible should not feel that they are being cheated out of something absolutely necessary.

For those who do plan a honeymoon, there are some reasonable guidelines based on the experience of other couples. First of all, the feeling of being rested and relaxed is important. Most are naturally a bit apprehensive about starting anything new. Newlyweds sometimes feel that everything they do or say in the first days and weeks of the marriage is crucially important to the establishment of lifetime patterns. They may feel that they are under pressure to be perfect in all areas, especially on the honeymoon. Perfection is, of course, impossible. In their sexual relations the couple will need time to learn what is pleasing to themselves and to each other. A relaxed schedule helps the couple to avoid building up unnecessary tensions.

A sense of humor comes in handy when travel arrangements turn out to be less than perfect, or when we or our mate makes a social blunder. The ability to defuse tensions by laughing at our own or the world's imperfections is a valuable quality to bring to marriage. It is usually best to plan the honeymoon around the proven interests of the couple. If you have never experienced foreign travel, with its problems of passports, visas, communicating with persons who do not speak your language and so forth, this is probably not the best time to attempt it. There will be other opportunities for travel later, and the honeymoon should be a time for learning about each other.

The honeymoon should provide the couple anonymity. Even if you have not seen your Aunt Martha for ten years, this is not the time to visit her, or to stay with relatives or friends. They will be there when you return. In a hotel or resort, or at a camping ground, you will appear no different from any other guest. No one need know that you were married only yesterday, and you will be free to keep the schedule which best suits yourselves. While it is customary not to tell everyone where you intend to honeymoon, you should leave an address or phone number with a trusted relative, so that you can be reached in case of emergency.

The primary purpose of the honeymoon is for the bride and groom to have some relaxed time together away from the cares of the workday world, during which they can begin to create their own marriage life style. Honeymoons, like weddings, do not bestow perfection on couples who participate in them. The wedding and the honeymoon give a couple the opportunity to begin married life by expressing their love before the community and to each other. Whether their love and their ability to express it grows or does not depends on how carefully they have cultivated their relationship before marriage—and on the effort they make to develop it afterwards.

Before you go on . . .

1. Until our century the _____ significance of marriage was stressed.

2. What aspects of marriage receive the most emphasis today?

3. In most states a couple can pick up a license to be married in the same day they apply. True or false?

4. What two types of marriage vows are in common use?

5. Every couple must be married by an official recognized by the state. True or false?

6. The honeymoon should ideally be planned around _____.

7. Who usually pays for the honeymoon?

Answers:

1. Religious.

2. Most emphasis is placed on personal satisfaction and fulfillment.

3. False. Most states require a blood test and a waiting period of several days before a license is issued.

4. The traditional religious and civil vows, and vows composed by the couple themselves.

5. False. This is not required if it conflicts with religious beliefs or in common-law marriages.

6. The interests shared by the couple.

7. The groom usually pays for the honeymoon, while the bride or her family pays for the wedding.

The State of Being Married

The basic change in the relationship between two people who get married is that they enter a life of **joint** rather than **individual** activity. This involves a commitment to accept each other's shortcomings as well as strengths, to compromise on problems for the good of both partners, and to work to preserve and continue the relationship on a permanent basis. This change of focus profoundly affects old habit patterns. Some of them must be discarded in favor of behavior that can lead to marital happiness.

In general, a team approach to living supplants a self-centered approach. In sexual relations, for example, objectives must often be redefined. The single man may have sought many women for his sexual gratification. But after marriage, he must turn his attention toward encouraging and satisfying his wife's desires as a source of his own pleasure. He is expected not to look outside of marriage for sexual satisfaction. The woman who may have been shy or reluctant to participate freely in sexual exchanges now has complete freedom to express her sexual desires, and the responsibility to please and satisfy her husband.

In day-to-day living, a division of labor develops. The wife becomes responsible for some household tasks and the husband for others. Decisions must be made about how money will be earned and how it will be spent. The solutions may vary from couple to couple, but the more similar their expectations, the smoother their relationship will run.

Changes in roles after marriage occur in several ways. We become known as each other's spouse. Comments like "Oh, you're Mary's husband" or "You're Peter's wife" may at first jolt our sense of individuality. But these demonstrate society's recognition of the "team" nature of marriage. The married person takes on a new identity as a spouse rather than as the child of his or her parents. When we marry, we must shift our emphasis and consider our spouse's needs and wishes ahead of other family ties. This requires not only changes in our perception, but also a changed orientation on the part of our parents and other relatives.

We must also learn a new set of relationships with the family of our spouse—our in-laws. This can often be a source of problems for young married people. However, the arrival of a child may help to establish good in-law relationships.

Many challenges and irreversible changes arrive with the first baby. New parents may be insecure in their new roles, and worries and anxieties may cause strains between husband and wife. The attention showered on a child may threaten a parent who does not feel secure about the marital relationship. Questions about money, religion, educational aspirations, distribution of time and energy, and relations with in-laws are all highlighted and more critical when they involve a child. But couples who have worked out their marital relationship satisfactorily before having a baby will find it easier to make the transition from being a married couple to being a parent-child family.

Over the years, there have been changes in society's concepts and expectations of marriage. These changes result from the shift from rural to urban living, the change from an agricultural to an industrial economy, the increased availability of higher education, and the growing independence of women. The patriarchal family, in which the husband had full control over family decisions and discipline, has given way to a spirit of more equality between husband and wife. And marriage, which was once considered a lifelong commitment, is now ending in divorce at an ever-increasing rate.

In the past, sexual fidelity in marriage has been more often expected of women than of men. In many working-class families, the husband's casual sexual encounters with other women are tacitly accepted, but the wife is expected to remain faithful. In some upper-class families, both partners can engage in extramarital affairs, provided they are discreet. In short, the spouse as exclusive sex partner has not existed as often as it has been talked about. But today greater equality is developing in extramarital sex relationships. A growing number of middle-class families feel that the wife has as much right as the husband to engage in extramarital sex, and that if one is not expected to, neither is the other.

Financial independence has always been considered an important prerequisite to marriage. This used to place a heavy burden on the husband, since women were expected to remain at home after marriage. But in recent years, women in increasing numbers are entering the job market. In many families, sharing economic responsibility is becoming the norm.

Another recent trend stems directly from the longer period of education needed to prepare young people for professional and technical positions. Some young people are marrying while they are still in school, and depending on their parents for financial support.

The parents often regard this as an investment in the future of their children and grandchildren. But such arrangements often lead the young couple to feel less than truly married. Rather, they are "playing house" until they can be economically self-sufficient.

With the trend toward urban living, the traditional division of duties between husband and wife has been revised. On farms, husband and wife worked in and around the home. The woman usually did the homemaking and contributed economically by preserving foods, making clothing, cooking, cleaning, and so on. The husband's responsibilities included the major farm chores and providing protection and economic necessities for his wife and children. Children were usually supervised by both parents. The mother taught her daughters household skills, and the father taught his sons to help with the farm work.

But in urban areas, fathers went outside the home to work and were separated from their families for long periods of time during the day. Children were no longer economic helpers. They spent their time in school preparing for work in the urban business world. Women devoted themselves largely to homemaking and child-rearing. Members of the urban family looked to each other for emotional support, and the home became a refuge from the impersonal outside world. Companionship between husband and wife became an increasingly important part of the marriage relationship.

Among middle-class families, a new life-style has emerged in which many women continue careers on a full-time or part-time basis. Many factors have contributed to this change—the availability of labor-saving devices and convenience foods, a system of public education that relieves the woman of child care responsibilities for much of the day, and the family's rising needs and expectations to consume a wide variety of manufactured goods and services. This new trend is accompanied by women's increased awareness of their human right to a full and rewarding life of their own. Many marriages today are undergoing changes in the balance of power between husband and wife. Some of them show signs of stress even though they benefit from the wife's increased independence and her economic contribution. Children are being raised with a greater awareness of the equality of the sexes. In the future, it is very likely that this middle-class phenomenon may spread to the rest of American society.

Before you go on . . .

1. After marriage, which relative should be given first consideration, a person's spouse or a person's parent?

2. What is a husband's responsibility in his sexual relationship with his wife?

3. What will make it easy for a married couple to decide which household tasks each one should do?

4. Which relationship might the birth of a child improve for a married couple?

5. What factors have encouraged women to work outside the home?

6. In moving from a farm to city life, why did the father's control over his family diminish?

7. In which social class do we find the greatest independence of women?

Answers:

1. Spouse.

2. To encourage her desires and satisfy her sexual needs.

3. Similarity of expectations and attitudes about household chores.

4. In-law relationship.

5. Labor-saving devices at home, the long time children spend at school, and the needs of the family for material items.

6. He had to spend long periods of time each day away from home.

7. The middle class.

Family Life Style

Marriage, of course, involves a union between two persons. But too often we forget that they remain distinct individuals. In a satisfying marriage, two people can become more fully developed human beings and can discover happiness in their togetherness. This does not happen automatically, but results from an ongoing process of growth, a process that each of the partners must work at in cooperation with the other.

The partners of each couple relate to each other in a characteristic way. The way they relate can lead to general harmony, to a resigned ability to put up with each other, or to continual antagonism. How the relationship works out depends both on their basic personalities and on how they develop their relationship together. Let us look in more detail at these factors.

Each person shows a good deal of consistency in personality. Alfred Adler, a leading psychologist of the early twentieth century, called this personal consistency the individual's "style of life." Though practical aspirations and actual projects often vary through the years, the style of life is formed at an early age, and generally remains unchanged. By "style of life"

we mean characteristic ways of perceiving, thinking, and acting. We try to develop a style of life that allows us to make full use of our potential and be appreciated by others.

Many elements in our style of life are concerned with very commonplace, habitual things. For instance, we all have characteristic patterns of movement. Some of us move quickly, others slowly. Similarly, some of us are eager to start new projects, some consider a decision carefully, others hesitate to try anything new, and still others will not break their ordinary routines.

Another factor in the style of life stems from the different ways we perceive ourselves, other people, and the world. For instance, one person may rely mainly on vision to understand reality, while another interprets the world more through what she hears. Perception also involves a basic orientation toward living. We can view life either from a fundamentally optimistic perspective or a fundamentally pessimistic one. The realistic optimist can see obstacles to the fulfillment of his or her goals, but has the self-confidence and courage to overcome them. The pessimist, on the other hand, becomes easily discouraged. Finally, our memories are selective. We remember what it is to our advantage to recall, what fits our goals and our life styles. Most of us remember what we regard as our strengths and disguise our weaknesses.

The style of life also includes the ways we relate to people—whether we are outgoing and friendly, a bit cautious, indifferent, reserved and shy, manipulative, or hostile. Our style of life includes our manner of approaching problems. Some people immediately tackle a problem in a direct and well-planned way; others charge at it without sufficient evaluation or planning; others hesitate or evade it. Still others depend on someone else to overcome their problems, or to help them carry the strain.

Thus our individual style of life, guided by the goal of a satisfactory way to achieve our potential, results in a fairly consistent pattern of movement, ways of perceiving, manner of relating to others, and approach to problems. We learn this pattern early in life, through interaction with persons such as our parents, brothers and sisters, teachers, and other caretakers.

Ideally, by the time two people are ready to marry, they will each have developed a degree of maturity. The life style of the mature person provides an **identity**, a sense of who one is and what one can do in life. Having an identity and knowing ourselves opens us to being intimate with another person and faithful to him or her. The mature person focuses not only on self, but has "social interest"—that is, respect and care for others. Such a person is considerate and warm with others, and wants to contribute positively to the wider community.

But not only does each person have an individual life style. There are also "family life styles," the distinctive way in which each family fits together.

The two potential marriage partners, having grown up in different families, are sure to have learned different family life styles, perhaps even conflicting ones. If a couple do not think and talk about the similarities and differences in their family patterns and individual life styles, they may experience frictions that they do not understand. A partner who grew up in a family that was reserved in showing affection may seem cold to the other, who was raised in a demonstrative family and expects a great deal of affection. At best, these untalked-about differences will cause unpleasant episodes; at worst, they will generate heated conflict and eventually disrupt the relationship.

Forming a relationship gives two people the opportunity to create a new family life style satisfying to them both. Creating a family life style demands honest reflection on oneself, respect for the other person, courage to make decisions and carry them out, and thoughtfulness about planning well for the future. Often we like certain aspects of our families, but not other aspects. Marriage provides the chance to construct a family life style that enables the partners to move, perceive, act, relate, set goals, and solve problems in a manner bringing fulfillment to themselves and others too. But all this does not simply happen. Especially if the individual life styles of the partners are markedly different, it takes work, understanding, and patience. Consider, for example, the problems faced by one couple, the Garlands:

Laura Garland recalls that at the age of three years she went with her father for a walk in the park one Sunday. A storm came up, and they took shelter in a greenhouse. The wind blew fiercely, threatening to break through the glass walls. After that incident, her parents had trouble getting her to leave the house. At five she remembers that she disliked going to school; at least once her mother actually pushed her to make her go. A third recollection is of a misfortune at her high school graduation, when she fell down the stairs in front of the audience in her first pair of high heels. She was horribly embarassed and fled in tears, though her friends sympathized with her afterwards.

Dave Garland recalls that at three he had a great time in his grandfather's bakery. The smell of bread turned him on, and he liked to watch his grandfather open up the big tub full of rising dough. He learned to love bread. At eight he made wine with his father, and enjoyed sticking his hand in the wine barrel. At ten, he was fascinated by the sight of a calf being born on his aunt's and uncle's farm.

We see quite a contrast in the tone of these memories, and the contrast reflects something important in the two persons' life styles. Laura comes across as very frightened, as needing a great deal of protection and encouragement, and as not at all adventurous. Dave, on the other hand, is active, eager to become involved in many projects, and good-naturedly goes along with whatever is happening. This difference has led to great dissatisfaction in their marriage. Laura worries, is always anxious and embarassed about her place in the community, and is unwilling to adapt to new situations. Dave simply fails to perceive many of the problems between him and Laura, and does not communicate his own feelings very much; but he runs a profitable business and has many friendly associates in the community. Their individual life styles differ markedly, and they have not cooperated well in building a mutually gratifying family life style.

Setting out to create a rewarding family life style challenges two persons to grow to their fullest potential. Before technology became so widespread, and when daily life was more physically demanding, many people married for economic reasons—to have someone to share the labor of making a living. Many people probably still do marry for economic reasons but for others economic necessity is no longer the main reason. Today many people marry because it is expected, or because they fear loneliness, but they do not share their intimate selves with each other. They live out approved roles, doing what is expected and what is popular in the wider society. A deep loneliness persists in them, because they do not share their most personal thoughts and feelings, or grow together through helping each other reach their fullest potential.

Only those who risk being known totally, who can trust enough to be vulnerable to their partners, and who make a real effort to grow together in their relationship are likely to experience the satisfaction of full relatedness. These people have created a family life style, not fallen into one. They will explore what they have in common, and the distinctive elements that each brings to the marriage. They will discuss ways of building each other's strengths and of solving problems. The challenge (and happiness) of marriage lies not in just knowing what a style of life consists of, but in actually constructing a mutually fulfilling family life style together.

Before you go on . . .

1. List some of the ways a married couple can relate to each other.

2. Our characteristic ways of thinking, perceiving, and acting make up our _____.

3. Our selective memory enables us to recall our strengths as well as our weaknesses. True or false?

4. When do we learn our individual life style patterns?

5. Development within a marriage requires an ongoing process of _____.

6. Many dissatisfactions within marriage are aggravated by lack of communication. True or false?

7. At one time many people married for _____ reasons.

Answers:

1. Their relationship may be harmonious; it may be resigned; or it may involve continual antagonism.

2. Life style.

3. False. We tend to suppress memory of our weaknesses.

4. Early in life, though interaction with the people close to us.

5. Growth.

6. True.

7. Economic.

Conflict, Change, and Growth

14

Any two people who marry will have some differences of opinion. Their different backgrounds and experiences have given them somewhat different values, attitudes, goals, habits, and expectations. For example, if a wife's mother was dominant, active, and outgoing but her husband's mother was submissive, passive, and shy, their attitudes toward the wife's role are very likely to be different. The word "wife" has a different meaning for each of them. Such differences are a built-in source of possible misunderstanding in any marriage. Husband and wife may also have different personality traits. They may differ from each other in dominance or submissiveness, introversion or extroversion, activeness or passiveness, whether they are outspoken or reticent, habitually optimistic or pessimistic, whether they prefer intellectual, athletic, or creative outlets for their energies, and in many other traits. These differences can add interest to the relationship or they may be a source of conflict.

Situational factors may also be irritating. A marriage which was harmonious may enter a period of conflict when a major situational change is made—for example, when a change in one partner's work forces the other to move, or when an elderly and ailing parent moves in with the family.

The sources of conflict we have discussed so far are external, but sometimes internal factors cause unhappiness in marriage. They can be harder to deal with because they are less visible. **Tensions** within one of the partners may cause friction between them. For example, a husband may wish to be a pleasing sexual partner to his wife, but may unconsciously feel that mature sexual behavior is too aggressive and somehow "not nice." This internal conflict may cause him to overwork, drink excessively, stay up late or go to bed very early to avoid sexual intercourse with his wife. But he is unaware of the source of the conflict, and probably believes that his overwork or fatigue are the real reasons he cannot find time for lovemaking. If she accepts his reasoning, there may be endless arguments about his long working hours. Only when he discovers and admits that the real problem is his conflicting feelings about sex can he begin to work on a solution.

One of the commonest factors in internal

conflict is **immaturity**, coupled with lack of experience. This can be a problem when a person's experience as a child is an inadequate guide to mature behavior. Another common factor is a poor self-concept. For example, a wife may feel inadequate in comparison to others and spend money extravagantly in an attempt to make herself and others feel that she is valued and valuable. Jealousy is another common way of expressing this type of insecurity.

Frustration is an important source of conflict. A husband may feel frustrated because he is not a success at his work. A wife may be frustrated at work or if housework and children are taking up too much of her time and energy. Individuals or couples may understand what is frustrating them, or they may just feel generally unhappy and irritable. If they are unaware of their problem or if it seems too big to handle they may try to avoid it altogether or find themselves acting defensively.

Defensiveness is a way of expressing internal conflict. There are several common **defense mechanisms. Displacement** occurs when anger is displaced from its source onto another person or situation. A husband, for instance, may be angry at his wife and yell at the children instead. People who feel guilty about their own attitudes or behavior may unjustly accuse their mates of what they themselves are doing or would like to do. A domineering man may accuse his wife of being bossy whenever she makes a suggestion. This is called **projection.** One or both partners may refuse to admit to behavior which is inconsistent with the self-image they wish to keep.

One of the most difficult defense mechanisms to detect is that of the person who never seems to get upset, but always sees the good side of everything. These persons, with their unrealistic Pollyanna attitude towards life, are protecting themselves from painful or uncomfortable realities. Because they deny their true feelings they are incapable of a full, authentic relationship with their marriage partners. For other people, defensiveness takes the form of a constant struggle for power. These persons may be very surprised to find that others see them as being very strong, because they see themselves as weak and taken advan-

tage of. All defense mechanisms tend to mask the true source of conflict.

A married couple should learn to appreciate conflict for what it is—an acknowledgement of their differences and an opportunity for growth. Conflict is feedback. Conflict says that something important is happening within an individual or between the couple.

Some couples never engage in open conflict. They appear to have a perfect relationship, but in fact they have a non-relationship. The children of such couples often suffer from serious personality disorders. Couples who are always in conflict are also destructive of the mental health of their partners and of their children. Emotionally healthy couples, though, can expect both to have a lot of good feelings about each other and to go through some times of conflict.

People also change in more basic ways. They may adjust their relationships to these changes, or they may drift away from each other. If a married couple fail to grow together as they change, either the marriage will collapse or the couple will retain only the formalities of being married while they live in separate psychological worlds.

Our motivation for marriage may also change. Initially, we may marry to escape parental domination, because social pressure encourages it, or to fulfill our romantic ideal. But these earlier motivations may not last, either because we become disillusioned with them or because more opportunities for growth become available. We may not be "tuned in" to our partner well enough to keep us interested in a life-long relationship, or another potential partner may seem more attractive than our spouse.

The impressions we have received about our parents' marriage may affect our attitudes, either consciously or unconsciously. For example, a woman who fears that her husband will loaf in a rocking chair for the last twenty years of his life as her father did may push him to achieve beyond reasonable expectations. Or a man may reflect on his parents' way of living and decide to change earlier patterns or roles. These personal attitudes will directly or indirectly influence a relationship. Often the growth of the partners is discouraged because the family, as a system, resists and refuses to recognize or encourage any deviation from a norm of behavior and belief.

Circumstances can also change a marriage. If hopes for financial success fail to materialize, the relationship may become strained. A move to a higher social class can create difficulties and unease in dealing with a different pace of life. The wife who works to put her husband through school but who does not continue her own education runs the serious risk of being dropped in favor of a woman with higher educational background. Children may affect the marriage relationship by detracting from the couple's time together or exaggerating gaps and antagonisms already present. Couples who create opportunities to nurture each other and who take time for each other are better able to stimulate the full development of their children and also to model a happy and fulfilling marriage relationship for them.

The bride and her Prince Charming don't always live happily ever after. Marriage coun-selors and advice columns report the conflicts and disillusionment of frustrated couples. But most marriages fall somewhere between these extremes. At some point, most people reevaluate what they want from marriage. Many women, for instance, want to continue their educations and careers. They question whether the traditional housewife role is really fulfilling their potential. Returning to school or resuming a career implies that the tacit contract regarding the roles each partner will play in a marriage will have to be renegotiated. Many men view female advancement as a personal threat. Others will support their wives' decisions. Flexibility in making such changes leads to greater fulfillment for each, and for increased happiness between them. But resentment caused by incompatible viewpoints can smoulder and poison a relationship or disrupt it altogether. Maintaining an ongoing process of growth, in the long run, is the most effective way for a couple to deal with the problems of conflict and change.

Before you go on . . .

1. Couples who never argue are emotionally healthier than those who argue occasionally. True or false?

2. The man who is angry with his boss but yells at his wife is using a defense mechanism called _____.

3. People who use defense mechanisms to cope with conflict may not know what the real conflict is. True or false?

4. People who yell and bluster often have a weak _____ .

5. An occasional_____ can help clarify the issues a couple disagree about.

6. Nearly all married couples play their original marital roles throughout their lives. True or false?

7. Couples may differ from one another in personality traits such as dominance or _____ and activeness or _____ .

Answers:

1. False. Emotionally healthy people feel free to express their differences.

2. Displacement.

3. True. Defense mechanisms mask the true source of conflict.

4. Self-concept.

5. Argument.

6. False. Most of them shift their roles as personal perspectives and circumstances change.

7. Submissiveness; passiveness.

Relating to In-Laws

Our folklore is rich in jokes about in-laws. Typically, in-laws are cast in a poor light. They are portrayed as domineering or dependent, as meddlesome and intruding.

Our discomfort with our in-laws has probably increased as the nuclear family has developed into the predominant pattern in our society. We are not suggesting that in-law problems are a new phenomenon. But in earlier times, when we were primarily an agricultural society and large families were necessary to do the work needed to support a family, extended families were very common. In an **extended family** one or more grandparents or other relatives live under the same roof with a married couple and their children. This is still seen in some parts of our society. A good number of black Americans, for example, live in extended families today.

In the extended family, the in-laws who share the residence are an integral part of the family. They are part of the "in-group," not outsiders. Of course, they may take part in and may even initiate family quarrels. But since they are considered part of the family, disputes that involve them can be handled in much the same

way as disputes between husband and wife. They are settled in the context of the family, and the solution finally agreed upon is the one most agreeable or least disagreeable to all concerned. In the **nuclear family**, which sees itself as an economically and psychologically independent unit, we are tempted to settle in-law quarrels by sending a troublesome visiting in-law packing.

Problems with in-laws are partially shaped by how we define the problem. Women are particularly featured in our popular stereotypes about in-law problems. But sons, too, may be overly attached to their mothers. And fathers-in-law may be dependent, domineering, or meddling. A young man who is pleased by his own parents' offer of material or emotional support may be upset when his wife's parents make a similar offer, and may be genuinely shocked to learn that she views his parents as interfering.

In one study of couples who had been married for an average of twenty years, women ranked in-law relationships second and men ranked them third in a list of the most serious problems they had encountered in achieving marital harmony. In another survey of university student couples, relations with in-laws were ranked as their most difficult marital problem. These studies indicate that establishing harmonious relations with in-laws is more difficult for most couples during the early years of the marriage. It may be less troublesome in later years because the couple are more certain of their relationship to each other. They have had more time to work out suitable solutions, or time has removed the problem through the incapacitation or death of the offending relative.

In the early years of marriage a young couple's financial dependence on one or both sets of parents is a frequent source of in-law friction. The couple may feel that they need and should have their parents' support while one or both are finishing college degrees. Their parents may share this point of view and may genuinely not intend to exert power over the young couple. But their very generosity, especially if they offer anything more than is asked for, may be seen as a wish to keep their son or daughter "tied to the apron strings."

In some cases one or both sets of parents are possessive. They may be unwilling to let go of the active parenting phase and to move on to other interests. This problem is further complicated when the son or daughter is immature and still overly dependent on the parents. Frequent complaints in such a situation are "You're going to see your mother again? Don't you two ever get tired of each other?" or "Do you have to consult your father about everything? Can't you trust my judgment just once?"

In the later years of marriage the tables are sometimes turned. The parents may become financially and emotionally dependent on their children. Mother may now come home to daughter, unable to cope with living alone after the death of her spouse. And daughter may become overprotective of her mother. This, too, can be burdensome for the mate. New programs such as Medicare have helped the elderly to be more independent, and have provided some financial relief to their families.

Personal insecurity in husband, wife, or an in-law can make it very hard to develop a warm relationship. If jealousy is added, a pleasant relationship becomes almost impossible. Problems with in-laws are rarely the only problems a couple must face. Financial and other difficulties often interact with these problems, and solving them may require a multiple approach.

Can in-law problems be avoided? Probably not entirely, just as marital problems cannot be avoided. But they can be anticipated, discussed, confronted, and worked out. Perhaps the best time to begin working on them is before the marriage. Couples should discuss the similarities and differences between their families, their reactions to their future in-laws, and how they plan to interact with their in-laws after marriage. This is particularly important if either partner already has difficulty relating to either family. In mixed marriages in-law problems can be especially troublesome. Marriage, in itself, is very unlikely to solve the problem. But the couple who sincerely try to solve or at least minimize in-law problems can do so.

The primary task of the newlywed couple is to form a new union, an enduring and harmonious relationship between themselves. Parents, brothers, and sisters are now secondary. Problems that arise between a couple are better solved between themselves, or in consultation with a disinterested party such as a counselor or minister. Too much advice from in-laws, especially as a marriage is just getting started, can interfere with the primary relationship between husband and wife. It is important that a couple learn early in their marriage to trust their own capacity to solve their problems together.

Before you go on . . .

1. An increase in the prevalence of in-law problems may be due to the predominance of the _____ in our society.

2. Studies indicate that most couples have problems relating to their in-laws. True or false?

3. In a survey of student couples, relations with in-laws ranked as their _____ problem.

4. What is an extended family?

5. Married couples usually have fewer in-law problems during the early years of the marriage. True or false?

6. Solving in-law problems combined with other difficulties may require a _____ approach.

7. The time to begin working on in-law problems is just after the couple is married. True or false?

Answers:

1. Nuclear family.

2. True. In-law problems often make it difficult to achieve marital harmony.

3. Primary.

4. A family in which other relatives share a residence with the husband, wife, and their children.

5. False. In-law problems seem to be worse at the beginning of the marriage and to improve over the years.

6. Multiple.

7. False. This problem should be considered before the marriage.

Money In Marriage

Money management is one of the most frequent sources of marital conflict. A 1967 study by Landis and Landis observed three groups: 581 happily married couples, 155 couples receiving counseling, and 164 divorced individuals. All three groups listed finances as either the first or second cause of marital problems. For other couples, money management is a challenge that can be met. Whether it will be a source of friction depends on who earns the money and the amount of income, the personalities and experience of the partners, how much they know about finances, what stage of development the family is in, and how the money is managed.

Traditionally the husband was the primary breadwinner. But in recent years the wife's salary has become more significant. This is most often true during the early family stage when the wife works before the children are born, and in the later period when the children are school age or older. Today many women are working, and some belong to the work force for 25 or more years. The high rising divorce rate has made the woman the primary breadwinner in many families.

The backgrounds of the spouses are significant in terms of spending patterns. A spouse from a poor, struggling family may feel insecure about money and be inclined to save and be frugal. One from a more affluent family may have a freer attitude toward monetary investments.

The parents' spending pattern is a model that children may follow even as adults. The couple's maturity may also affect wise spending. Couples should consider whether to buy impulsively or to save for long-range priorities. They should try to avoid using money as a weapon, a method of retaliation, or a means of control or power. Spouses from different backgrounds will set different priorities and have varying attitudes. Such differences should be explored and discussed as the couple prepares to marry or sets up initial living arrangements.

A family may go through several distinct financial stages. In the first stage, both partners may be working. There are several major purchases they must make to begin housekeeping—a bed, table and chairs, and a sofa. They begin to set priorities for other purchases. The young couple is pressured by the mass media to "need" certain items and to achieve a certain status by "keeping up with the Joneses." In our society, we are taught to consume products with a built-in obsolescence. Often special "come-ons" are directed toward the newlyweds.

The second stage can be quite difficult. The couple may begin to have children and be trying to purchase a home. Perhaps the wife has stopped working to care for the children. The husband's earnings may not have increased significantly, since he may be still early in his career. This factor may be changing, since more educated women often have children at a later, more stable point in their careers.

As the children complete elementary school, more women return to work for their own satisfaction and bcause the expense of raising children increases as they grow older. The family may extend their credit buying beyond their ability to pay, because of the increasing costs of clothes and appliances.

The next stage, when there are college-age children, may be the most expensive. Fortunately, it usually comes at a time when the husband is reaching his maximum earning potential. During this stage, most wives are working. A spouse may work at a second job to pay a specific large expense, such as the children's college education. It is often difficult to give up this additional income once the expense is covered, but extra time to spend with the family may be more rewarding than the money.

The next stage occurs after the children have left home. This is a stage of relative financial security. Expenses connected with the children are diminished or completely gone, and other major expenses, such as the house mortgage, are completed. During this period the couple can begin to save for retirement.

The final stage occurs after retirement. The couple is usually eligible for Social Security, the Medicare program, or some private retirement plan. Planning is crucial, since an unfortunate number of elderly people live below the poverty level of income. Social Security is not enough because of the high rate of inflation and increased medical needs. Some form of financial assistance may be needed from children or other family members.

How the money is managed is just as crucial as the stage of family development. There are five major systems that families use to allocate money. In the first two, one person manages the finances. In traditional families this person is often the father. There can be a "dole" system in which money is allocated to family members a little at a time. This system can easily cause resentment, and can lead to manipulation or deceit if both spouses have not agreed to the arrangement. A second method provides for a family treasurer. Personal allowances are planned, but the "treasurer" pays the bills.

Other methods allow shared responsibility

A. Monthly Income

    Source   Amount

                    Total: _____

B. Monthly Fixed Expenses

    Item   Amount

                    Total: _____

Total Monthly Income (A)   _____

Total Monthly Fixed Expenses (B) _____

C. Difference (A minus B):   _____

D. Monthly Discretionary Expenses

    Item   Amount

                    Total: _____

A sample budget sheet. Fixed expenses should include rent, utilities, insurance, loan payments, and any other amounts you are committed to pay. Item (C) is the amount available for other (discretionary) users, such as savings, new clothing, or entertainment.

for finances, and these methods become more prevalent as women increase their earning power. Studies show that as women become professional and exert control outside the family, they also exert more control within the family. In some families, expenses are divided. The husband pays for certain expenses such as cars and insurance, and the wife pays for such things as food and clothing.

When both the husband and the wife work, the fourth system provides for a joint account where either spouse can pay expenses. For this arrangement to succeed, both spouses must be responsible and the income must exceed the expenses. The system often does not provide for emergency expenses, such as those connected with serious illness, which may create an avoidable financial crisis.

A fifth method, budgeting or planned spending, seems to suit the majority of middle-class families. A **budget** is a plan for spending, not just a way to accrue savings. Joint decisions are made about major expenses, and excess amounts are saved or spent by mutual consent.

One advisory spending guide for families in the $10,000 to $15,000 income range suggests that about 27 percent of income goes for housing. The second largest expense, food, absorbs 22 percent. Transportation and clothing are 16 percent and 12 percent of the income respectively. The remainder is divided among medical care, recreation, education, and savings.

Couples must set their own priorities for spending. They can receive budgeting assistance from some banks or from adult education courses that deal with household financing.

Before you go on . . .

1. During the _____ and _____ periods of marriage, many wives work outside the home.

2. The stage _____ offers many couples their greatest financial security.

3. Unless mutual solutions are worked out, the way our parents handled finances can largely shape our own approaches. True or false?

4. Because of inflation, Social Security alone is usually _____.

5. The financial level of the family is pretty well fixed by how well it begins. True or false?

6. Couples can benefit from agreeing on their _____.

7. Managing money does not have much effect on family functioning. True or false?

Answers:

1. Initial; later. They usually do not when the children are young.

2. After children leave home.

3. True. Parents are a model for later spending habits.

4. Insufficient to support the elderly.

5. False. Family income frequently goes through several stages, and can vary in each.

6. Priorities.

7. False. Money management is the first or second most common source of disagreement between spouses.

Financing the Future

The safest way to finance expenditures is with cash or savings. But many couples use one of the three basic types of credit. **Open credit** requires payment at the end of the billing period without extra charges; it builds up a credit rating at no extra cost. **Profit-making credit** involves finance charges, but promises the borrower a financial return, such as tools or an educational loan. **Non-profit-making credit** also carries finance charges, but without any economic return.

There are many sources of financial credit. In a credit-installment plan the consumer and dealer legally agree to delay payment. This includes interest charges, service charges, insurance coverage for the amount, and the cost of the item. But there are pitfalls to credit-installment purchasing. The dealer may repossess the item, if payment isn't made as agreed. He may then sell the item, and if this doesn't cover his expenses, the customer will have to pay the difference. If the customer refuses to do so, the dealer may legally attach his wages. If the contract provides for add-ons, all items bought by the customer may be added on to the first contract, with finance charges applicable to the sum of debts outstanding, and repossession applicable to all items bought under that contract. The **holder in due course** clause provides for the contract to be sold to a finance company. The finance company is under no obligation to guarantee the item sold, but can repossess it if payment is not made. This affects many poor people who receive low-quality merchandise. The **balloon payment** clause provides for a very large final payment.

Pawnbrokers provide a quick but expensive source of money. The interest rates can be as high as 50 percent a year, and the borrower doesn't receive the item's full value.

A **small-loan company** may charge an interest as high as 36 percent or more, per year, but it will also take greater risks than other sources. The greatest pitfall of the loan company is "flipping" one loan on top of the other for the same borrower, and then charging interest for the total sum of all loans.

A bank credit card cash-advance service, such as BankAmericard, furnishes fast but costly service. The annual interest rate for the service can range between 12 percent and 24 percent. But a bank checkway credit, instant credit, or balance plus can be as fast as a credit card service, and the annual interest rate is usually 18 percent.

A **revolving charge account** usually charges 18 percent annual interest. But shoddy business practices have given it a bad reputation, and such accounts should only be opened at a reputable store.

A **second mortgage,** in which the borrower uses his home as collateral, gives the borrower the use of the money for a period of three to ten years at an annual interest rate of 12 to 14 percent.

Personal loans from commercial banks are useful when buying a car, boat, furniture, or even a piano. Their interest rates, ranging between 11.5 and 13.5 percent a year, are lower than for installment credit.

An excellent way to borrow for purchasing non-profit-making items is to use a savings account, life insurance policy, or investments such as bonds or stocks as collateral. In this way the interest charges are offset by the interest received from the collateral.

Credit unions provide an excellent and practical source of credit, but only for those eligible as members. The interest rate is usually between 10 and 12 percent a year. No collateral is needed up to a certain union-fixed amount for any personal loan.

Refinancing, or "opening up the end of a mortgage," provides an inexpensive and excellent source of money. An individual becomes eligible only after paying off a large part of his home mortgage. The interest rate of refinancing is usually between 7.5 to 9 per cent per year.

The decision to rent or buy a home is a difficult one, and involves considering the alternatives. Renting a furnished room pays when the couple has no furniture and no way of buying it for the moment. But since the rent includes use of the furniture, it is much higher than for an unfurnished room of the same quality. In renting an unfurnished apartment, it is not economically feasible to pay a rent higher than the weekly income of the couple.

In buying a home, the total housing payment (including taxes, insurance, and upkeep of the home) should not exceed one-fourth the monthly income of the family head. It is advisable not to buy a house that costs more than two and one-half times the annual income of the family head, unless the couple can make a very large down payment. The couple buying a house should appraise the soundness of its structure, the room arrangement, capacity for expansion, and its possible future value. Social and transportation considerations must also be agreed on.

Should we buy a new car or a used car? A new car's value decreases 25 to 30 percent the first year, 18 percent the second year, 14 percent the third, and 11 percent the fourth year. It has no value after ten years. A new car's repair costs begin rising after the fifth year. The point at which a not-so-rich consumer can get a well-functioning car at a consumer-saving price is after two years of use. The buyer can then drive it for three more years, before its repair costs begin rising.

Term life insurance pays the face value of the policy in the event of death anytime between signing of the contract and the expiration of the **term** (usually 5 years). The policy can be renewed after each term, at a higher premium corresponding to the insured's higher death risk. At age 65, the policy is paid up, cancelled, and not renewed. Term insurance is practical, fair, and offers maximum protection for the money.

There are many types of **insurance plus investment**, but they are all basically the same. A higher premium is paid for the face value of the policy plus a savings investment. It does not have to be renewed, and the premiums are constant. But the cash value of the policy cannot be touched unless one cancels the life insurance, and the interest gained annually is only 2.5 percent (less than a savings account). Money can be borrowed against the policy's cash value, but this depletes the value of the policy.

A good **home insurance** policy should cover two basics: property damage due to fire, flood, and vandalism; and liability insurance for anyone that gets hurt while in the house. The best insurance covers these basics for a reasonable maximum value. **Car insurance**—collision, comprehensive, or liability—should cover a reasonable minimum of the following basics: bodily injury liability; property damage liability; and insurance against uninsured drivers. According to experts, a reasonable minimum of these basics would be in the neighborhood of $100,000 for one injured person involved; $300,000 if more than one person is involved; and $50,000 coverage for property damage.

A couple should not rely on Social Security benefits or a retirement pension as their sole source of income during their later years. These provide only a supplementary income. The best plan of action for couples interested in their future financial safety and security includes the following points:

They should have a practical life insurance policy.

They should save and invest regularly during their working years.

They should be aware of the possibilities and the balance of safety, yield, and growth of a potential investment of savings plan. If the yield is less than the rate of inflation, there is no growth.

Many United States citizens who fill out their own income tax forms pay more taxes than they should. This happens either because they use the short form (which allows for only 13 per cent deductions) or because they are unaware of savings opportunities. If a couple are interested in learning more about their income tax rights, a $1 manual entitled *Your Federal Income Tax* can be ordered from the U.S. Superintendent of Documents, Washington D.C., 20402, or they can refer to Lasser's annual *Income Tax Guide*.

It may be worth the money!

Before you go on . . .

1. What is profit-making credit?
2. In a _____ plan, customer and dealer make a legal agreement to delay payment.
3. A small-loan company will not take as many risks as a commercial bank. True or false?
4. _____ are an excellent source of credit for eligible members.
5. The best time to purchase a used car is when it is _____ years old.
6. Insurance plus investment policies provide the maximum amount of protection for the money. True or false?
7. Couples can make the most effective preparation for retirement by

_____, _____, and
_____.

Answers:

1. Credit that promises the borrower a financial return.
2. Credit-installment.
3. False. The small-loan company will usually take more risks.
4. Credit unions.
5. Two.
6. False. Term insurance is more economical.
7. Saving; investing; purchasing a good life insurance policy.

ADJUSTING TO MARRIAGE *Chapter Review*

1. All of the following may be mechanisms of withdrawal, with the exception of (a) sleeping; (b) fantasizing; (c) fear of illness; (d) yelling.

2. The honeymoon is a good time for the bride and groom to (a) visit relatives; (b) get in some educational travel; (c) expect perfection of themselves and each other; (d) relax together.

3. Jealousy is often related to a poor self-image. True or false?

4. Many people no longer feel that marriage is a lifelong commitment. True or False?

5. The people most often featured in in-law jokes are (a) cousins; (b) men; (c) women; (d) children.

6. Marriage serves all of the following purposes except (a) preservation of moral standards; (b) protection of property rights; (c) providing a sure source of economic security; (d) determining the legitimacy of children.

7. The maximum legal interest per year on a revolving charge account is (a) 3 percent; (b) 6 percent; (c) 9 percent; (d) 18 percent.

8. A budget is a plan for _____ as well as a means for saving money.

9. Credit unions usually charge 18 percent annual interest. True or false?

10. The stage in a family's life which offers the most financial security is frequently the stage (a) after retirement; (b) just before retirement; (c) when the children are young; (d) before the children are born.

11. The wife who is angry at her husband but yells at the children is using a defense mechanism called (a) projection; (b) denial; (c) displacement; (d) withdrawal.

12. Dr. Alfred Adler referred to the individual's characteristic ways of perceiving, thinking, and behaving as one's

_____.

13. The average middle-class family can expect the percentage of the family income spent on housing to be about (a) 20 percent; (b) 30 percent; (c) 40 percent; (d) 50 percent.

14. People who are always happy are psychologically healthier than people who sometimes get upset. True or false?

15. A person's style of life is generally formed at an early age but usually changes once or twice. True or false?

16. Traditional families often either use the dole system or have a family _____ to allocate their money.

17. In terms of their income, many elderly persons live below the _____ level.

18. Research seems to indicate that married couples usually have more in-law problems in the earlier years of their marriage than they do in later years. True or false?

19. While the most common normative pattern in the United States is the _____ family, where only a couple and their children live together, some Americans live in _____ families, in which they share their living quarters with grandparents, aunts and uncles, or cousins.

20. Projection, denial, displacement, and withdrawal are all ways of expressing _____.

21. The mature person is not focused only on self but also has

_____.

22. All of the following are usually required when one marries except (a) a medical examination; (b) a marriage license; (c) two witnesses; (d) the exchange of rings.

23. It is always best to purchase a new car instead of a used one. True or false?

24. Churches stress the religious aspect of marriage, but divorce is based on the _____ marriage contract.

25. It is best to have a house that one is considering buying appraised by an inspector to determine the condition of the building before purchasing it. True or false?

26. In the past, when most families lived on farms, large families were more typical since children were needed as
_____ helpers.

27. Children today are being raised with greater awareness of the potential equality of the sexes. True or false?

28. What purposes does a honeymoon serve?

29. What factors have helped married women today enter or remain in the labor market?

30. What are the potential sources of conflict that are built into most marriages?

To find the answers, look at page 191.

GENERAL REVIEW *Chapters One through Three*

1. What functions does dating fill for young people in our society?

2. Husbands of the white race are more likely to accept their wives' taking on a career and a more active role in the family than are black husbands. True or false?

3. What are the four ways to end a marriage?

4. Every individual must fill certain _____, when he or she must act in certain expected ways.

5. Another name for women's liberation is _____.

6. People who live in a (a) nuclear; (b) extended; (c) companionate; (d) conjugal family carry on most of their interpersonal relating within the family circle.

7. Marriage is both a social _____ and a dynamic _____ between persons.

8. Although there has been some relaxation in Catholic policy toward interfaith marriages, the Catholic partner in an interfaith marriage must still promise to raise the children as Catholics. True or false?

9. In West Africa, the place where most Afro-Americans originate, the family structures are stable, strong, and supportive of personal development. True or false?

10. Orthodox rabbis are unwilling to perform interfaith marriages. True or false?

11. For housing, families in the $10,000 to $15,000 income bracket can expect to spend what percentage of their income? (a) About 20 percent; (b) About 30 percent; (c) About 40 percent; (d) About 15 percent.

12. The characteristic ways a family think, perceive, and behave may be called the _____.

13. Most of the women who work are single. True or false?

14. Why do defense mechanisms make marital adjustment more difficult?

15. What is the most important purpose of the wedding ceremony?

16. What happens to sex when conflict arises in a marriage?

17. The highest legal interest rate on a revolving charge account is (a) 9 percent; (b) 18 percent; (c) 6 percent; (d) 2 percent.

18. What are the six "Cs" that provide a firm basis for a marriage relationship?

19. Traditional families are likely to use one of two systems for allocating their money: _____ or _____.

20. People who are loud, aggressive, and bullying usually have strong and positive self-images. True or false?

21. List and describe briefly the stages of dating.

22. Why are teaching, nursing, and social work referred to as semi-professions for women?

23. How may a husband and wife need to redefine their sexual objectives after marriage?

24. Research has shown that many elopements and secret weddings end in failure. What are some of the reasons for this?

25. Why do most couples have more in-law problems in the earlier years of marriage but fewer in later years?

To find the answers, look at page 193.

CHAPTER FOUR

REPRODUCTION

Leading thoughts:

- ■ Women and men are basically the same in anatomy. Even the sex organs are very much alike in structure

- ■ Conception—starting the development of a new life—brings about many changes in the mother's body. These make it possible to carry out early tests for pregnancy

- ■ During the nine months of pregnancy the fertilized egg develops by stages into a functioning infant

- ■ During this time the couple should take special care for the mother's health and nutrition, to avoid damage to the baby and the mother

- ■ For many women, childbirth can be a deeply rewarding experience

Male Sexual Anatomy 18

Females and males differ most obviously in their sexual organs or genitals. Both sexes can use their sexual parts to obtain pleasure, and genital contact serves as the ordinary way for starting the development of a baby. Since sexuality plays an important part in a marital relationship, a solid understanding of the appearance and workings of both the female and male sexual organs can increase satisfaction for both partners.

In both sexes some of the sexual organs are visible externally, and some are concealed within the body. In the male the two external parts—the **penis** and the **scrotum**—can be seen hanging below the abdomen and between the legs. The penis, shaped like a tube, enables the male to eliminate urine, semen, and to enter the female body through the vagina in sexual intercourse. The penis has two main sections: the **glans** or rounded tip and the **shaft**. The glans is covered by the foreskin at birth. The process of circumcision removes the foreskin;

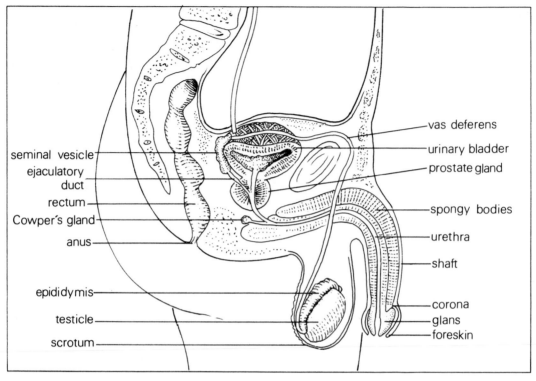

Male sexual anatomy

this prevents the accumulation of smegma, an odorous cheesy substance secreted by glands in the penis. Circumcision probably does not reduce sexual pleasure during intercourse, and may even increase it. The shaft is the portion of the penis, about three-quarters of its length, that extends between the glans and the rest of the body. Between the glans and shaft runs a lengthwise ridge known as the **corona**. The corona and glans are extremely sensitive to touch, and hence to sexual stimulation and pleasure; the shaft is less sensitive.

The **urethra** runs the length of the penis and ends in an opening at the tip. Through this channel flow both urine and the fluids secreted during sexual arousal. The penis is composed of spongelike tissue surrounding several large cavities. Most of the time these cavities are empty and the penis remains limp and soft. But during sexual excitement, the cavities fill with blood, so that the penis swells and stiffens, becomes erect, and extends outward from the body. At the same time, a muscle valve prevents urine from entering the urethra until after the erection has subsided.

Behind the penis hangs the scrotum. The scrotum contains two **testicles**, one slightly larger than the other. The testicles produce sperm or **spermatozoa**, the male reproductive cells that can unite with female reproductive cells to start the development of a baby. Each testicle contains several hundred winding and tightly coiled **seminiferous tubules** that manufacture the spermatozoa. Each tubule, if uncoiled, would be about one to two feet long, and placed end to end they would stretch for about half a mile. Once produced, the spermatozoa mature in the **epididymus,** a chamber in the back and upper part of the testicle. The spermatozoa need a steady temperature, and too much heat can destroy them. In fact, this is why it is necessary for the scrotum to hang below the abdominal region as it does. The normal temperature inside the body is too high for the spermatozoa, but the smaller, more exposed scrotum is cooler. The scrotum offers additional protection by changing size in response to changing temperatures; in a hot atmosphere it lengthens, removing the spermatozoa further from body heat, and it draws closer to the body's warmth in the cold. Even with this protection, the spermatozoa live for only thirty to sixty days and then die, so new ones are constantly being made. In addition to spermatozoa the testicles also produce testosterone, the male hormone that triggers the development of masculine body build, a deep voice, and increased body hair.

The epididymus is connected to the **vas deferens,** a tube about eighteen inches long that goes up into the abdomen and eventually leads to the urethra. The vas deferens provides a passageway for spermatozoa. Before the spermatozoa leave the body (are ejaculated), they are mixed with other fluids from the **prostate gland** and the **seminal vesicles.** These fluids give the spermatozoa some protection against acids and other dangers in their environment as they travel through the urethra and on into the body of the woman. Sometimes when the penis is erect, a few drops of fluid may seep out even before ejaculation; this clear fluid, which serves as a lubricant, comes from two other glands, located at the base of the penis. It may contain a small number of spermatozoa.

To summarize what we know about spermatozoa: they are the male reproductive cells, produced in the seminiferous tubules and maturing in the epididymus of the testicles. When ejaculation is about to take place, they travel through the two vasa deferentia. They are mixed with fluids from the prostate gland and the seminal vesicles to form **semen**. The semen then enters the urethra and is expelled from the tip of the penis. Semen looks milky white, and its consistency ranges from thick and gelatinous to thin and watery. A teaspoonful of semen contains from 200 to 500 million spermatozoa.

Since life as we know it needs water, spermatozoa can survive only in a liquid environment. Within the body they are immersed in fluid. If semen is ejaculated into the open air, the spermatozoa die quickly. The penis acts as a protecting link between the male body and the moist receptivity of the female body. Once in the female body spermatozoa may live from three to five days.

Before you go on . . .

1. The male external genital organs are the _penis_ and _scrotum_.

2. The two main parts of the penis are the _urethra shaft_ and the _glans_.

3. Circumcision reduces sexual pleasure during intercourse. True or false?

4. What is the function of the urethra? _provides for urine flow & sperm flow_

5. Too much heat destroys spermatozoa. True or false?

6. Prior to ejaculation, spermatozoa are mixed with fluids from the _prostate gland_ and the _seminal vesicles_

7. Semen and spermatozoa are the same thing. True or false?

Answers:

1. Penis and scrotum
2. Glans and the shaft.
3. False. It may even increase pleasurable sensations.
4. It serves as a duct for the passage of both urine and spermatozoa.
5. True. The testicles are slightly cooler than the rest of the body.
6. Prostate gland and the seminal vesicles.
7. False. Semen is a combination of fluids, which contain the sperm cells.

Female Sexual Anatomy

Parts of both the external and internal female anatomy serve sexual and reproductive functions. The external female genital area is known as the **vulva**. The most visible part of the vulva is the **mons pubis,** a slight mound of fatty tissue that in the mature woman is generally covered with pubic hair. Behind the mons pubis are two large vertical folds of skin, the **labia majora** (larger lips), which overlap the remaining organs. The labia are a "homologue" of the scrotum in the male. That is, although they look different in the mature organism, they originally grew out of the same tissue in the developing baby. Inside and parallel to the labia majora run the **labia minora** (smaller lips), which are thin, pink, hairless folds of skin.

At the top of the labia minora lies the **clitoris,** the homologue of the male penis. The clitoris is loaded with nerve endings and probably constitutes the only organ in the human body devoted exclusively to pleasure. Ordinarily the clitoris is hidden by the top part of the labia minora. During sexual arousal it fills with blood, becoming erect and extremely sensitive to stimulation.

The **urethra** of the female is not connected to the sexual organs, as in the male; it serves only for the transport of urine. Instead, the woman's body has a passageway called the **vagina,** which opens between the labia minora. The vagina is composed of thin, elastic, muscular walls, which encircle the penis during sexual intercourse and stretch greatly during the birth process to allow the baby to pass through. When the female is sexually aroused, the vagina becomes lubricated with mucous secretions, making it easier for the penis to enter.

Most females are born with a piece of tissue called the **hymen** partially closing the vaginal opening. Normally the hymen is broken at the time of first sexual intercourse. Thus it used to be thought that a broken hymen was a sign that a woman was no longer a virgin. Actually, the hymen varies so much in size, structure, and thickness that this is a very unreliable sign. In some women the hymen can remain unbroken after intercourse or even after childbirth; in others it is so delicate that it is broken long before sexual intercourse occurs. For most women the breaking of the hymen will

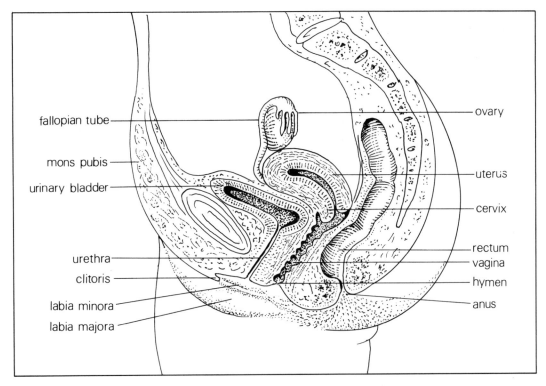

fallopian tube

mons pubis

urinary bladder

urethra

clitoris

labia minora

labia majora

ovary

uterus

cervix

rectum

vagina

hymen

anus

Female sexual anatomy

cause some slight bleeding. This provided the basis for the practice, in various traditional cultures, of showing a bloodstained cloth on the morning after the wedding as a demonstration of the bride's virginity. If a medical examination reveals that the hymen will not break easily, the woman may have it stretched or surgically cut, if she so desires.

The vagina leads from the vulva to the **cervix** or entrance of the **uterus** or womb. The uterus is normally quite small—about the size and shape of a pear—and expands to become the place where a baby develops during the nine months of pregnancy. From each side of the top of the uterus a **fallopian tube** runs about four inches to the **ovaries.** There are two ovaries, each the size of a large almond, located deep within the abdomen, somewhat below and on each side of the navel. The ovaries produce the female reproductive cells.

Females are born with all the reproductive cells, about 50,000, they will ever have. These are still immature, and are contained in tiny **follicles** in the ovaries. From the time the female reaches sexual maturity, a follicle ripens about once every twenty-eight days. The ripened follicle then bursts, releasing a newly matured **ovum,** an egg that can be fertilized by a sperm. The newly released ovum is caught by the finger-like projections of the upper end of a fallopian tube. It then travels down the fallopian tube toward the uterus. If sperm are present, it is during this journey that they are most likely to meet and fertilize the ovum. If the ovum does not encounter a sperm, it continues on to the uterus, where it dies after about 48 hours.

If a baby is to grow from a tiny fertilized ovum, it needs a safe and nurturing place to develop until it can survive on its own in the external world. This is the role of the uterus. Each month, as the follicle ripens, it produces the hormone **estrogen,** which stimulates growth of the uterine lining—a thick mesh of tissue saturated with small blood vessels. As soon as the matured ovum is released, the empty follicle begins to produce another hormone, **progesterone,** which further stimulates growth of the uterine lining. If the ovum is fertilized, it implants itself in the lining, where it is nourished and protected. If the ovum is not fertilized, progesterone production stops, and the uterine lining begins to disintegrate. The disintegrated tissue, which is mostly blood, drains out through the vagina as the monthly menstruation. In the meantime, a new follicle begins to mature and the cycle prepares to repeat itself.

The menstrual flow usually lasts about four days, but its length and the amount of the discharge may vary from woman to woman. Some women experience various discomforts during menstruation (abdominal cramps, headaches, fatigue, and nausea). Some of these complaints may have a definite physical cause, and a physician may be able to give some assistance. But there seems to be an important emotional element as well, for women who are satisfied with being female and who feel generally fulfilled in life tend to experience fewer menstrual discomforts. As with many other situations, what a woman has learned to expect will affect her menstrual experiences. If she has been taught to anticipate an uncomfortable and uncontrollable experience, this may produce tension which will actually bring about greater discomfort.

Many women also report mood swings during the menstrual cycle. Two researchers, Ivey and Bardwick, studied these fluctuations. They found that women tend to feel relatively confident—satisfied, hopeful of success, able to cope—during the middle of the cycle. This is the time when estrogen tends to be plentiful. Just before menstruation some irritability, tension, and depression seem common, and this is when the estrogen level is at a low point. However, these mood swings are not usually extreme, and a woman who is aware that they have a physiological cause can usually learn to deal with them without undue distress or guilt.

Ivey and Bardwick discovered that hormone levels appear to change the tone but not the nature of the woman's experiences. For example, if a student were to learn that she had done well on one examination and poorly on a

second, she would probably feel glad about the one and sorry about the other no matter when she received her grades. But during the middle of the cycle, when her estrogen level would be high, she would probably be more elated by the good grade than upset by the bad one. Just before the menstrual period, when the estrogen level would be low, disappointment over the bad grade would probably loom a good deal larger in her mind. Men may go through similar cycles of hormonal and mood changes, and research is being done on this topic, but clear indications such as menstruation are not available to guide the search.

In addition to its effects on menstruation and mood, estrogen is responsible for the development of the female's secondary sexual characteristics—enlarged breasts, widened hips, pubic and underarm hair. Most of these characteristics do not serve a direct function in reproduction, but in many cultures they are associated with sexual attraction. The female breasts, for instance, are sensitive to sexual stimulation, and may be stimulated in lovemaking (though in a few cultures the woman's brother may fondle her breasts, and it is taboo for the husband to do so!). During sexual arousal the breasts become fuller and more sensitive, especially the nipples. And the breasts, of course, provide the milk which, under natural conditions, is the entire nourishment of the newborn.

Before you go on . . .

1. ___Vulva___ is the term applied to the female external genital area.

2. The labia minora are inside and parallel to the labia majora. (True) or false?

3. The ___clitoris___ is the female counterpart to the male penis.

4. The passageway that opens between the labia minora is called the ___vagina___.

5. In the past, a broken hymen was thought to be proof that a woman was not a virgin. (True) or false?

6. A woman's primary sex organs are the ovaries. (True) or false?

7. What is the function of the uterus? *a place for the baby to stay*

Answers:

1. Vulva. This is the outermost area of the genitals.

2. True.

3. Clitoris. This is the only human organ that serves exclusively for pleasure.

4. Vagina.

5. True. This is now known to be false.

6. True. They produce the egg cells, or ova.

7. It provides a safe place for the fertilized egg to develop.

Conception and Tests for Pregnancy

20

A new human life begins when two sex cells—a sperm and an ovum, or egg cell—join together. The transfer of sperm from the male to the female normally occurs by inserting the penis into the vagina during sexual intercourse. The stimulation of intercourse causes the penis to contract rhythmically and to squirt semen into the upper part of the vagina, near the cervix of the uterus. The sperms—about 100 million of them—use their **flagella,** or tails, to propel themselves along the moist surface of the cervix and uterus up to the fallopian tubes. A sperm can travel about an inch in twenty minutes. Only about 100 of the sperms finally reach the fallopian tubes. Meanwhile, the egg, or ovum, is also being guided toward the tubes. If an ovum and a sperm are to meet, it is most likely to happen here, in the upper third of one of the fallopian tubes.

When the ovum first meets the sperms, it is protected by a layer of follicle cells. However, contact with the sperm cells sets off a chemical reaction that dissolves the follicle cells. A single sperm can then penetrate the wall of the egg cell. The sperm then unites with the ovum, and we then say that **conception** has taken place. After conception, the ovum wall is sealed against the entrance of any other sperms. The nucleus of the ovum and the nucleus of the sperm then join together to form the nucleus of a new cell, which is called a **zygote**. The zygote is capable of multiplying into the millions of cells necessary for the development of a new baby.

As the zygote continues to move down the fallopian tube to the uterus, it divides into two cells, then four, eight, sixteen, and so on. By the time the zygote arrives in the uterus it has multiplied into at least 200 cells. It is now called a **trophoblast.** Meanwhile, the lining of the female's uterus has become thickened by the growth of new tissue, filled with blood vessels. For a couple of days the trophoblast drifts within the uterus. Then it digests away part of the thickened uterine lining, forming a sort of nest around itself in the wall of the uterus. By about 10 to 12 days after conception, the trophoblast sends out tiny tendrils called **chorionic villi,** which draw oxygen, nourishment, and protective antibodies from the mother. At this stage the trophoblast becomes an **embryo**.

Several important structures develop at this time. The **umbilical cord,** containing two arteries and one vein, links the embryo to the mother's bloodstream. The **placenta** is a disc-shaped organ that takes up a large area of the wall of the uterus. The placenta is where the exchange of nutrients and waste products takes place between the mother and the fetus. The placenta is designed to permit the exchange of these materials without actually allowing any blood to move between the bodies of the mother and the child. The **amnion** is a sac that fills with salty, watery fluid. This **amniotic fluid** protects the embryo from temperature changes and physical injuries. Most fertilized ova embed themselves within the uterus. Sometimes, how-

ever, one will lodge in a fallopian tube. As the embryo grows, it eventually becomes so large that it ruptures the thin walls of the tube. This usually results in severe internal bleeding which can be fatal to the mother. It is necessary to terminate such **tubal** or **ectopic** pregnancies by surgically removing the embryo.

What are the earliest signs of pregnancy?

During the first two weeks, a woman has no way of knowing if she is pregnant. After that time, missing a period may suggest a possible pregnancy. This is not a reliable sign, however. A late or missed period may be caused by emotional upset, nervous shock, illness, tumor, or even aging. Also, a woman may bleed slightly, at about the time of her normal period, for a month or two.

Body temperature may be a good clue to the start of pregnancy. A woman's basal temperature normally varies by about half a degree Fahrenheit during the monthly cycle. Usually there is a drop in temperature just before ovulation and a rise shortly afterward. Thus, if a woman's temperature stays as high as 98.8 to 99.99 F for 16 days, 97 percent of the time it means she is pregnant.

Other signs may also be indicative. During pregnancy the breasts feel fuller and heavier, the nipples and the surrounding areas (the areolae) become darker, and the breasts become more sensitive to touch. Some women feel nausea and loss of appetite in the morning ("morning sickness"). Because major changes are going on inside the body, many pregnant women feel fatigue, and may find they need some extra sleep. During early pregnancy the growing uterus does not leave adequate space for the urinary bladder, and many pregnant women find they have to urinate quite often.

An accurate determination of pregnancy usually requires a laboratory test. The tests are of two basic types: those that use laboratory animals and those that employ only chemicals. All the tests are based on the fact that a particular hormone—HCG, or human chorionic gonadotropic hormone—is found in the urine of a pregnant woman. Pregnancy tests that were developed in the 1930s and 1940s examined the effects of the woman's urine when it is injected into immature animals. If HCG is present, the ovaries of a virgin female mouse or rat will ovulate within 24 to 48 hours. This is the Ascheim-Zondek (A-Z) test. The Friedman test used rabbits for the same purpose. More recently, frogs have been used, because they take only six to 18 hours to ovulate. All of the tests that use animals are time-consuming and expensive, but several chemical tests are available that cost less and work more quickly. These tests are similar to the test for blood type. Red blood cells, coated with two sets of chemical compounds, can be added to the woman's urine in a test tube. The two compounds are the

hormone (HCG) and a related substance (anti-HCG) that reacts very differently. If the red blood cells clump together, the woman probably is not pregnant. If the red blood cells settle in a characteristic ring in the tube, she probably is pregnant. This test takes about forty-five minutes. A less accurate test, also using a drop of urine, but with latex particles in the place of the red blood cells, requires only three minutes. Used together, these two tests will give an accurate prediction of pregnancy in 98 percent of the cases.

Before you go on . . .

1. When a sperm and an ovum unite, we say that
   ___Conception___ has taken place.

2. About 100 out of some 100 million sperms finally reach the fallopian tubes. True or false?

3. The sperm and the ovum join to form a new cell called a
   ___Zygote___ .

4. When a fertilized egg reaches the uterus, it has multiplied into at least 200 cells. True or false?

5. What is the trophoblast called after it has developed for several more weeks? Embryo

6. The disc-shaped organ that takes up a large area of the wall of the uterus is called the ___placenta___ .

7. Pregnancy tests that use animals are more reliable than those that use only chemicals. True or false?

Answers:

1. Conception.

2. True. They can live there for as long as five days.

3. Zygote. The zygote develops into the fetus.

4. True. It is now called a trophoblast.

5. It is called an embryo.

6. Placenta. It permits exhange of nutrients and wastes between mother and embryo.

7. False. Most chemical tests are just as accurate.

Stages of Fetal Development

The zygote passes down the fallopian tube, arrives in the uterus, and embeds itself in the uterine lining. It grows a protective sac called the amnion, which fills with fluid. At this stage of development the zygote has become an **embryo**.

By the end of four weeks the embryo, about the size of a pea, lies curled with its head and tail almost touching. The fluid-filled amnion protects it. The early embryo possesses gill pouches like those of fish and a tail-like structure, both of which trace the path of human evolution. The brain, eyes, and stomach have begun to form, but the embryo does not yet look distinguishably human. The heart beats about sixty times a minute.

During the second month, clumps of tissue that look like paddles appear where the arms and legs will grow. The gill pouches and surrounding areas change into a recognizable neck and face. The ears are taking shape. The nerves and muscles are far enough advanced so that the embryo can move, but neither mother nor doctor can detect this movement. The liver is manufacturing blood cells, and the kidneys are extracting waste products.

Sexual characteristics now become apparent. Both chromosomes (X or Y) and hormones are essential for sexual differentiation. If the embryo is to become a male, the testes will secrete male hormones. If male hormones are not produced, female sex organs will develop, even if the embryo has a Y chromosome. If an embryo with only X chromosomes receives androgens (as sometimes happens when women are given progesterone to prevent miscarriage), it will develop male sex organs. At the end of the second month the embryo is called a **fetus**. It is now about two inches long and weighs approximately half an ounce. The head makes up almost half its length. The eight-week-old fetus has reflexes. Its entire body

will move if its mouth is touched lightly.

During the third month the arms and legs lengthen and nails are growing on the fingers and toes. Teeth, vocal cords, and ears have appeared. The external sex organs can be easily differentiated. The head is still extremely large in proprotion to the remainder of the body. The fetus moves its body and limbs, but is still so tiny—about three inches and weighing approximately one ounce—that neither mother nor physican will notice the movement. During the next six months the fetus will change mostly in size, although some organs still need to reach their full development. The rudimentary nervous system continues to develop reflexes. The mouth will make sucking movements when something touches it, and the Babinski reflex is now present (stroking the sole of the foot causes the toes to fan up and outward).

By the end of the fourth month the fetal heartbeat can be heard through a stethoscope. Hearing the heartbeat of their unborn child gives prospective parents one of their first thrills. During the following month, after the fetus's muscles have become more mature, mother and father can both feel the fetal movements that are often called "kicking." By this time facial features are more distinct, and eyebrows and eyelashes are appearing.

During the fourth month the fetus doubles its length to six or eight inches and gains in weight to five or six ounces. It can now open and close its fist, move its thumb independently, and even suck its thumb. Only the specific area touched will respond to stimulation, and facial expression changes when the cheek is touched.

The four-month fetus swallows reflexively and sometimes inhales the amniotic fluid. This causes no harm, because it is receiving its oxygen supply through the umbilical cord. The fetus also draws nourishment from the mother and expels waste products through the blood

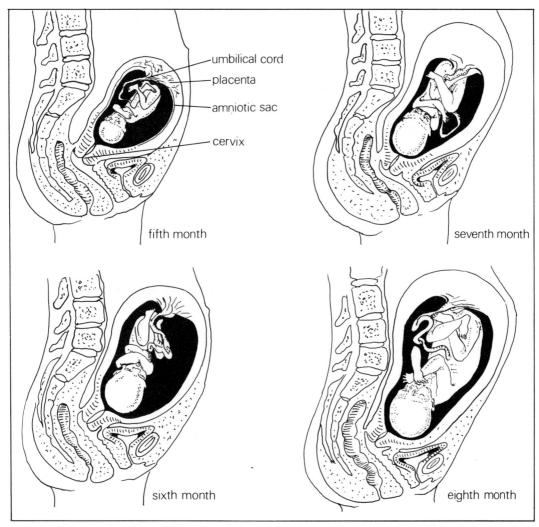

umbilical cord
placenta
amniotic sac
cervix

fifth month

seventh month

sixth month

eighth month

Four stages of fetal development. By the fifth month the fetus weighs about a pound and has all the major internal organs. In the sixth month the weight is about two pounds, and reflex behaviors can be seen. During the seventh, eighth, and ninth months the nervous system, respiratory system, and temperature-regulating mechanisms have their final development. The weight in the eighth month is 5 to 8 pounds. A child born at this time is capable of surviving on its own.

vessels in the umbilical cord. The blood vessels of baby and mother adjoin each other at the placenta. The heart is now pumping 25 quarts of blood a day. The placenta has begun to produce enough progesterone to maintain the pregnancy, so the corpus luteum withers away. Antibodies from the mother reach the fetus through the placenta. These antibodies will protect the newborn against certain diseases during the first months of life, and additional protection will be gained from the mother's milk.

By the fifth month the fetus occupies the entire uterine cavity. The expanding uterus crowds the mother's other internal organs. She needs to urinate more often, and is able to eat less food at one time. Blood cell formation in the fetal bone marrow commences. The skin is fully developed, nails are at an advanced stage, sweat glands are present, and head hair may appear. The internal organs have assumed positions comparable to those of the newborn. The fetus has periods of sleep and wakefulness, and may even hiccup. By the end of the fifth month it is ten to twelve inches long and weighs about one pound. Dead skin cells mix with a fatty secretion from glands in the skin, forming a cheesy substance that will cover and protect the skin until it is cleansed after birth.

During the sixth month the fetus opens and closes the eyelids, and moves its eyes around. The fetus may now weigh two pounds and be about fourteen inches long. Vigorous and frequent fetal movements make the mother well aware of life within her. The premature infant of six months can cry weakly and grasp an object firmly. It will retain the "grasping reflex" during its first few weeks of extrauterine life—a hold so tight that it can support its own weight up to a minute while hanging on to some object like a parent's fingers. But the six-month fetus cannot regulate its breathing and temperature, and if it is born prematurely it has little chance of survival.

During the last three months of pregnancy the brain grows at a particularly rapid rate. Though pregnancy in general requires solid nutrition, fetal brain development in particular requires proper nourishment. If the brain does not develop properly during this critical period, it will never again be able to do so. Brain development brings extended and refined control over body systems.

In the seventh month the fetus's eyes can distinguish light from dark. The testes of the male descend from the abdomen into the scrotum at some time between now and birth. At this time the fetus has proportions much like those of the average newborn. By the end of this month it may weigh three pounds and measure sixteen inches. The fetus may now be able to survive outside the womb under proper conditions if precautions are taken against infection. If premature birth occurs, overcautiousness about infection can lead to social deprivation. Premature infants prosper, as all babies do, from cuddling, talking, crooning, and rocking. Move-

ment, such as the fetus experiences in the uterus, is so important to the premature baby that some hospitals now have incubators that rock continuously. Since a fetus has a chance of surviving outside the womb after the sixth month, the courts in the United States consider it "viable" after this time, and abortions are restricted to cases endangering the mother's life.

By the eighth month most of the organs are functioning. Since the fetus gains up to about eight ounces a week, the mother must adjust her posture to compensate for her abdominal burden. The characteristic stance of an expectant mother, with a very straight back, inspired Shakespeare to call it "the pride of pregnancy." The fetus acquires most of its antibodies from the mother during the last couple of months. It can now perform many of the activities that it will perform as a newborn. Some liquid passes through the digestive tract, and the fetus urinates a little each day. It continues to move, though late in pregnancy it is usually too cramped to turn completely around. But it can really wallop the mother's abdominal walls with feet, head, and elbows—the pregnant woman may imagine that her abdomen has become a miniature football field. The fetus is nearly ready to be born, and most mothers are more than eager to relieve themselves of a cumbersome weight and to meet the new member of the family.

Before you go on . . .

1. After the amnion forms the zygote is known as a(n)
   Embryo .

2. Sexual characteristics of the fetus develop from the fourth month on.
   True or false?

3. Under what circumstances can an XX fetus develop male sex organs?
   [handwritten: If mother was given drugs to prevent miscarriage (androgens)]

4. During the last months of pregnancy the fetus changes mostly in
   size .

5. The fetal heart begins to beat during the fourth month. True or false?

6. The unborn child is considered viable after the
   _6th_ month.

7. _Nutrition_ is essential for proper fetal brain development.

Answers:

1. Embryo.

2. False. Sexual characteristics begin development during the second month.

3. If the mother has received androgens during pregnancy to prevent miscarriage.

4. Size.

5. False. It begins beating at about four weeks, but cannot be heard through a stethoscope until the fourth month.

6. Sixth.

7. Good nutrition.

Prenatal Influences and Nutrition

22

The fetus depends on its mother for survival and nourishment. Small amounts of blood may pass between them through the placenta. This may cause a problem involving Rh incompatibility.

In most people the blood contains a substance called the **Rh factor**. Those with the factor are Rh-positive; those without, Rh-nega-

tive. If some blood from an Rh-positive fetus mixes with the blood of an Rh-negative mother, the mother will produce antibodies against the Rh factor. In later pregnancies, these antibodies can attack the blood of an Rh-positive fetus. The mother may miscarry, or the newborn may have severe jaundice. The development of antibodies in the mother may be prevented through treatment prior to pregnancy. Tests can now determine whether antibodies are present in the mother's blood. Babies born with jaundice are given total transfusions of new blood. A similar, but not as serious, condition may result from blood-type incompatibility (among the ABO group) between mother and baby.

Toxemia is the build-up of waste products in the pregnant woman's body. Swelling and puffiness caused by retention of excess fluids can signal the beginning of toxemia, which may produce convulsions and severe damage to both mother and fetus. Extra rest and elimination of salt from the diet overcomes most cases of toxemia.

Some bacteria, viruses, and chemicals can pass through the placenta from mother to fetus. **Rubella,** or German measles, is one of the most common viral infections. If the mother catches it during the first three months of pregnancy, the baby will probably be born with defects such as deafness, heart disease, cataracts, and damage to the central nervous system resulting in mental retardation. Young girls should either be exposed to rubella or receive the new vaccine against the disease. Since the vaccine contains a live virus, it is not safe for pregnant women or those about to conceive.

The viruses and bacteria that cause mumps, measles, polio, typhoid, influenza, and diptheria can also harm or kill the fetus. If untreated before the eighteenth week, syphilis may cause miscarriage, death shortly after birth, deformity or mental retardation. Diabetes in the mother frequently induces miscarriage or stillbirth. Physicians recommend that an expectant mother take no unprescribed medicine. The thousands of babies born in 1961 with deformed arms and legs, hearts, blood vessels, digestive tracts, and ears after their mothers had taken the tranquilizer Thalidomide serve as an urgent warning that pregnant women should never take drugs not thoroughly tested for side effects.

The fetuses of heroine or morphine addicts become addicted also. They undergo withdrawal symptoms of fever, tremors, and convulsions right after birth. They often have low birth weights—possibly due to malnutrition—

and are more likely to be miscarried or die at birth. Methadone also will produce addiction in the fetus. Even drugs taken some time before conception may have effects on fetal growth.

Nicotine can pass through the placenta and accelerate the fetal heartbeat. Most research shows that smoking leads to a greater rate of prematurity and lower fetal weight, which may endanger the health of the child. Small amounts of alcohol do not seem to affect the fetus adversely. But excessive drinking depresses the fetus and makes it less responsive after birth.

Listening to Beethoven or riding horseback will not automatically make the child a lover of classical music or an equestrian. But a mother's moods may affect her unborn child, because her emotional state alters the level of various hormones that reach the fetus through the placenta. Many emotions are accompanied by biochemical charges, such as the familiar fear–adrenalin sequence. Some of the chemical components penetrate the placenta and affect the fetus, but the degree and types of effects are not fully understood yet. Excessive radiation can harm the parents' genes before conception or harm the fetus during pregnancy. So X-rays should be taken only when absolutely necessary.

Every pregnant woman must have adequate nutrition, to protect her health and allow the fetus to develop to its fullest potential. Good nutrition greatly lowers the chance of miscarriage or prematurity, and results in a healthier baby. Proper nutrition is also essential for nursing. An adequately-nourished mother will have more stamina and will produce healthier children. When a man is well nourished he produces healthier spermatozoa.

Good nutrition is determined more by the quality than the quantity of food. Foods are interdependent. Eating one nourishing food may not help as fully as possible unless we eat a second food. For example, we need protein. But unless we also have some fat with it, especially the unsaturated types, a good deal of the protein will be used to produce immediate energy rather than to build up our body tissues.

We need four types of nutrients: carbohydrates, such as grains, breads, fruits, vegetable cereals, and legumes; proteins, including meat, fish, eggs, milk, whole grains, nuts, and vegetable proteins; vitamins, which are present in most foods; and fats. We can normally obtain the nutrients we need by daily eating several selections from each of the four food groups: grains and cereals; meat, fish, and eggs; milk and dairy products; and fruits and vegetables.

Since protein is the basic building material of cells, the pregnant woman should consume from 75 to 90 grams of protein daily, to ensure that her child develops to its fullest capacity. Here are some examples of the protein content in various foods: 1 quart whole milk = 33 grams; 1 serving meat, fish or fowl = 12-24 grams; ½ cup wheat germ = 13 grams; 1 cup navy or lima beans = 6-8 grams; ½ cup cooked soybeans = 22 grams; and ¼ cup yeast = 20 grams. The vitamins A, C, D, E, and K and all those in the B group are essential. Fresh fruits and vegetables are the best source of vitamins, but some types of commercial processing may remove vital nourishment. Whole grains contain the B vitamins and vitamin E, but the refining and bleaching process used to manufacture white flour destroys these vitamins. Thus whole grain breads are more nourishing than white bread. Excessive artificial supplements of vitamins A, D, and K can cause harm to mother and fetus.

Our bodies require a balance of trace minerals such as magnesium, copper, zinc, and iron. Only natural iron prevents anemia. Artificial iron salts destroy vitamin E which in turn can cause anemia to develop.

During pregnancy an expectant mother may gain 25 to 30 pounds. Some years ago this much gain was discouraged. But research now indicates that weight gained by proper nutrition tends to lead to healthier babies, improved brain development, and a better preparation for nursing. A weight gain of 28½ pounds would be distributed like this: infant (7½); placenta (1½); amniotic fluid (2); enlarged uterus (2); increase in blood volume (4); increase in breast tissue (½); normal increase in body fluids (3); and fat stored for nursing (8). Most of this is lost shortly after delivery.

We have already noted that solid nutrition is essential not only for the baby's general health, but for the development of its brain and intelligence. Pregnancy, with its focus on good nutrition, can be a time when couples learn about good nutrition and actually prepare themselves to live healthier lives as they age. Frequently, magazines in the obstetrician's office have interesting and informative articles on nutrition.

Before you go on . . .

1. How is a newborn with Rh jaundice treated? transfusions

2. Toxemia _____ is caused by the buildup of waste products in the pregnant woman's body.

3. Pregnant women should always be vaccinated against rubella. True or false?

4. Women with ~~a~~ diabetes often have miscarriages or stillbirths.

5. Addiction _____ are frequent in children born to heroin-addicted mothers (withdrawal)

6. The pregnant woman should gain as little weight as possible. True or false?

7. The four types of nutrients are _Proteins_____ ,
   _Carbo_____ , and _Fats_____ .

Answers:

1. The infant's blood is entirely replaced by a transfusion of new blood.

2. Toxemia.

3. False. The rubella vaccine is made from live virus, and can damage the fetus as badly as the disease itself.

4. Diabetes.

5. Withdrawal symptoms.

6. False. Weight gained through proper nutrition promotes improved brain development and produces healthier babies.

7. Proteins; carbohydrates; fats; vitamins.

Childbirth and Nursing

Childbirth is the natural process in which a fetus leaves the mother's body. The mother can take an active part in the process. Contractions of her uterus expand the cervix so the fetus can exit, and force the baby down through the vagina. The mother's discomfort can be lessened if she works with her body rather than against it. Relaxing the rest of her body during each contraction results in less discomfort, while tensing adds to her distress. Childbirth involves hard work—labor—but the woman who understands what is happening and actively cooperates with the birth process will have less fear and may experience an easier delivery.

Labor occurs in four stages. During the first stage, **effacement,** uterine contractions cause the muscles of the cervix to become thinner, so that the baby can pass through to the birth canal (the vagina). The first contractions are very mild; they may begin almost unnoticed several days before delivery. A contraction feels like a hardening and tightening of the abdominal muscles, followed by a period of relaxation. These early contractions last from 30 to 60 seconds. They are separated by intervals of five to twenty minutes or even longer.

During the second stage, **dilation,** the cervix opens to about 7 centimeters. The contractions become stronger, but it is possible for the mother to control them by relaxing and working with, rather than against, these preparations for delivery. Contractions during this stage last about 60 seconds and come about every one to three minutes.

The third stage, **transition,** is the most difficult but also the shortest. The cervix opens to a full 10 centimeters. The contractions are extremely strong, lasting from 60 to 90 seconds with only a minute in between. This stage usually lasts no more than a half hour.

In the fourth and final stage, **expulsion,** contractions last about a minute and occur every one to three minutes. This stage may last from 30 minutes to two hours. As the baby's head descends into the birth canal, the mother feels an intense urge to bear down with her abdominal muscles and push it out. Most babies emerge head first. The baby rotates so that first one shoulder pops out and then the other. The rest of the body follows easily. The doctor immediately uses an aspirator to suck mucus from the baby's mouth, so that it can breathe easier. Once the infant begins to breathe, the doctor ties off and cuts the umbilical cord a couple of inches from the abdomen. Continued contractions expel the placenta, after which the doctor examines the woman to ensure that it has all come out and to detect any possible irregularities.

Even if a woman prefers to be put to sleep during delivery of her child, she must still carry the child during the last months and be conscious through the first couple of stages of labor. Knowledge, exercise, and good nutrition make childbirth easier. Medication during labor may affect both mother and fetus. Babies born to heavily-anesthetized mothers may remain drowsy for a couple of days after delivery. However, an anesthetic may be medically indicated. But the less medication the mother takes, the more alert her baby will be and the better she can participate in the delivery process.

Exercise during pregnancy keeps the mother's body in good shape and makes childbirth easier. Many women can continue any type exercise they are used to, such as tennis or swimming, although it may be wise to discontinue very vigorous sports. The weight of the growing fetus puts an extra strain on the back and abdominal muscles. A number of specific exercises are designed to strengthen these muscles. Many helpful exercises are described in *Preparation for Childbirth,* by Donna and Roger Ewy.

The pregnant woman can practice contracting part of her body while relaxing the other parts. This works best if she has a partner to check whether the uncontracted parts are really relaxed and limp. The baby's father is the most natural partner. An increasing number of couples are making the whole childbirth process

a partnership. The father helps conceive the child and takes part in raising it, so helping in the birth process brings him closer to both the child and his wife. Being together during childbirth allows the couple to share a deeply rewarding experience. When they have been trained to work together with a medical team, the wife derives a great deal of assurance from an encouraging and comforting husband.

The expectant mother can use several breathing techniques to make labor less uncomfortable. The different stages of delivery call for different responses. Effacement may pass practically unnoticed. During dilation deep, rhythmic breaths will keep her attention focused on breathing and relaxing rather than on becoming tense. When she feels the urge to push, she can take shallow breaths and pant to prevent the diaphragm from forcing the baby's head against the pubic bone. During the expulsion phase, pushing helps. She can take a deep breath, exhale part of it, and then push. These methods of breathing work more effectively, especially in the later stages, when the husband is present to coach and encourage his wife.

Emergency situations, such as giving birth in a taxicab, occasionally happen. But most expectant mothers can plan the type of delivery they want in advance. Some husbands do not want to participate in the childbirth process. Some wives and doctors object to the father's presence. A woman should consider her feelings about being with her husband during labor and delivery, about medication, about nursing, and about having her baby in the same room with her or in a general nursery. On this basis she can choose an obstetrician and a hospital that will accomodate her viewpoint. If a couple choose to work together or if a woman wants to become better informed, training classes are available through local maternity groups. The "natural childbirth" approach of Grantley Dick-Read concentrates solely on having a positive attitude. The Lamaze method advocates the use of breathing and relaxing techniques. An informed and prepared woman will be able to work in any circumstances as a team member with her husband, her doctor, and the nurses.

Many women fear childbirth, but it can be a positive and controllable experience. An expectant mother can prepare for this challenge. A positive attitude coupled with training can lessen and control, but not completely eliminate, the discomfort. Some medication and surgical intervention may be necessary, but minimizing its use adds to the well-being of both mother and child. The active, confident, and knowledgeable woman can give birth in a dignified and fulfilling way. Sharing this unique and beautiful experience with her husband promotes both their mutual closeness and a fuller appreciation of life.

During pregnancy the mother's breasts fill with **colostrum.** This is a liquid very rich in antibodies against disease, and at least five times richer than milk in vitamins A and E. Within a few days after birth, the breasts begin to secrete milk that is more nutritious and better suited for most babies than cows' milk or formula. The baby's nursing stimulates milk production. Successful nursing does not depend on breast size, but on small milk-producing glands. The baby does not suck the milk out, but squeezes it out by pressing down on the areola around the nipple. At first the mother's breasts may feel sore, the milk may not flow easily, or it may flow too heavily. Nursing goes best in a relaxed, leisurely atmosphere. Gradually mother and baby adapt to each other. Breastfed babies have fewer allergies and are generally healthier. Because breastfeeding has been unpopular in recent decades, many women are uninformed about the process. Groups of experienced nursing mothers belonging to the La Leche League exist in many cities. The League can be located through the telephone directory or through La Leche League International, 9616 Minneapolis Ave., Franklin Park, Illinois, 60131. A mother who does not want to nurse will be given synthetic estrogen to stop milk production. However, nursing provides the baby with emotional warmth as well as high-quality nutrition.

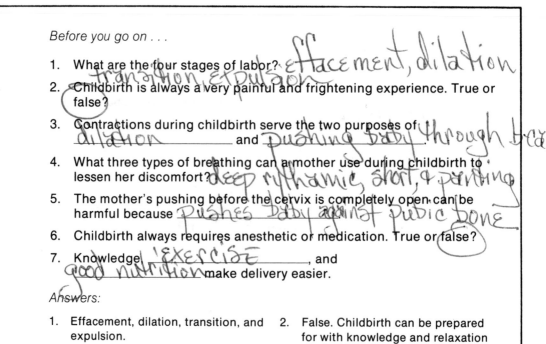

Before you go on . . .

1. What are the four stages of labor? effacement, dilation transition, expulsion

2. Childbirth is always a very painful and frightening experience. True or false?

3. Contractions during childbirth serve the two purposes of dilation _____ and pushing baby through birth canal _____.

4. What three types of breathing can a mother use during childbirth to lessen her discomfort? deep rythamic, short, & panting

5. The mother's pushing before the cervix is completely open can be harmful because pushes baby against pubic bone

6. Childbirth always requires anesthetic or medication. True or false?

7. Knowledge, exercise _____, and good nutrition make delivery easier.

Answers:

1. Effacement, dilation, transition, and expulsion.

2. False. Childbirth can be prepared for with knowledge and relaxation techniques.

3. Opening the cervix; forcing the baby through the birth canal.

4. Deep rhythmic breathing, short breaths, and panting.

5. It forces the baby's head against the mother's pubic bone.

6. False. Some mothers can do without them, especially when they are prepared for the experience of childbirth.

7. Exercise; good nutrition.

REPRODUCTION *Chapter Review*

1. The embryo is surrounded by the _____ that cushions it against injury. (a) chorionic villi; (b) amniotic fluid; (c) body stalk; (d) gills.

2. The male's _scrotum_ contains two testicles that produce spermatozoa.

3. A teaspoonful of semen contains about 23,000 sperm. True or false?

4. For a fetus to become a male, its testes must secrete male hormones during the _____ month of pregnancy. (a) second; (b) fourth; (c) sixth; (d) eighth.

5. Spermatozoa are hardy and cope well with extreme temperatures. True or false?

6. Just as the penis is very sensitive to touch, so the female's clitoris brings her the most sexual pleasure. True or false?

7. During sexual excitement the vagina becomes _lubricated_ to allow the penis to penetrate more easily.

8. Spermatozoa mix with fluids from the prostate gland and seminal vesicles to form (a) epididymus; (b) smegma; (c) glans; (d) semen.

9. Sexual intercourse occurs when the male _____ enters the female _____. (a) testicle; vagina; (b) penis; vagina; (c) epididymus; uterus; (d) penis; clitoris.

10. Identical twins resemble each other closely because _they're both in one egg_

11. If a woman's temperature remains as high as 98.8 to 99.9 F for 16 days after ovulation, she is pregnant in _____ percent of cases. (a) 23; (b) 86; (c) 97; (d) 45.

12. The fetal heartbeat can be heard through a stethoscope during the ____4th_____ month of pregnancy.

13. The vagina is connected to the uterus by the _____.
    (a) cervix; (b) labia minora; (c) clitoris; (d) fallopian tube.

14. Women vary greatly in their moods, depending on whether or not they are menstruating. True or false?

15. "Morning sickness" is less common among women who want to be pregnant and are well nourished. True or false?

16. Premature babies can suffer from ____social_____ deprivation if they are not related to warmly.

17. The rapid growth of the brain during the ___last 3_____ months of pregnancy requires good nutrition.

18. Childbirth is invariably a frightening experience. True or false?

19. Women who are satisfied with life and content with being female often experience less discomfort during menstruation. True or false?

20. _____ enables the fetus and baby to take full advantage of genetic potential. (a) Chromosome; (b) Rubella; (c) Nutrition; (d) Bilirubin.

21. The four types of nutrients a healthy body needs are ___fats, carbo, proteins, vitamins_____

22. The fetus displays reflexes such as sucking and grasping objects. True or false?

23. During a _____ period, development must take place or it never will. (a) developmental; (b) maturational; (c) menstrual; (d) critical.

24. The fetus becomes viable, or able to survive outside the womb, around the _____7th_____ month.

25. Most research shows that nicotine from smoking leads to a greater rate of prematurity. True or false?

26. For the first few days after delivery a woman's breasts secrete _____ a liquid that is rich in nutrients and antibodies. (a) villiosum; (b) colostrum; (c) ductine; (d) bilirubin.

27. Chemical tests on a woman's _blood_ and _urine_ can generally determine whether she is pregnant.

28. What are the advantages of nursing a baby? *nutrition, less emotional allergies*

29. Discuss pregnancy and childbirth as a partnership between the parents.

30. How does a baby develop? *sperm fertilez egg*

To find the answers, look at page 195

CHAPTER FIVE

SEXUALITY

Leading thoughts:

- ■ Our expectations about sex have a great influence on the success of our sexual activities

- ■ Sexual partners should each make an effort to learn what kinds of sexual stimulation please the other

- ■ The physical reactions during sexual arousal and intercourse are divided into four well-defined stages: excitement, plateau, orgasm, and resolution

- ■ Growth within a sexual partnership requires time, understanding, and effort on the part of both members

- ■ The most common form of male sexual dysfunction is premature ejaculation

- ■ Nearly all women suffering from orgasmic dysfunction can be taught how to achieve orgasm

Expectations about Sex 　24

Our experiences are affected by our expectations. This principle is as true for our sexual experiences as for any others. Sexuality involves our physical selves, our emotions, and our ideas. Sex has a meaning of more importance than most other physical processes. Sexual activity fits into the context of the person's ongoing life, it is not merely an isolated event. It provides both a way of individual expression and a way to express an orientation towards others.

At some point during the preschool years,

the child becomes aware of the differences between females and males, in a way peculiar to each child. Children notice that females and males behave somewhat differently. Glimpses of parents partially or totally unclothed, or the child's bathing with other children, demonstrate that some physical differences exist.

The child is no more naturally intrigued with sex than with any other part of life. But children are curious and they pick up the emotions that adults communicate. If parents acknowledge a child's perceptions and comments about sex, answer questions clearly and without deception, and are affectionate with both the child and each other, the growing child will accept sexuality as a positive and untroubled aspect of life. Most of us can remember when our curiosity first prompted us to find out about sex differences with the neighborhood kids. We probably had the impression that it was rather special, that adults might not approve, and that there was some fascinating sensation about exploring the genital areas. At that age we did not comprehend exactly why females and males differ. But we were nevertheless building up our impressions and feelings about sexuality.

Unfortunately, some parents punish their children for touching their genital areas. This is a normal part of a small child's discovering new parts of his body, much as hands and feet were discovered earlier. Some parents show no affection within the family, refuse to discuss sexuality, or regard all sex as dirty or immoral. Each family has its own style of demonstrating affection and of dealing with sex. Family attitudes toward sex range along a continuum from open, expressive, and acceptant to repressive and regarding sexual activity as unmentionable and immoral. Children pick up and build upon these sentiments that their parents communicate about sex directly or indirectly. As they grow older, a growing sense of modesty prompts them to regard their sexual parts as private.

Adolescence extends our self-image. Bodily changes promote more pronounced awareness of ourselves as sexual beings. There are some obvious changes during adolescence. Boys get erections easily and sometimes find their bedclothes moist after a "wet dream" —the ejaculation of semen during sleep. Girls develop breasts and begin to menstruate. Many members of both sexes notice that the genital areas respond pleasurably to touch in masturbation. Peer group pressure among adolescents pushes toward conformity to its norms, whatever they may be. "Kissing is O.K. for dates, but petting is for steadies," "Do it, you'll like it," "Save yourself for marriage," "Prove yourself," or "Heavy petting is permissible only during engagement." The media, too, present us with images of what liberation supposedly means, how to be a "real" woman or "real" man, and how a lady or a gentleman should act.

No single one of these factors—family background, physical changes, peer pressure, or the media—defines exactly how each individual responds as a sexual being. We all want some privacy. Sexuality seems like a special part of ourselves—a part on which we stake a good part of our self-image, self-respect, dignity, and reputation. Nobody wants to be simply a mechanical reflection of societal expectations.

Sex involves our private selves, but at the same time it is fundamentally oriented towards another person. How do we bridge this gap? Understanding and affection can change disgust to desire, repugnance to revelation, and lust to love. A sense of commitment to another person with whom we can share trust, mutual support, and reciprocated closeness changes the sexual aspects of a relationship. Activities that are considered wrong, prohibited, obnoxious, or immoral in other circumstances now seem appropriate, sanctioned, right, and meaningful.

Some people say that they can engage in sex, without any commitment to the other person, and without guilt. Most people, however, choose to express themselves sexually only in an ongoing relationship or in marriage. The attentive and considerate lover demonstrates caring and giving of self to another person. Traditionally, males were expected to be interested in sex, to initiate sexual activity whenever they could, and to assure themselves of gaining pleasure. Ideal females were taught to protect themselves against male advances, that it is not ladylike to be interested in sex nor to be assertive or initiate sexual activity, and to draw the line when the male went too far. Research shows that both sexes are capable of sexual interest, arousal, enjoyment, and fulfillment. But these more positive aspects of sexuality can flourish only in an atmosphere that the couple choose as appropriate and meaningful.

Moving from unawareness about or uninvolvement in sex to a sexual relationship requires a psychological reorientation for both individuals involved. Prior to sexual involvement, unawareness, religious or ethical restraints, or personal inhibitions may have held the individual back. Change will not occur at the snap of a finger. Even if we suddenly decide to become sexually involved, we must learn how to obtain maximum gratification with our particular partner.

Sex is a way of relating. In a sexual relationship we first want security in knowing that we are appreciated. Second, we want to cooperate with another person. Finally, we wish to obtain genital satisfaction. Time is needed to develop all three aspects. During this time we learn through discovery, exploration, and pleasuring. In our initial sexual encounters we discover our sexual reactions and feelings. Knowledge of basic sexual anatomy, and willingness to try and learn, are necessary for a positive experience. Mutual exploration of each other's bodies at a pace and under circum-

stances both partners consider comfortable leads to satisfaction. A sexual relationship can be defined by the extent and intensity of exploration. With mutual exploration, the couple interested in a satisfying sex life learn to give and receive pleasure. Pleasuring one's partner brings the special enjoyment of giving satisfaction to another very special person.

Inability to give and receive pleasure in an intimate, caring way is the major cause of sexual frustration, dissatisfaction, and dysfunction. Even if an individual has had prior sexual experience, discovery, exploration, and learning to pleasure are necessary in relation to the particular person one is involved with. Tastes and preferences vary with individuals. Different relationships can bring out unknown aspects of ourselves. Learning about sex will seem strange at first—it can be either exhilarating or frightening. Sometimes we may feel unsure, anxious, or a bit guilty about our early sexual experiences as we become more intimate in touching, kissing, hugging, and unclothing. But understanding, appreciation, concern, and commitment make us yearn to know our partner in many ways, including the sexual dimension. For those who have learned to cooperate, communicate, and copulate together, sex may bring a great deal of pleasure at the same time it enriches a relationship.

Before you go on . . . *exploring the body*

1. What are the main steps in learning to build a sexual relationship?

2. Time is necessary to build a sexual relationship. True or false?

3. In a sexual relationship, we seek _security_, _cooperation_, and _satisfaction_.

4. The ability to _give pleasure_ leads to sexual satisfaction, and its lack prevents sexual fulfillment.

5. Sex is more meaningful and fulfilling within a relationship of trust, cooperation, and commitment. True or false?

6. During adolescence the individual's ___body___ and ___self-image___ are changed by sexual development.

7. A person with prior sexual experience really has nothing to learn and can jump right into a new sexual relationship. True or false?

Answers:

1. Discovery of sexual reactions; bodily exploration; learning to pleasure.

2. True.

3. Interpersonal security, interpersonal cooperation, genital satisfaction

4. Give and receive pleasure.

5. True. Most people find sex more satisfying this way.

6. Anatomy; self-image.

7. False. Each person varies in sexual responsiveness and expectation; each couple needs time to discover the best way to achieve pleasure together.

Sexual Stimulation 25

In popular terms "having sex" means "engaging in penile–vaginal intercourse." Actually "sex" encompasses a broader range of physical contact. Sexual intercourse usually occurs within an ongoing, meaningful relationship. It involves some lovemaking in addition to the actual act of intercourse. We can become sexually aroused in ways that do not lead to intercourse. And a full sex life makes use of various means of stimulation even when we intend to engage in sexual intercourse.

The fascinating thing about sexuality is that sexual arousal occurs spontaneously and naturally in both sexes. But what we learn about sex has a great influence on how our sexual processes function. When we discuss sexuality, we must take into consideration both the spontaneous and learned aspects of sex. Sexual

arousal—erection of the penis in the male, and erection of the female clitoris and nipples accompanied by lubrication of the vagina—will occur automatically with emotional and tactile stimulation if no other factors interfere. However, some factors can impede spontaneous sexual arousal. A person may consider sexual contact in general, or in a particular instance, immoral, sinful, dirty, wrong, distasteful, or unappealing. In such cases the person will probably not enjoy the sexual contact. He or she may be indifferent to it, repelled by it, or simply unable to function in the customary physical manner. Inhibiting attitudes toward sexuality may have arisen from stern religious instruction, from socialization by parents who regarded sex as wrong, harmful, or frustrating, or from personal shyness, reluctance, ignorance, or fear. And some women may connect menstrual discomfort with sex, and never realize the pleasure available through sexuality.

People who are inhibited about sexual contact will not appreciate sexual stimulation, and they will resist discovering it. Being inhibited is not the same as being unaware. The person who is generally unaware of sexual stimulation because of lack of an appropriate opportunity, and the person who is sexually active but does not know all the intricacies of sexuality, can learn how to be a more enjoyable sexual partner. Statistics about who is doing what are not that helpful. Sex remains an activity of individuals with values, feelings, expectations, and experiences. In fact, norms and peers can sometimes pressure people into doing what they find objectionable. But knowledge about the range of sexual possibilities can be of great help. The sexual partners can choose what they consider appropriate for themselves at this particular time, while leaving the door open for exploring other alternatives, if they wish, at a later time.

During lovemaking partners may find all parts of each other's bodies interesting. Each can find enjoyment in touches, caresses with the hands and tongue, and kisses all over the body. Certain parts of the body are especially sensitive and responsive to touching and caressing. The penis is the male's main organ for pleasure. A man can have either a "cerebral" or a "reflex" erection. In a cerebral erection, erotic thoughts cause blood to engorge his penis. The reflex erection occurs in response to touch. The penis's homologue in the female is the clitoris, the only human organ devoted exclusively to pleasure. Popular opinion used to consider the vagina more sensitive than the clitoris, and to regard it as more suitable for stimulation than the clitoris. Actually, only the outer third of the vagina has much sensitivity. The clitoris is much more sensitive, and should be stimulated along with the vagina. A man who really cares for a woman will see that she receives stimulation in all areas of the body that will please her. Both females and males have the same nerves and blood supply systems to the penis and vaginal-clitoral areas. The sensations arising from touch and the congestion of blood in these tissues give both partners a delightful experience. The

perineum, an area of skin midway between the vagina and anus in the female and at the back of the scrotum in the male, responds pleasurably to touch. The nipples of both sexes produce pleasurable sensations from stroking. The female breasts and clitoris can become irritated if contact is too rough or grating, but moistening these areas makes the touch smoother and more pleasurable. The anus also has a number of nerve endings that respond with pleasure to touch.

Many people first discover by **masturbation** the pleasure that can come from the genital areas. In masturbating, the individual touches his or her own genital areas until pleasure is obtained, usually in the form of orgasm. A number of people continue to masturbate when married, especially if the spouse withholds sex, is not sexually satisfying, or is unable to engage in sexual relations. During masturbation the individual often experiences a variety of erotic fantasies.

Genital areas and female breasts are our most intimate and private body parts. They can give us the most pleasure, but they are not the first portions of our bodies that we normally share with others. The ears, back of the neck, and thighs also show more sensitivity to caressing than do some other parts of our bodies. Actually, any part of our bodies can be stimulated by stroking. Giving close attention to several parts of the body pleasures one's partner in several ways and leads nicely to the climax of intercourse.

Touching the partner intimately on the breasts, thighs, and genital areas is called **petting**. Many couples who are serious but have not progressed to sexual intercourse, or those who intend to postpone sexual relations until after the wedding, engage in petting. Petting activity—intimate hugging and caresses accompanied by kissing—does not cease when the couple engages in sexual intercourse, but makes a stimulating prelude that is known as **foreplay**.

Young males feel an especial urgency about obtaining sexual release. Many think at first that the quicker they ejaculate the better. The female can become sexually aroused almost as quickly as the male (he can attain a full erection in three seconds, and her vaginal walls can become moist within 10–20 seconds). But most females take a longer time to build up to the point where they are ready to enjoy intercourse. Females experience pleasurable sensations that increase and decrease gradually. Male excitement, however, can peak quickly and fall off immediately after ejaculation. Females prefer to engage in foreplay—kissing, hugging, and caressing—and often do not desire an immediate concentration on the genital area. Men should learn to prolong their own enjoyment in foreplay and to derive emotional and interpersonal satisfaction from pleasuring their partners. For a couple to enjoy sex together, the male must learn to prolong his erection until his partner reaches the climax of her excitement, and to pay attention to her even after he ejaculates. People who enjoy sex engage in it not out of duty, or obligation, or because of a right, but to please themselves and each other.

Most couples do not begin immediately engaging in sexual intercourse. But interest in each other and feelings of sexual attraction often lead them to express affection by hand holding, light kissing, and hugging. The next stage often involves touching the chest, breasts, and thighs. Touching the lower abdomen and genital areas signals a further degree of intimacy. Undressing or allowing oneself to be undressed shows greater trust and vulnerability. Engaging in sexual intercourse represents the greatest intimacy and sexual sharing possible.

Serious or full sexual involvement usually requires time for trust and commitment to develop. Most partners enjoy sexual stimulation more within a relationship that promises security, commitment, and permanence. Research shows that the social–emotional context is almost necessary for the woman to gain full sexual satisfaction, and that a man can derive greater satisfaction from sex within an ongoing harmonious relationship. Most women take from one month to a year of marriage to experience the full sexual satisfaction of orgasm, so time with a respected and caring partner is essential for mutual pleasure. Especially with those who have not participated in serious lovemaking, expecting the best on the wedding night is setting too high a standard that may be disappointed. Sexuality usually matures, ripens, and blooms later, in an ongoing growth of togetherness.

Before you go on . . .

1. The most sexually sensitive parts of the body are the
   Penis of the male and the
   Vagina and _clitoris_ of the
   female.

2. Statistics about sexual activities are helpful guidelines for the average couple. True or false?

3. Since males can gain sexual satisfaction _quicker_
   while females gain it _gradually_, the male should learn
   to pace his activity.

4. The nipples of the female only are sexually sensitive to touch. True or false?

5. Our sexual functioning is affected by both the _emotional_ and the _physical_ aspects
   of sex.

6. Both men and women tend to find the _Emotional_ aspect of sex, as well as the physical, essential to complete satisfaction.

7. Sexual inhibition and unawareness are very difficult to overcome. True or false?

Answers:

1. Penis; clitoris; vagina.

2. False. These statistics do not take into consideration the social, emotional, and sexual attitudes of the individual.

3. Quickly; gradually.

4. False. The nipples of both sexes are sexually sensitive and can become erect during sexual arousal.

5. Learned; automatic.

6. Social–emotional.

7. False. In a secure and loving atmosphere with a caring partner the individual can quickly overcome either of these problems.

Sexual Intercourse

26

Until just over a decade ago, no scientifically-based information on sexual functioning was generally available. In 1966 Dr. William Masters and Virginia Johnson published their first book on human sexuality. Their research has been thorough in its exploration of how sexual responses occur and why they sometimes fail.

Masters and Johnson have observed more similarities than differences in female and male sexual responses. Both sexes pass through four distinguishable stages in their sexual response cycles: excitement, plateau, orgasm, and resolution. In both sexes, sexual arousal is evidenced by vasocongestion or retention of blood in the genital tissues, and by increased muscle tension.

During **excitement** in the female, blood gathering in the tissues of the vagina causes it to become moist or lubricated. Blood rushing into the labia and the clitoris faster than it can leave expands these tissues. The skin flushes, and the breasts swell. The vagina enlarges and stretches as it becomes ready for penetration, giving a feeling of muscle tension.

During the **plateau** phase, the outer third of the vagina becomes especially congested with blood. The clitoris becomes erect and rises above the folds of skin which usually cover it. The uterus retains blood, increases in size, and lifts slightly within the abdominal cavity. Blood floods the genital tissues, forcing the vagina to become increasingly lubricated. The fully aroused woman feels that she has reached her maximum capacity for excitement.

During **orgasm,** the tissues can stand no further inflow of blood. The muscles, especially those of the vagina and the uterus, contract forcefully and rhythmically to push the excess blood back into the veins. These contractions give an intensely pleasurable feeling of peace and release. Many women are capable of having several orgasms in succession.

During **resolution** the body returns to its non-aroused condition. Blood drains out of the engorged tissues, and muscle tension relaxes. If the woman does not achieve an orgasm, her tissues will gradually regain their unstimulated state, but sexual tension may persist. Unresolved sexual tension occuring too often can be very frustrating to a woman.

In the excitement phase in the male, blood rushes into the penis faster than it can leave. The penis becomes stiff and erect rather than hanging loosely as it normally does. The testicles rise up somewhat in the scrotum. The skin flushes, and the man may feel warm and perspire a bit.

During the plateau phase blood is contained within the genital areas to the maximum extent possible. Some fluid, particularly from the Cowper's glands at the base of the penis, may leak out. This fluid may contain a few spermatozoa. As this stage ends the man feels a pleasurable sensation indicating that orgasm is inevitable and cannot be stopped.

The orgasmic phase occurs in two stages, at least for younger males. First, rhythmic contractions of the prostate gland give the man the pleasurable feeling of the inevitablity of orgasm; this lasts for 2–4 seconds. During the second stage there are pounding contractions in the penis and groin. Semen containing spermatozoa produced in the testicles and fluids from the prostate gland and seminal vesicles is ejaculated from the penis through the urethra. During sexual intercourse the contractions of the vagina gently massage, squeeze, and stroke the penis. Penile contractions during orgasm stimulate the vaginal lips and clitoris, and force semen up into the vagina near the cervix.

During the resolution phase, blood drains out of the genital area, and the muscles lose their tension. A man experiences total and refreshing relaxation. The penis will remain semi-erect from blood congestion. Before the male can have another orgasm, he passes through a **refractory** period. Though these reactions change somewhat with age, the couple who enjoy good health, maintain interest in each other, and engage in intercourse, can enjoy sex at least into their seventies.

Some of the description in this section may sound rather technical and dispassionate. Lovers will not notice all these specific changes during lovemaking, nor do they have to know all of these facts. In fact, they would be distracting in the form presented here. Concentrating on pleasuring one's partner and enjoying the sensations in one's own body bring the most delightful sexual sensations. But these physical processes must go on for sexual pleasures to occur, and these processes will just happen naturally, if we allow them to.

We have focused on what happens to us during lovemaking. Yet we are not passive. People *make love.* Thus our discussion is tied to the previous one on sexual stimulation. We actively participate in relating to our partners, so that the natural, spontaneous sexual reactions will happen to us. Kissing, hugging, stroking, caressing, and licking provide the stimulation that arouses us during the excitement and plateau phases. Tender words, erotic thoughts, and an atmosphere considered appropriate by both partners add to the stimulation. Manipulation of the clitoris and vaginal containment of the penis finally set off the automatic responses of orgasm.

Concentration on the physical facts of sex and means of sexual stimulation can leave the impression that successful sex requires a mastery of technique. Yet satisfying lovemaking does not result only from techniques. It requires an artistic approach. The art called for here concerns the interpersonal relationship between the sexual partners. As with all art, tastes and preferences vary. Sexual partners need sensitivity to what pleasures the partner. They must also have awareness of their own sexual reactions, the capacity to communicate about a mutually satisfying sexual pattern, and the generosity to give themselves in order to please each other. Technique can improve the art of relating. For example, a woman may conclude intercourse without orgasm, and consequently miss full sexual satisfaction, because she has not received clitoral stimulation. The couple can learn about clitoral stimulation, talk together about what pleasures her, and use these techniques to enhance their sexual relationship.

Some conditions make full sexual satisfaction more likely. Looking forward to sexual relations with someone we enjoy being with can add to our delight. Promises or hints, often in the couple's own private language, can fill the imagination with pleasurable emotions and thoughts. Meaningful signals can add atmosphere to lovemaking. Cleanliness, too, makes each partner more attractive. Regular bathing will remove hygenic objections to contact with all areas of the body.

A person may feel physically stimulated and decide to make love with a beloved. Or,   .

emotional closeness may lead to the physical closeness of sex. Some women feel opposed to intercourse during their menstrual periods. Orthodox Jews are forbidden sexual contact at this time. Other women may object to intercourse because menstruation reminds them of the discomfort of childbirth. However, there is no intrinsic medical objection to intercourse at this time. In fact, the congestion of the genital tissues stimulates some women physically towards sexual release. Some women report their strongest sexual urges just before menstruation and others just afterwards. Orgasm can give some relief from the pressure of tissue congestion. When the partner is gentle during penetration, intercourse can be fun during menstruation too. The essential factor is that the couple should have an open, accepting attitude about sex, now as at other times.

Before you go on . . .

1. What are the four phases of sexual stimulation? *EXCITEMENT, plateau, orgasim & resolution*

2. The two signs of sexual excitement are _*Muscle tension*_ and *rushing of blood*

3. The male has a delay period after orgasm, whereas a female can have multiple successive orgasms. (True) or false?

4. At the end of the plateau phase, the sexually stimulated person feels that *Orgasm* _____ is inevitable.

5. Male and female sexual stimulation and responses are more different than similar. True or (false?)

6. An *erection* _____ in the male and a *lubricated vagina* in the female serve as psychological-physical invitations to the partner for sexual intercourse.

7. Describe the physical events that make up orgasm. *rythmatic contractions*

Answers:

1. Excitement, plateau, orgasm, resolution.

2. Vasocongestion; muscular tension.

3. True. This is called the refractory period.

4. Orgasm.

5. False. Masters and Johnson's research has shown that male and female sexual responses are more similar than different.

6. Erect penis; lubricated vagina.

7. The muscles of the genital area contract forcefully and rhythmically to push blood out of the tissues of the engorged genitals, giving pleasurable sensations.

Growth in Sexuality 27

Sex is a partnership, and partnership is a process that requires learning and growth together. Sexual satisfaction can and does increase when the partners work together to share themselves totally as persons and as sexual beings. An individual can know all the anatomical facts and stimulating sexual techniques and still not find satisfaction. Gratifying sex occurs within a meaningful relationship. Once the partners have a solid relationship, as persons who feel emotionally and intellectually fulfilled with each other, the physical aspect of sex can mature.

Growth as sexual partners will not happen in one night, nor even in a couple of weeks. Partners need time to become accustomed to bodily exploration, undressing, lovemaking, and copulating. They may start during engagement, or may prefer to save serious lovemaking until after marriage. Unless the couple enjoy privacy, authentic closeness, total willingness, and freedom from moral or pregnancy fears, premarital intercourse cannot really serve as a test of sexual compatibility. Within a deeply-felt, caring relationship in which each partner is patient and understanding with the other, sexuality can and will develop at a pace appropriate for each couple.

In general, females and males differ in their expectations about sex. But we must also remember that sexuality involves personal experience for each individual. Statistics and popular norms may indicate what a lot of people are doing. Still, each person will learn about sexuality and choose to be sexually active or to refrain from sexual involvement in his or her own way and at his or her own pace. Individuals of either sex may be outgoing and adventurous, or shy and reserved about sex. Men become more noticeably aroused by erotic stimuli. Imagining closeness or lovemaking with a woman, looking at pictures of women, or watching or making physical contact with a woman can cause blood to rush into the man's penis, giving him an erection and a sexy feeling. Such activities can make the woman's vagina moist and rouse her interest. But many women do not notice the vaginal lubrication and profess not to have as automatic an interest in sexual stimulation. Women usually report that they become sexually stimulated more readily within a social–emotional relationship in which they feel respected and appreciated as persons.

Younger men become quickly stimulated and can perform sexual activity with greater frequency than older men. But mature women experience more sexual awareness and greater satisfaction with sex than do younger women. However, sexuality involves more than just physical performance. It also expresses a dimension of a relationship. Sexuality can be a battleground between the sexes, a demonstration of inadequacies in both partners, or an expression of pleasure, enjoyment, and satisfaction found in fulfilling togetherness.

Games between people—giving sex as a reward for acceptable behavior, withholding sex as punishment for faults committed, using sex as a bribe, competing for orgasms—prove less than totally satisfying. Interest in the other person, enchantment, and wanting to share a good feeling through sex in a straightforward and honest relationship bring the greatest all-around fulfillment. Fatigue, overwork, illness, worry, or serious emotional upset can render a person incapable of sexual interest or responsiveness. A caring partner can offer comfort without forcing sex on the other person. In a real give-and-take relationship, each is free to initiate sexual activity. But the couple will have a mutual agreement that each can say when a particular time is not right, and that one will not try to coerce the other. However, in a loving and sensitive relationship, refusals happen rarely. Continued refusal indicates a problem in the relationship.

Growth together through the years keeps a couple interested in each other sexually. Partners committed to each other learn and use the techniques of sexual stimulation, and they also try to grow in their total personal relationship. They know how to arouse each other and take advantage of their opportunities. They understand their possibilities (that women can have multiple orgasms) and their limitations (that males experience a refractory period during resolution and that both sexes undergo changes with aging). They maximize their enjoyment by making sure that the vagina is thoroughly lubricated before the penis penetrates. They can communicate on several levels: physically (an erect penis and a lubricated vagina express invitations for sexual union); emotionally (they grow in their interest in each other); and intellectually (they work at communicating what pleasures each person and how to improve their sex lives).

Experience and flexibility lead couples to experiment with new ways of stimulation and with a variety of positions for intercourse. Oral-genital contact can be exciting when couples agree that it is appropriate. Traditionally in our society the man lies on top of the woman during sexual intercourse. But in some cultures this position is never used. The woman can also lie on top. The couple may sit facing each other, or the man may enter the vagina from the rear. Masters and Johnson recommend a way of lying side by side facing each other as the best method to obtain pleasure, because it allows each partner maximum freedom of movement. Interested and sexually responsive couples will try to discover their own most satisfying ways of obtaining sexual pleasure.

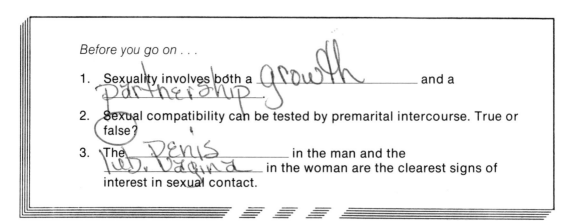

Before you go on . . .

1. Sexuality involves both a _growth_ and a _partnership_.

2. Sexual compatibility can be tested by premarital intercourse. True or false?

3. The _penis_ in the man and the _vagina_ in the woman are the clearest signs of interest in sexual contact.

4. Refusals of sex rarely happen in a harmonious relationship. True or false?

5. Under what conditions can sexual activity be less than totally rewarding? *fatigue, illness worry etc.*

6. Sexual satisfaction increases when the couple work together at their sexual relationship. True or false?

7. What factors can make an individual temporarily unable to respond sexually? *sex as bribe, reward, punishment*

Answers:

1. Partnership; growth process.

2. False. Sexual compatibility cannot be easily tested in brief encounters, especially if the partners are not totally comfortable with the situation.

3. Erect penis; lubricated vagina.

4. True. Continued refusals are a sign of a problem.

5. When sex is used to reward, punish, or bribe the partner.

6. True.

7. Illness, emotional stress, fatigue, or mental disturbance.

Sexual Dysfunction in the Male 28

We have discussed the way our bodies are intended to function sexually, and some of the ways in which partners can improve their sex lives. If the psychological, emotional, and interpersonal factors are conducive to making love, partners who actively participate in pleasuring each other usually find that the biological aspects of sexuality function automatically. Unfortunately, not all individuals find that sex works as smoothly and as easily as Eric Berne humorously describes the process: "Insert widget A into sprocket B and clamp down gudgeon C, and presto! There will be a baby on Christmas morning." Some individuals cannot enjoy sex because they have learned ways of thinking and behaving that inhibit their sexual expressions. Other people are just basically unaware. With a little information, patience, and willingness to try they can mature in their sexual responsiveness. Some people, luckily only a small percentage, find themselves frequently or always unable to engage in satisfying sexual relations. Thanks to Masters and Johnson and other serious sex therapists, many persons with sexual inadequacies can receive treatment and achieve sexual fulfillment.

In this section we shall look at the major sexual inadequacies, the physical and possible psychological reasons for them, and ways to overcome them. We will discuss the factors that interfere with normal sexual functioning. We have chosen to discuss sex among the aging in a later section because we cannot call the changes that older people go through in their sex lives abnormalities. Older people can find sexual fulfillment by adapting to the altered state of their bodies. Here we shall focus on some general considerations and then turn to some particular inadequacies and ways to deal with them.

Effective sexual functioning involves several general factors. First, satisfying sexuality involves pleasurable sensations. A person who cannot enjoy pleasure, because it is seen as forbidden for social or religious reasons will not find sexual activity gratifying. An essential part of Masters' and Johnson's sex therapy consists of convincing couples that there must be a "sensate focus" in lovemaking. They insist that the couple experiment with discovering how to pleasure the whole body of the partner. Couples getting to know each other sexually can begin their bodily explorations through petting, undressing each other, or giving each other baths or massages. It is important for couples to communicate verbally and non-verbally to each other what activities give them pleasure.

Second, an individual who concentrates on and constantly thinks about how he or she is performing sexually can run into sexual inadequacies. Thinking does not give an erection, lubricate the vagina, or cause an orgasm for either partner. These processes happen automatically when the partners become involved sexually with each other. Enjoyable sex is not a spectator sport but an active sport.

Finally, each person has a sexual value system. By this we mean that each person considers certain sensations to have an erotic meaning and that he or she finds these sexual feelings appropriate under certain circumstances and with a suitable person. The sexual value system may be articulated or unconscious. But if a particular partner or circumstance does not fit in with one's sexual value system, sexual inadequacies may result.

There are five basic types of sexual dysfunction in males—premature ejaculation, ejaculatory incompetence, primary and secondary impotence, and dyspareunia. **Premature ejaculation**—ejaculating during foreplay or earlier than is desirable after inserting the penis into the vagina—is the most common type of sexual dysfunction. Some descriptions of premature ejaculation speak of a specific time period in determining whether the man ejaculates prematurely. Masters and Johnson have criticized this "stopwatch" approach because it emphasizes individual performance rather than the sexual partnership. A better definition states that more than fifty per cent of the time a man does not satisfy his female partner while his penis is contained within her vagina because he cannot wait to ejaculate until she is sufficiently stimulated. Thus a man who really intends to pleasure his partner, but who occasionally becomes overstimulated and cannot wait to ejaculate, need not worry that he will fall into the syndrome of premature ejaculation. The female partner's understanding of how easily the man becomes excited, and her sympathetic acceptance of these episodes, can also help to prevent its occurence, except on rare occasions. Bringing the female partner to a high level of excitement before inserting the penis into the vagina removes some of her need for prolonged intravaginal containment before orgasm.

Besides being the most common male sexual dysfunction, premature ejaculation responds the most easily to treatment. Typically, the male had his first sexual experiences in situations that prompted hurried release and little regard for the female's response—with a prostitute, in a parked car, in a by-the-hour motel, or while fully clothed. A wife, frustrated by premature ejaculation, may put up with the condition until the children are raised and then either discourage sex or become demanding and possibly drive her mate to impotence (the inability to have an erection). Masters and Johnson have found two techniques successful in correcting this condition. Basically, the male needs to learn how to receive penile stimulation without ejaculating immediately. First, the "squeeze technique" allows the male to achieve ejaculatory control. When the man feels that he may ejaculate, the partner places her thumb on the frenulum (where the foreskin was or is attached on the underside of the penis) and the first two fingers on either side of the corona on top, and squeezes fairly strongly for three to four seconds. This makes the man lose his desire to ejaculate instantly. In the second technique, the female assumes the superior position and kneels over her mate with her knees at about his nipple level and inserts the penis into the vagina at about a 45-degree angle (does not sit on it directly). This position is less demanding sexually than the male-above position. The couple may later change to the "lateral coital" position described by Masters and Johnson.

Ejaculatory incompetence is the opposite of premature ejaculation. Here the man fails to ejaculate in the vagina. This usually stems from extreme fears of contamination by sexual contact he considers dirty or immoral, from disdainful contempt for his partner or women in general, or from an unreasonable fear of impregnating the woman. In this condition the male needs to be forced into ejaculation through the manual manipulation of his penis by his female partner. Once she brings him pleasure, he can identify with her as a pleasure symbol, and not see her as threatening or somehow objectionable. The next step involves learning to ejaculate within the vagina.

Primary impotence means that a man has never been able to maintain an erection sufficient to establish a coital connection. **Secondary impotence** implies that a man has successfully established coital connection at least once, but has failed to have an erection on other occasions. Unusual fatigue or distraction can cause erective failure. This does not become a definite syndrome until it reaches about twenty-five percent of coital attempts. Sometimes the causes of impotence may be physical (e.g., Hodgkin's disease, diabetes mellitus). More often psychological factors precipitate the condition—alcoholism, extreme religious orthodoxy, or homosexuality. Contrary to some popular opinion, alcohol is not a stimulant, but a depressant. In excess, it depresses and slows down sexual responsiveness. Radical religious orthodoxy that prohibits the expression of affection, forbids the discussion of sexuality except in occasional harsh terms, and looks down upon sexual pleasure, can induce impotence. Since an erection cannot be forced, therapy does not try to make the male have an erection. Rather, treatment focuses on the couple, and ways for them to experience pleasure together, so that an erection will occur automatically. Some men also suffer from **dyspareunia** (pain during intercourse). Medical assistance should be sought to correct this disorder.

Before you go on . . .

1. _Preme Ejaculation_ is the most common form of sexual dysfunction in males.
2. Sexual dysfunction is usually caused by a physical problem. True or false?
3. List several potential causes of male sexual dysfunction. Alcohol, religion, homo,
4. In _primary impotence_, the male has never been able to maintain an erection long enough for intercourse to take place.
5. Fear of contamination by sexual contact may result in _impotence, Ejac incompetence_
6. Secondary impotence is characterized by the inability to achieve an erection in at least fifty percent of attempts made. True or false?

7. Pain during intercourse is known as _dysparenuia_

Answers:

1. Premature ejaculation.

2. False. Most cases of sexual dysfunction stem from psychological problems.

3. Fear of contamination, dislike or contempt for the partner, fear of impregnating the partner, alcoholism, radical religious orthodoxy, latent homosexuality.

4. Primary impotence.

5. Ejaculatory incompetence.

6. False. The figure is at least twenty-five percent of the time.

7. Dyspareunia.

Sexual Dysfunction in the Female

The major female sexual dysfunctions include being non-orgasmic, vaginismus, and dyspareunia. **Orgasmic dysfunction** is the most common female sexual complaint. Because of the traditional focus on male sexuality and the woman's capacity to conceive without orgasm (whereas the man cannot deposit semen without ejaculation), orgasmic dysfunction did not receive proper attention until very recently. Now, however, an increasing number of women are eager to experience orgasm. The non-orgasmic woman is sometimes referred to as "frigid." However, frigidity sounds permanent, and many non-orgasmic women can learn to achieve orgasm.

Cultural bias, prejudice against females, and ignorance of female sexuality have contributed to the neglect and repression of women's sexual responsiveness. Few women experience orgasm during their initial act of sexual intercourse. But over half do so by the end of the first

month of marriage, and eighty percent by the end of the first year. This leaves a sizable percentage who take a longer time, or who never reach orgasm at all. Female and male genital stimulation and orgasm are similar. Both sexes seek their partners selectively and want to gain positive regard, affection, some sense of personal identity, and pride from their sexual encounters. Why, then, do not all women experience orgasm?

Basically, women are psychologically handicapped by the double standard. Men are expected to seek sexual release, while women are usually taught to be restrained and not too interested in sexual matters. Consequently, a woman is not as likely as a man to pin her psychological and social self-identity and personal expectations on sexual responsiveness. Many women develop a "good girl" facade that conceals their potential for sexual fulfillment. Girls are not instructed nor permitted to value their sexual feelings in anticipation of appropriate or meaningful opportunities for sexual expression. During their formative years, most non-orgasmic women had parents or religious instructors who deliberately omitted sex instruction or who admonished them about the negative nature and consequences of sex. The non-orgasmic woman probably grew up on a protective vacuum where she was not encouraged to develop her sexual feelings. She may say "I don't feel anything," because ignorance, fear, or authoritarian directives cause her to repress sensual awareness. If orgasmic dysfunction persists, the wife will probably feel that her husband is not fulfilling her expectations. In some cases this may very well be true. Studies by Masters and Johnson show that many non-orgasmic women are married to men who ejaculate prematurely.

A woman needs security in a relationship, an attachment to her partner, and warm expression of mutual emotional responsiveness in order to enjoy sexual intercourse. The treatment of orgasmic dysfunction must, therefore, involve both the social–emotional and biological levels. The female sexual value system requires commitment, tenderness, respect, and sensitive attention before the biological processes of sex can function spontaneously to their fullest. Within a relationship of trust, warmth, and mutual admiration, a woman can permit herself to let go and surrender to the orgasmic experience, fully receptive, open and responsive to her partner. Without this intimate psychological attachment, she often feels too vulnerable and too "used" to relax her emotional control.

On the biological level, the non-orgasmic woman must first identify, through mutual exploration, her bodily areas of sensitivity. She must permit herself to enjoy the touches of her lover. The next step leads to discovering the pleasures of clitoral stimulation, which in turn sets off vaginal lubrication. The final step involves sexual union in an erotic, non-demanding atmosphere.

Being an active participant in lovemaking rather than a spectator helps overcome orgasmic dysfunction. The woman needs non-demanding thrusts of the penis within her vagina to fully appreciate her sensations. This is initially accomplished most comfortably through the female-superior position we discussed earlier. Both partners may then enjoy switching to one of the other positions available. The lateral-coital position described by Masters and Johnson is only one of the possibilities. The couple who are willing to experiment with a variety of positions for intercourse may add an entirely new dimension to their lovemaking. Some of them may take a little practice, but are ultimately rewarding.

Vaginismus is a relatively rare occurence. The vaginal muscles contract so tightly that the male penis cannot penetrate. A woman who suffers from vaginismus often has a background of extreme religious orthodoxy that allows only very limited instruction in sex and that condones intercourse only for conception. She may have suffered a psychosexual trauma such as rape, or a history of painful intercourse (dyspareunia). Or she may have a latent homosexual orientation. Treatment consists of dilating the vagina to relieve spasms, imparting solid sexual information, and encouraging the woman toward sexual cooperation with her partner.

Dyspareunia is painful or difficult intercourse in either sex. A few women experience pain, burning, or aching during or after intercourse. These reactions can be caused by torn tissues, infection, sensitivity to contraceptive chemicals or douches, diminishing amounts of hormones in the older woman, the use of radiation in the vagina, or insufficient vaginal lubrication. Tissues may be torn or badly scarred during childbirth. A poorly performed total or partial hysterectomy can leave the vagina too short or gravely scarred. Thus a woman will do well to choose her obstetrician and gynecologist with care. Medical or surgical treatment can correct most physical bases for dyspareunia. Contrary to popular opinion, douches are never medically necessary after intercourse because the vagina returns to its normal chemical balance within several hours. Douches can wash away the vagina's natural protection, leaving a woman prone to infection.

Before you go on . . .

1. _orgasmic_ _dysfunction_ _____ exists when a woman rarely or never achieves orgasm during sexual intercourse.

2. A woman's achievement of sexual satisfaction is based on both social–economic and biological factors. True or false?

3. Stimulation of the _clitoris_ _____ is extremely important to a woman's enjoyment of sexual intercourse.

4. In _vaginismus_ , abnormal muscle contractions of the vagina prevent penetration by the penis.

5. Douching is usually desirable after intercourse. True or false?

6. List several physical bases for dyspareunia in woman. _infection_ _not enough lubrication, scar tissue_

7. Most non-orgasmic women can learn how to achieve orgasm. True or false?

Answers:

1. Orgasmic dysfunction.

2. True.

3. Clitoris.

4. Vaginisimus.

5. False. The vagina soon returns to its normal chemical balance, and douching may lower the vagina's resistance to infection.

6. Infection, torn or scarred vaginal tissues, sensitivity to contraceptive chemicals, lowered hormone level in older women, insufficient vaginal lubrication.

7. True.

SEXUALITY *Chapter Review*

1. Parental attitudes about sex can influence a person's own attitudes in later life. True or false?

2. Recent research shows that males are, on the average, more interested in sex than females. True or false?

3. Sexual arousal can be inhibited by (a) religious ideas; (b) tactile stimulation; (c) emotional stimulation; (d) all of the above.

4. A _reflex_ erection occurs in response to tactile stimulation whereas a _cerebral_ erection has more to do with emotional stimulation.

5. The _clitoris_ of females corresponds to the penis of males.

6. The most sensitive part of a woman's body is her vagina. True or false?

7. The region in front of the anus in both sexes which is sensitive to stroking is called the _perinium_.

8. Touching one's own genitals to achieve an orgasm is called (a) foreplay; (b) reflex reaction; (c) ejaculation; (d) masturbation.

9. A woman's perineum is more sensitive to touch than are her breasts. True or false?

10. Caressing and kissing are called _petting_ when not followed by sexual intercourse. The same behavior, when followed by sexual intercourse, is called _foreplay_.

11. For a fully satisfying sexual relationship there must be (a) affection and trust; (b) security; (c) a favorable social–emotional context; (d) all of these.

12. During sexual arousal, the tissues of the male's penis and the female's vagina fill with blood when certain blood vessels undergo a change called _vaso congestion_.

13. According to Masters and Johnson, in the _orgasm_ stage of sexual intercourse blood is pumped out of the genital tissues, but in the _resolution_ stage it gradually flows out.

14. Spermatozoa (or sperm) are produced in the (a) seminal vesicles; (b) prostate gland; (c) testicles; (d) Cowper's gland.

15. The resolution period is the time it takes before a man can have a second orgasm. True or false?

16. Stimulation of one's sex partner is achieved by emotional as well as physical activities. True or false?

17. Copulation should be put off until a woman has completed her menstrual cycle. True or false?

18. In general, younger males can copulate _More Easily_ than older males.

19. The most common position for sexual intercourse is (a) man on top; (b) partners sideways; (c) woman on top; (d) none of these.

20. The most common male sexual inadequacy is _premature ejac_

21. The most common female sexual dysfunction is (a) inability to have an orgasm; (b) vaginismus; (c) dyspareunia (d) secondary impotence.

22. A sexual value system is a person's set of beliefs concerning sex. True or false?

23. Premature ejaculation can be prevented by (a) the squeeze technique; (b) making the sex partner a pleasure symbol; (c) the female assuming a superior position during intercourse; (d) both a and c.

24. Secondary impotence means that a man cannot have an erection and has never had one. True or false?

25. The sensate focus is (a) nonverbal communication; (b) exploring what gives pleasure to the sex partner; (c) the orgasm; (d) all of the above.

26. _Dyspareunia_ refers to an abnormal condition of pain during intercourse.

27. Vaginismus is caused by bacteria. True or false?

28. Compare male and female sexual responses. _The two are physically very similar but attitudes may differ._

29. Describe some differences in sexual arousal between men and women. _Men reach orgasm quicker_

30. What are some of the most important causes of sexual unhappiness? _lack of sexual sincerity_

To find the answers, look at page 197

CHAPTER SIX

FAMILY PLANNING

Leading thoughts:

- Prospective parents should ask themselves whether they really want children, and evaluate their reasons for wanting to be parents

- Contraception (birth control) includes a variety of methods for avoiding pregnancy or spacing the births of children

- Several methods of birth control are available, so that nearly every couple can choose the method that is best suited to them

- Genetic counseling can assist people who carry genetic defects in making their decision whether or not to have children

- Infertility is present in nearly 15 percent of all couples, but in many cases it can be medically corrected

- Couples who want to adopt children usually face a long, drawnout legal process, but adoption of a child can be immensely rewarding

Do We Want Children?

Before effective contraceptives were developed and made readily available, the question "Do we want children?" had little meaning for married couples. If people married, they had children, unless there were physical problems that prevented conception.

Many married couples still think of parenthood as though it is an inevitable result of marriage. They marry and have children because they believe it is expected of them. But today a couple may choose to have children or not to have them. Although society may still raise its eyebrows at couples who decide not to have children, increasing numbers are making that decision.

Let us look at some of the arguments for and against having children.

Why do some couples choose to become parents? Those who decide they will have children give personal and social reasons for doing so. They mention many of the following points. Children increase the number of primary, intimate relationships that a couple share. As society becomes more impersonal and we become increasingly mobile, it is becoming more and more difficult to maintain life-long intimate relationships. One's husband or wife and one's children travel with one through life. Warm, intimate relationships give a sense of security and well-being. In a home where children are wanted, loved, and respected, warm relationships are built which nourish both parents and children. Children give their parents the opportunity to grow in other important ways, too. Accepting the responsibility for the care of a small, weak human being and leading it slowly towards independence gives the parents experience in building warm, workable human relationships. By teaching their children, parents are helping to weave the fabric of society.

A couple may choose to have children because they want to extend themselves into the future. This seems to reflect the feelings of competence and of self-worth in the parents, and to be an optimistic expression about the world in general. Such parents feel that they can influence what is happening about them. They like to think of their children and grandchildren taking an active part in shaping the world of tomorrow. Closely related to this is the feeling that we achieve a kind of immortality by having children. Death seems less final if we can leave behind a chain of offspring who are part of ourselves. Finally, some people choose to be parents because they believe they have a talent for parenting. They find that caring for children is a personally satisfying and worthwhile activity.

These reasons all seem to be beneficial to both parents and their children. But sometimes a couple decide to have a child for reasons that mainly benefit the adults. They may feel that parenthood establishes their mature status, or

proves their fertility. Sometimes an unhappy couple will have a child in an attempt to hold together a troubled marriage, but often the stresses connected with the care of the baby contribute to the final break-up of the marriage. Such motives give little thought to the needs of the child.

Why do some couples choose not to have children? The reasons given by those who decide to not have children include biological, personal, and ecological concerns. One or both parents may carry a physiological or genetic defect which they do not wish to risk passing on to a child. Sickle-cell and Tay-Sachs disease are among the defects which are hereditary. Certain emotional and mental deficiencies are also thought be be hereditary.

Today couples who are worried about defects that could be passed on to their children can seek the advice of a genetic counselor. Genetic counselors are knowledgeable about genetically-transmitted diseases. In many cases a couple is relieved to learn that a defect in a member of either family is not a problem of heredity, but was caused by other factors. In other cases the counselor can help a couple who carry genetic defects to examine alternative ways of becoming parents, if they wish. These include artificial insemination (if the father carries the defect) and adoption.

A relatively new medical test called **amniocentesis** can often determine whether a child that has already been conceived is likely to be born defective. In some instances, parents may decide to terminate a pregnancy in which it seems rather certain that the unborn child is developing abnormally. On the brighter side, couples who wish to have children but have not conceived after a year's time can often be helped by new medical techniques.

Personal reasons for not having children often relate to the parents' careers, especially that of the wife. A very demanding career simply may not leave enough time to raise physically and emotionally healthy children. And some couples simply are not interested in having children, preferring a lifestyle that centers around adult interests. The ever-increasing cost of raising children may cause couples to delay having children until they feel they are financially able to support them. Or, they may decide to have fewer children than they would prefer. The economic factor may account for the fact that families are generally smaller than they once were.

Many couples are becoming increasingly concerned about world population growth. Young people, especially, are concerned with ecology—the environment we live in and its capacity to support ever-growing numbers of people. Some people believe that our goal should be **zero population growth**. To achieve this, most couples would have to limit themselves to two or at most three children. Carefully controlled population growth would allow us to plan the environment—our cities, our use of land and other resources—to fit the needs of a stable population rather than struggling to stretch our

resources to meet the needs of an expanding population. Family planning allows us to decide how many children we wish to have, and when. The family-planning approach to population control, however, is less rigorous than the zero-population-growth approach. Couples who plan their families may still wish to have more than three children.

While the decision to have or not to have children may be influenced by others, the final decision rests with each couple. Couples find themselves in different circumstances. They have differing values, expectations, personalities, career orientations, and genetic make-ups. Because of these differences it seems reasonable that some will make a wise choice in deciding to not have children, while others will just as wisely decide to have them.

Before you go on . . .

1. Couples who are worried about transmitting a hereditary defect to their children would be advised to consult a ___genetic counselor___

2. Having a child may help to lessen tensions in a troubled marriage. True or false?

3. List some valid reasons for choosing to have children. *satisfaction or*

4. ___Sickle cell___ and ___Tay-Sachs___ are two known genetically transmitted diseases.

5. Zero population growth calls for families to limit themselves to four children at most. True or false?

6. A new technique that helps to determine whether an unborn child is developing normally is called *amniocentesis*

7. List some of the expenses you can think of that are connected with rearing children. *food, clothing, health, education, shelter, sometimes only one pay check*

Answers:

1. Genetic counselor.

2. False. The stresses connected with care of a new baby may be the final straw that causes the marriage to break up.

3. Desire to extend the intimate hus-

band-wife relationship to include children; desire to add new individuals to future society; desire to achieve a kind of immortality by leaving children; desire for the sheer satisfaction of raising children.

4. Sickle-cell anemia; Tay-Sachs disease.

5. False. Zero population growth would require limiting families to two or three children at most.

6. Amniocentesis.

7. Costs of prenatal and obstetrical care; costs of food, clothing, and medical care; costs of camps and schools; loss of the mother's salary.

Genetic Counseling

Every expectant parent hopes for a normal, healthy child. But six out of every 100 babies born suffer from some kind of defect or malformation. These defects may be minor, such as a large birthmark. Often, however, the defect is either immediately or eventually lethal. Nature reduces the number of defective children born. Ten to 25 percent of defective fetuses are aborted spontaneously within the first three months of pregnancy.

Some defects occur because the fetal blood system receives damaging substances from the mother. These will be discussed in a later section. Many other defects are caused by genetic irregularities. The genes contain the information that directs the development of the body. Not all genes express themselves in obvious ways. This is because some are dominant and others recessive. **Dominant genes** produce apparent characteristics. **Recessive genes** influence development only when the fetus receives a recessive gene for a particular trait from each parent. For example, genes for brown eyes are dominant and those for blue eyes are recessive. So a person with blue eyes received recessive genes from both parents.

Recessive genes are often responsible for abnormalities. The abnormality will appear only if two recessive genes are present, or if the person does not have a dominant gene to combat the abnormal recessive gene. Thus, a person can have a recessive gene for a defect and not actually suffer from it. Such a person is called a **carrier** and can transmit the defect to his children if he marries another carrier.

Muscular dystrophy, involving the weakening and wasting away of the muscles, results from defective genes. The most severe form usually affects males. It is caused by a defective gene on the X chromosome received from the mother, and the male has no normal X chromosome to combat it. The extreme cases are confined to wheelchairs as youngsters. They usually die in their 20s or 30s from heart failure or lung infection.

Certain genetically-caused diseases affect specific groups of people. **Sickle-cell anemia** occurs mostly in persons of African origin. Their hemoglobin, the oxygen-carrying red pigment in the blood, contains one wrong amino acid. As a result, their red blood cells take on a sickle shape, and cannot carry enough oxygen. Clumps of sickled cells can cause abnormal blood clotting, especially in the lungs, central nervous system, and long bones. The affected person suffers from episodes of fever and severe pain. Unless both parents have contributed a gene for the sickling trait, the offspring will not have the condition. An estimated 2,500,000 Afro-Americans have a gene for this trait, but only one in 400 has the disease. Half of those with the disease will die by age twenty.

Eastern European Jews are susceptible to the hereditary **Tay-Sachs disease**. A chemical substance that breaks down fat in the nervous system does not develop in the fetus. The baby seems fine for six months. Then the fat builds up, causing damage to the nervous system and brain, which kills the child before it reaches five years of age. Carriers of this recessive gene can be identified by blood tests, and the condition of the fetus can be determined by amniocentesis.

Cystic fibrosis is found mostly among Caucasians and affects one of every 2,000 Caucasian babies. A defective gene causes the production of excessively thick mucus. This mucus clogs the lungs and pancreas, interfering with breathing and digestion. The victims rarely survive past their teens. **Diabetes** (a metabolic abnormality that makes the victim unable to utilize glucose) and **hypertension** (high blood pressure) have a tendency to run in families, but the exact genetic abnormalities involved have not been pinned down.

Abnormalities can also result from genes being broken or combining with others during the production of sex cells in the parents. One of these is **Down's syndrome**, which results in a retarded child with short stubby ears, a protruding tongue, a tendency toward leukemia, and an Oriental-looking eye fold. It is caused by the presence of an extra chromosome, and occurs once in every 600 births. The incidence of Down's syndrome, also called "mongolism," is very much higher in babies born to mothers over the age of forty. Mongolism in the fetus can be detected by amniocentesis.

Worry about whether they will produce healthy children plagues some parents. This is especially true when the family medical history, the use of questionable drugs, or the presence of some disease in a parent indicates a possible defect. Medical technology now makes it possible for some prospective parents to determine before having children whether they are carriers of a genetic defect. The possibility of genetic problems creates stress and may put a severe strain on family relations. Self-blame about defective children is natural and very common. But parents can often be helped by genetic counseling that provides accurate medical diagnosis and psychological support during a crisis or in making decisions about childbearing.

Three methods help to identify possible genetic problems. First, a detailed account of the family medical history can give indications of whether a defective recessive gene or a predisposition to an abnormality exists. Second, in some cases blood tests can determine whether a developing fetus is defective or normal. In **amniocentesis** the mother is given a local anesthetic, and a hypodermic needle is used to draw some of the amniotic fluid out of the uterus. This fluid contains some dead cells and waste products from the fetus, which can be examined for abnormalities. If a defect is evident, the parents may abort the fetus, or can at least prepare to deal with an abnormal child.

Genetic counseling provides a valuable service to those who wish to bear only healthy children. But it also raises religious and ethical problems for those who believe that sex should be oriented toward procreation or who find abortion morally objectionable. The possibility of predicting genetic defects also creates an ethical and legal dilemma. Should society try to prevent the births of defective children? Or does the individual have the right to procreate even when it is certain a defective child will be produced? These are only two of the many questions concerned with the problem of genetic defects, and it is possible that they may never be fully resolved. In the meantime, genetic counseling can at least provide a warning to those prospective parents who are likely to produce defective children, so that they can make an enlightened decision about childbearing.

Before you go on . . .

1. About what percentage of newborns are defective in some way? *6%*

2. If a person receives a _*X or recessive gene*_ for a trait from each of the parents, he will display that trait.

3. A carrier is a person who has a defective gene but cannot pass the trait on. True or false? *(false)*

4. What is Tay-Sachs disease? *Jewish - baby dies by 5yrs*

5. The incidence of Down's syndrome is very much higher in babies born to _*women over 40*_

6. All carriers of genetic defects can now be identified by blood testing. True or false? *(false)*

7. Genetic problems can often be determined by _*family history, blood test*_, or _*amniocentesis*_

Answers:

1. Six percent.

2. Recessive gene.

3. False. A carrier has a recessive gene for a defect. If he or she marries another carrier for the same trait, some of their offspring will display the defect.

4. Tay-Sachs disease usually affects Jews of Eastern European origin. It involves a defect in fat metabolism, and is always fatal within the first five years of life.

5. Mothers over the age of forty.

6. False. So far carriers of only a few defects can be identified in this way.

7. Investigating family medical history; blood testing; amniocentesis.

Birth Control 32

Birth control is the prevention or avoidance of pregnancy. The desire to plan or limit the birth of children stems from a wish not to have them, or from the feeling of being unable to cope with more children. Not wanting to overpopulate the world also influences the decision of some couples to plan their families. Legal and religious considerations may also enter into this decision.

The decision whether or not to have children is not always just a personal one. Some religious groups do not approve either of preventing conception or of facilitating conception by artificial means. And the norms of our society still push couples in the direction of having children. A couple who decide not to have children will probably have to defend their reasons to relatives, friends, and even casual acquaintances. But if they are in firm agreement about their decision, husband and wife can bolster each other's courage if they face the disapproval of others.

A number of **contraceptives,** or birth control methods, are readily available. Legal efforts are being made to provide family planning information to everyone who wants it. Some religious groups officially prohibit birth control, in their belief that the only moral sexual acts are those directed toward conception. Most Protestant denominations approve of artificial birth control. Reform and Conservative, but not Orthodox, Jews sanction family planning. The Roman Catholic Church at a hierarchical level opposes artificial birth control, terming it unnatural, intrinsically evil, and unjustified. Pope Paul VI, in reaffirming this position, based his conclusion on the minority rather than the majority report of the study commission he himself appointed. But many reputable Catholic theologians and the Second Vatican Council state that the responsibility for family planning lies with the parents.

The most effective way not to have a child is not to engage in sexual intercourse or any activity that may deposit spermatozoa in the vagina (sperm have been known to seep through panties). This method does not appeal to most married people, nor to the sexually active unmarried. Helping children to grow up to their full potential requires a great deal of time, energy, commitment, insight, and dedication. Unless the couple fully intend to conceive a child, the consequences to themselves and a possible child will be more favorable if they use an effective means of birth control. If a couple intend to engage in sexual intercourse, taking

responsibility for family planning demonstrates more maturity and common sense than the irresponsible, "Oh, I didn't think it would happen." This attitude is potentially devastating both to the couple and to the embryo that can become a child. Spontaneous sexuality is more rewarding in a context of mature responsibility. Though no child asks to be born, it is the child who is stigmatized as "illegitimate," not the parents responsible for its birth. Maybe we should redefine "illegitimate" to refer to parents who do not have the maturity to raise a child to his or her fullest potential.

Persons who are not entirely comfortable with their sexual activity are often embarrassed or shy about purchasing contraceptive materials. Those who have moral or religious doubts about their sexual activity may feel less guilty if they do not prepare for it by using a safe and effective contraceptive. Both satisfying sexual intercourse and parenthood demand the maturity and responsibility to be able to make effective decisions. The individual who does not want to have a child, but who engages in sexual intercourse without contraception just for the thrill of it, is probably very immature. Sexual intercourse by couples who do not want a child will be more enjoyable and more likely to bring them close together emotionally when they have used effective contraception.

A mature couple will assume contraceptive responsibility in a sexual relationship where children are not desired. They will decide through open and honest communication how to handle this. However, male chauvinism sometimes leaves this responsibility totally to the female. Since she is the one who will surely suffer any consequences of pregnancy, we shall discuss contraception among females first.

The most effective female contraceptive, **the pill,** is based on hormones. The most common type contains estrogen and progesterone in various combinations. The woman's body reacts in some ways as if she were pregnant; she cannot conceive. However, the woman continues to menstruate regularly, even if she was irregular before. The pill is only available by prescription. It may produce several side effects, including nausea, dizziness, and retention of fluid in the tissues. Research indicates that its use may cause certain types of cancer or abnormal blood clotting. Contraceptive pills also lower the acidity level of the vaginal tract, which may make it easier for a woman to contract venereal disease. The pill should be taken only under strict medical supervision. If not taken regularly, pregnancy may occur. A woman who wishes to become pregnant is advised to discontinue the pill for several months before starting the pregnancy, to allow the chemicals to leave her body.

A "mini-pill" using only progesterone is also being developed. A "vaginal ring" is in the experimental stage. It is inserted close to the uterus for 21 of every 28 days. It secretes artificial progesterone and has the same effects as the pill, with the added advantage of limiting the use of hormones to the uterine area. "Morning-after" pills that can be administered the day after intercourse are effective, but they cause unpleasant side effects and are emergency measures only. A once-a-year pill is in the early stages of development.

Mechanical devices are designed to block spermatozoa from reaching the uterus or to prevent conception. The **diaphragm** is a dome-shaped cup of thin rubber, which fits over the cervix. It may be inserted any time before intercourse and removed six to eight hours afterwards. The diaphragm must be fitted by a physician. When used with a spermacidal jelly, it has a 4 to 10 percent failure rate. The **IUD,** or **intrauterine device,** is a plastic object in various shapes that a physician inserts in the uterus. It is not yet known exactly how the IUD works, but apparently it prevents the embryo from implanting in the uterine wall. It may cause extra-heavy menstrual periods and has a 2 to 3 percent failure rate. Both the diaphragm and the IUD can be displaced by vigorous activity.

Nonprescription chemical methods of contraception include spermacidal foams and jellies placed in the vagina shortly before intercourse. Their failure rate is 20 to 22 percent, and they can interfere with spontaneity and oral-genital contact. Some women use a douche after intercourse to wash the sperm from the vagina. This is extremely ineffective, with about a 35 percent failure rate.

Some couples use the "rhythm method" of birth control. This system depends on an accurate calculation of when the woman ovulates. The main idea of this method is to have intercourse only during "safe periods" when no egg is available to be fertilized. But many women ovulate irregularly, and emotional and physical factors can vary the time of ovulation. Rhythm is the only method of family planning currently sanctioned by the hierarchy of the Catholic Church. Since it has a 14 to 35 percent failure rate, Catholic couples often refer to it as "Vatican roulette."

A woman can be rendered permanently sterile (incapable of future pregnancy) by a surgical method called **tubal ligation**. The fallopian tubes are tied, cut, or electrically cauterized, so that ovum and sperm cannot meet. Tubal ligation was formerly a major operation involving a large abdominal incision and several days of hospitalization. But a new technique, **laparoscopic sterilization**, is now becoming very popular. In this so-called "band-aid operation," tubal ligation is performed through one or two tiny incisions that are then closed with a single stitch and covered with a band-aid. The procedure must be performed in a hospital, but the woman can usually go home and return to full activity a few hours after the surgery.

Abortion is removal of the unborn child from the uterus before it can survive on its own. It differs from other methods of family planning since it takes place after conception when the cells have already begun to multiply and organize themselves. Thus legal and moral questions enter into a discussion of abortion. Abortion should be used only as a last resort: responsibility for pregnancy should begin before conception.

For the male the commonest form of birth control is the **condom,** a thin rubber shield that fits over the erect penis. The condom has the added advantage of providing effective protection against venereal disease. Used in conjunction with a spermacidal foam or jelly, the failure rate is about 10 to 11 percent. However, the condom may produce some loss of sexual sensation. A man may also practice **withdrawal,** removing his penis from the vagina before he ejaculates. This method is very unreliable with a failure rate of 8 to 40 percent.

Vasectomy is a relatively simple surgical procedure in which the sperm ducts are tied off, cut, or cauterized so that sperm cannot leave the testicles. The procedure can take place under local anesthesia in a doctor's office. Vasectomy, like tubal ligation, has the potential disadvantage of being irreversible. It does not interfere with the production of sex hormones, erection, or orgasm. Research is also being conducted into pills or injections for males that will curtail the production of spermatozoa. But these are not yet effective or safe enough for commercial distribution.

Before you go on . . .

1. Birth control is the termination of pregnancy. True or false?
2. The most effective way to avoid pregnancy is *not to have sexual intercourse*
3. Birth control methods are available only to females. True or false?
4. Spermicidal foams and jellies are available only by prescription. True or false?
5. The "morning-after pill" should be routinely used for birth control. True or false?
6. Vasectomy is a surgical procedure in which the fallopian tubes are cut or tied off. True or false?
7. *Rhythm* _____ is the only family planning method currently sanctioned by the Roman Catholic Church.

Answers:

1. False. Birth contol is the prevention or avoidance of pregnancy.
2. Complete avoidance of sexual intercourse.
3. False. Several methods are available to males.
4. False. These contraceptives may be bought over the counter.
5. False. This pill has very uncomfortable side effects and should be used only in emergencies.
6. False. Vasectomy involves tying off the vasa deferentia. The fallopian tubes are tied off by tubal ligation.
7. The rhythm method.

What If We Can't Have Children?

Some couples face an opposite situation to that of couples who use birth control—they want a child, but have not conceived one. Perhaps ten to fifteen percent of couples are involuntarily childless, and are thus considered **infertile**. Infertility has several causes, and the condition may be temporary or permanent. Illness, fatigue, poor nutrition, drugs, alcoholism, and emotional stress can all contribute to lowered fertility.

Many involuntarily childless couples would like to raise a family. If they experience social pressure from relatives and friends to have a family, they may feel like failures. And many couples who are happy with each other would like to share their love with children. Being unable to have children when they are wanted can lead to frustration, worry, and self-doubt. There are remedies for a large percentage of cases. If conception does not occur after a year of regular sexual intercourse without using birth control, a couple may benefit from seeing a gynecologist or a urologist working in the fertility field. They may be able to have a child, or at least they may discover why they cannot. In this section we shall consider several reasons for infertility and examine several remedies.

Because diagnosis is easier and less expensive for the male, we will look first at his situation. Unfortunately, men are more reluctant than women to approach a doctor about fertility. Many consider infertility a reflection on their masculinity. But males are just as likely to be the infertile partner, so it makes sense to do the easiest analysis first.

The most common cause of male infertility involves a **low sperm count** or impaired motility of the sperm. The condition of the sperm can be tested by a laboratory analysis of the semen. If the testicles do not descend from the abdomen before adolescence, either naturally or with surgical assistance, the internal body heat will destroy their sperm-producing potential. A common problem among infertile males is **varicocele.** In this condition the valves in the left spermatic vein are weak. Unpurified blood from the kidneys can back up into the testicles, thus injuring sperm production. A surgical procedure called varicocelectomy cuts the vein and stops the backflow of blood. Another remedy for a low sperm count is to allow only the first squirt or two of semen to enter the vagina, since this part of the semen is richer in spermatozoa. Increased intake of proteins, magnese, zinc, and vitamins A, B, and E may improve the production and condition of spermatozoa.

Some infertile couples turn to artificial insemination. If the sperm count is low, several specimens of semen can be collected and combined. This "enriched semen" is then placed in the vagina around the time of ovulation. If the husband's sperm still cannot induce conception, some of them may be mixed with those of an anonymous donor who matches the husband's physical features and blood type. Some couples may balk at using a donor's sperm. Artificial insemination from a donor raises legal, psychological, and ethical questions. Does the baby belong to the father and have a right to inheritance? Can the father accept the child as "his"? Sometimes the answer is no. Yet the same couple may adopt a child which is not biologically theirs. The child resulting from artificial insemination will definitely be the mother's biologically, and she will have the satisfaction of carrying it. Some religious groups question the morality of artificial insemination. Interestingly, many couples conceive a child after seeking medical assistance but before any treatment occurs, or after adopting a child.

The female may be infertile because she does not ovulate frequently, even though she menstruates regularly. The drugs Clomid and Pergonal have helped some women to ovulate. They both produce higher rates of miscarriage and many more cases of multiple births than the average, and they have some side effects. Emotional tension may also inhibit ovulation. The fallopian tubes may be blocked. **Rubin's test** blows some carbon dioxide gas through the tubes. If the pressure builds up, they are definitely blocked, but often the test itself may open them. Scars from gonorrhea can permanently close the tubes. If cysts on the ovaries or uterus are interfering with conception, they can often be surgically removed. The vagina may be too acidic or the uterus may be inhospitable to the implantation of the zygote. Chemical treat-

ment may relieve this condition. Radiation can cause infertility in either sex. Insufficient protein, eating too little, excessive amounts of refined sugar in the diet, smoking, and drinking can interfere with conception.

Couples who have not conceived over a long period of time or who find out that they are unlikely to have children may consider adopting a child if they are really eager for children. Some couples who are not that interested in children, unless they happen to come along by themselves, will simply let nature take its course.

Before you go on . . .

1. Infertility is _the inability to have children_.

2. Couples who want to have children but have not after a year of regular intercourse without contraception may obtain help from seeing a physician. True or false?

3. A low _sperm count_ is the main cause of infertility among males.

4. Diagnosis of infertility is easier and less expensive for males. True or false?

5. What is artificial insemination? _Placing it in the vagina using a doners sperm_

6. Rubin's test checks to see whether the _fallopian tubes_ are blocked.

7. Though she menstruates regularly, a woman may not be _ovulating_.

Answers:

1. The inability to have children.
2. True. Treatment is available for most kinds of infertility.
3. Sperm count.
4. True, although men are often reluctant to seek medical help.
5. Placing of sperm from the husband or a donor in the vagina around the time of ovulation.
6. Fallopian tubes.
7. Ovulating.

Adoption **34**

Many couples who are involuntarily childless eventually consider adoption. The federal government estimates that about 150,000 childless couples approach state or federal adoption agencies each year. Other couples turn to the so-called "gray market" where they can sometimes obtain an unwanted child by paying medical and legal expenses directly to a physician, attorney or the mother. Some couples adopt children from foreign countries. The number of foreign children who are adopted by American citizens has been increasing in the past fifteen years. It is estimated that nearly ten million Americans under the age of eighteen now live with adoptive parents.

In the past there were many more couples wishing to adopt than there were children available. Availability now depends upon a number of factors, but waiting periods are still long for couples who want healthy, white babies. However, agencies often have difficulty placing children with physical handicaps and those of mixed or minority group parentage.

Couples considering adoption must accept one fundamental principle: adoption in the United States is **child-centered**. The adoption process is designed to provide a permanent substitute family for a child deprived of a natural family. Providing children for childless couples is only a side advantage. Our laws have been developed primarily with the needs of the child in mind.

The first step in the adoption process deals with the termination of the rights and obligations of the natural parents. Sometimes courts will remove children from parents because of neglect or mistreatment. But more than half of the children available for adoption are those born to unwed mothers. In either case the court transfers responsibility for the child to a qualified social agency to make plans for adoption.

When a couple decide to adopt through an agency, they must undergo a screening procedure. If they want a healthy, white infant, for whom demand is great, they must meet certain minimum qualifications. Mothers are expected to be under thirty-five years of age, fathers under thirty-eight or forty. Preference is given to couples who have been married three to five years, are in good health and are reasonably secure financially. The agency may require medical proof of their inability to conceive, and may limit adoption to couples with no more than one child. Some adoption agencies are sectarian and are licensed to serve only people of a particular religion.

After the initial screening, the qualified couple are placed on a waiting list. Depending on availability of children, the waiting period can be as long as three to five years. During this period the agency studies the adoptive home and tries to find ways to help the prospective parents get ready to receive the adoptive child.

A child is initially placed in the home for six months to one year before final court action is taken. During this time adoption workers help the child and family to grow into a social unit. Two major problems can arise during this period. First, workers' visits often seem threatening to the adopting parents, since the agency still has guardianship of the child and can remove the child if conditions seem unsatisfactory. This situation causes many couples to emphasize their positive feelings. But by doing so, they lose the opportunity for the agency worker to give valuable assistance in dealing with real problems. Second, couples may not want to admit that there is a difference between adoptive and natural parenthood. They may view the adoption worker as a constant reminder of this difference.

Adoption requires special adjustments in addition to those that occur with any new baby.

Normally, a couple can know within a couple of weeks when to expect the baby. But with adoption there is no such specific time guide. When the agency calls with the news that there is a baby available, there may be very quick changes in their life style. For instance, a woman may leave her job on just a few days notice and go, at least temporarily, from a career orientation to full-time mothering.

The adopted child may have strong needs for security from both parents. Often the adoptive home is the second or third setting the child has been in, and at first the child may be disoriented by the change in caretakers. Most people can meet the adopted child's special need for security. But they should understand that it will often resurface in one form or another as the child grows.

As the relationship between adopted child and parents develops, the couple must eventually resolve four issues:

(1) What is their understanding of the differences between adoptive parenthood and biological parenthood?

(2) How do they feel about the child's biological parents? If the child was illegitimate, how do they feel about illegitimacy?

(3) How do the parents help the child to understand and accept his or her adoptive status?

(4) How do they let people outside the family—relatives, friends, neighbors—know (or not know) that the child is adopted?

A couple cannot realistically expect these issues to be resolved during the supervisory period, nor in some cases for years afterwards. If they should later have a natural child a new set of relationships will develop. Each child may then feel that the other is more highly valued by the parents. Sibling rivalry between an adopted and natural child may be exaggerated if parents are not sensitive to their own feelings about the needs of both children.

During adolescence, children normally become very concerned with the question of personal identity. At this period, the adopted child may begin to ask questions about his or her biological parents. Many begin extensive searches for a natural parent and for their origins. There is no standard way to deal with the effects this may have on the relationship between adoptive parents and the maturing adolescent. But parents should anticipate this period and not automatically assume that they are being rejected. As with any other set of close human relationships, the specific problems connected with adoption are best worked out in an atmosphere of open, honest communication.

Before you go on . . .

1. The number of Americans under the age of eighteen now living with adoptive parents is approximately __1 million__.

2. The children in greatest demand for adoption are those who are __white__ and __healthy__.

3. In the United States our adoption laws are written mainly in the interests of the __child__.

4. There are usually no age limitations set by adoption agencies for prospective parents. True or (false?)

5. After a child is placed in a home for adoption, how long must the parents still wait before final court action? __1 yr__

6. Do a couple who are adopting a child usually know exactly when the child will join their household? *no*

7. If an adopted child searches for his or her natural parents, it usually means that the child rejects the adoptive parents. True or (false)?

Answers:

1. Ten million.

2. White; without physical disabilities.

3. Child.

4. False. Most agencies specify an upper limit of 35 for prospective mothers and 38 to 40 for fathers.

5. Six months to one year.

6. No. The agency makes this decision, and there may be no specific time guide for the parents.

7. False. Many adopted children do this when they reach adolescence.

FAMILY PLANNING *Chapter Review*

1. Most couples who decide not to have children do so for biological reasons. True or (false)?

2. Sickle-cell and Tay-Sachs disease are examples of ___*heriditary*___ diseases.

3. A genetic counselor can be helpful only to couples who carry genetic defects. True or (false)?

4. The goal of zero population growth is (a) a stable population; (b) a decreasing population; (c) a small population; (d) family planning.

5. Three reasons why couples might not want to have children are ___*financial*___, ___*careers*___, and ___*genetic problems*___.

6. Another name for birth control is ___*contraception*___.

7. Birth control methods depend on the prevention or avoidance of ___*pregnancy*___.

8. Family planning is basically a woman's responsibility. True or (false)?

9. Complete avoidance of sexual intercourse is the most effective method of birth control. True or false?

10. The most effective methods of female contraception are ___*the pill*___ and ___*IUD*___.

11. The contraceptive pill often results in irregular menstruation. True or false?

12. Use of the pill does not require medical supervision. True or false?

13. A contraceptive method that prevents sperm from entering the uterus is (a) the pill; (b) the I.U.D.; (c) the diaphragm; (d) spermacidal jelly.

14. Surgical tying-off of the _fallop. tubes_ will prevent ova from reaching the uterus.

15. Lowered fertility is always due to physical illness. True or false?

16. "Infertility" refers to (a) voluntary childlessness; (b) permanent inability to conceive; (c) involuntary childlessness; (d) impaired ovulation.

17. The most common cause of male infertility is _low sperm count_

18. Inability to have children is almost always due to infertility on the part of the woman. True or false?

19. Infrequent _ovulation_ can cause infertility in a woman.

20. Artificial insemination always depends on the use of semen from a man other than the husband. True or false?

21. Nearly 15 percent of married couples are infertile. True or false?

22. Adoption agencies usually require a waiting time of ____3____ to ____5____ years.

23. A good adoption worker will want to know about the upbringing of the prospective couples. True or false?

24. What decides which child will be placed with an approved couple? (a) age of child; (b) education of woman; (c) occupation of man; (d) compatibility.

25. A child should be told that he was adopted. True or false?

26. Age of the prospective parents is not an important factor in agency adoption. True or false?

27. What are some problems a couple might expect to have in raising an adopted child? _overprotection; social pressures_

28. In a few sentences, compare family planning and zero population growth.

29. Discuss the attitudes of the major religious groups toward birth control. _Catholic & orthodox Jews against_

30. How does abortion differ from other methods of family limitation? _it takes place after conception_

To find the answers, look at page 199

CHAPTER SEVEN

THE CHILD IN THE FAMILY

Leading thoughts:

- When children come, the couple need to adjust to their new, demanding roles as parents

- More than anything else, the child of any age needs consistent, loving care; but family stresses often make this difficult

- Children pass through several stages of development—social, intellectual and moral—as they learn their roles in society

- Today some children are increasingly free from the sex-role stereotyping that was common in earlier years

When Children Join the Family

The arrival of the first child—is it a blessed event or a crisis? In our society there is a great deal of romanticism connected with the birth of a baby. Congratulations come pouring in, there are baby showers, and many preparations must be made. Very often the young couple are so involved in the fantasy of the new baby that they have no time to prepare themselves for the reality. Hence they are met with surprises when the baby actually arrives.

When children come, attention that recently could be directed toward each spouse now goes to the newborn infant. Rivalries may develop. One parent, usually the father, may feel left out. New demands are made on the couple, and they face new and different responsibilities. Time has to be shared. Often the available space must be divided. Extra financial burdens begin to be felt; the breadwinner may feel added pressure to earn a good living. If the husband and wife feel emotionally deprived, their ability to give to the newborn will be diminished; they may feel repressed resentment toward the child for intruding into their life.

Our culture makes the assumption that parenthood enhances personality, stabilizes the couple's position in the community, and strengthens the marriage. Many people believe that becoming a parent increases their maturity. Often, parenthood does bring these bonuses. But if they do not materialize as expected, and the responsibilities still mount up, one or both parents may become disillusioned and discouraged. Their reaction may be, "No one ever told me that it was going to be like this."

Parents who expected to love the new baby on sight may have a mixed reaction. "This screaming little red creature is my child?" They may find that the little bundle of joy is also a bundle of additional burdens and pressures. A new baby takes a great deal of time. New mothers and fathers often find that they have much less time for themselves or for each other. This is a period when much love, devotion, energy, and time are given to the new baby; and the returns often come in the form of dirty diapers, drooling, or a messy burp.

The father who comes home after a hard day at the office and wants to relax with his wife may find that she is exhausted by her new role and has little energy left over for him. He may find that she is occupied with the baby, and he may feel left out. She, on the other hand, may resent the fact that he does not involve himself more with the care of the new infant.

For a woman, the birth of her first child may create new conflicts. If she has had a career, it may be difficult for her to give this up, to stay at home with the baby. She may find that she has little time for herself. If she has invested much of her identity in her career, she may find that staying at home with the baby is not as gratifying as she had expected. Her self-image may suffer as a result. It is not necessary to get dressed up in the morning to take care of a new-born infant, as it was when she was going out to work. She may look in the mirror and see a tired, housedress-clad image reflected back. After spending the entire day at home, she may want to go out with her husband. She is looking for stimulation; he wants to relax. The different requirements may even cause the couple to have some doubts about their marriage.

The wife and mother who goes back to work when her child is still young faces other problems. Since she was raised in a society which considers woman's primary role to be that of wife and mother, she may be plagued with guilt feelings about leaving her young child with another person. If the child is sick, she will consider it her responsibility to deal with this and to take time off from work. When she comes home from work, not only will she have to look after the infant, but she might also deal with some of the housework or cooking. Instead of having one job, she has three—housewife, mother, and career person.

In order to make a good adjustment to these changes in the family, the household duties, tasks, and roles should be organized and reassigned, so that each partner can meet the needs of child and spouse without overlooking his or her own. How this is to be done will, naturally, differ in each family unit.

The "experts" are always trying to tell parents how to raise their children. Until the early decades of this century, the young couple would often live with in-laws. They got most of their child-rearing information from their families. Later, as young couples began moving away from their families, they began to turn to the "experts" for help. Unfortunately, parenting is one of the only roles in life for which there is no formal preparation. Many people grow up in families in which they receive little love and nurturing. Often their preparation is negative. They see their parents as unhappy in their roles as parents. They decide to raise their children differently. Instead, they often wind up doing the same things that were done to them by their own parents.

Being a parent is one of the most difficult challenges any individual can meet. Parents usually place heavy burdens on themselves. They assume that they have to be the "perfect" parents, and they often measure themselves against an ideal image. They feel that it is not enough just be be a mother or father. They have to be a "good mother" or a "good father." And often their concept of this is totally unrealistic. They often impose the same unrealistic demands upon their offspring, wanting an "ideal" child. They make unrealistic demands on their children, and have too high an expectation of their abilities and performance. Such parents may want to live vicariously through their children's performance. They want their children to accomplish all that they have failed to achieve. Some other parents do not take their children seriously. They may regard their child as a toy, thereby robbing her of dignity and self-respect. A common example of this is the parent who laughs at the child's misbehavior.

We can assume that no two parents will have identical ideas on childraising. The reason for this is that they usually come from different home environments and have had different early experiences. For example, one parent who grew up in a strict environment may want to raise the child strictly, while another from the same type of environment may want to be more lenient. Still another, having grown up in an unstructured environment, may want to set some definite limits for the child. Very often, such a difference in views can lead to conflicts between the parents.

To the growing infant, the family represents the society at large. All men are mirrored in "Father" and all women in "Mother." The child has a strong need to belong and to feel accepted. All her efforts are directed toward finding a place in the family. The child needs to feel a sense of achievement and mastery. She needs encouragement in facing challenges and in taking risks. She needs to feel loved and understood, and to develop a sense of independence and autonomy. It is important that the parents begin to help a child develop according to these needs from the very day of birth.

Before you go on . . .

1. When a new baby arrives, _conflict_ may develop between the parents.

2. Fantasies about the new baby are often very similar to the realities of caring for it. True or false?

3. Above all, new babies demand a lot of _time_ and _energy_.

4. A family may find it easier to adjust to the new baby by _sharing household + baby responsibilities_

5. What are some of the things all children need? _love, understanding_

6. All people have different ideas about raising children because of what they have read. True or false?

7. Parents may feel _guilty_ if they don't feel that they are _adequate parents_

Answers:

1. Rivalry.

2. False. Usually they have very little resemblance to reality.

3. Time; energy.

4. Recognizing their difficulties and reassigning household tasks.

5. A sense of achievement and mastery; encouragement; love; understanding; a sense of independence and autonomy.

6. False. Most of people's ideas about parenthood are based on how they were raised by their own parents.

7. Guilty; "perfect" parents.

Between Parent and Child

36

Children raised in democratic families, where decisions are made cooperatively, often feel closer to their parents and are better adjusted than children from authoritarian homes, where all decisions are made by one or both parents and the children are allowed no "backtalk." Children from laissez-faire homes, where there are few definite parental expectations, show the poorest social adjustment.

Most parents love their children and care for them to the best of their ability. But some parents abuse their children, and this violence seems to breed more violence. Parents who brutalize their children were almost certain to have been abused by their own parents. Neglect and mistreatment of children are legal offenses. Laws that require physicians to report child abuse have provided a new safeguard for infants and children.

Infants need consistent, loving care. Caring for their physical needs is not enough. They must be held and stroked and talked to. This helps them to develop an attitude of basic trust. If they do not have a person they can depend on to meet their emotional as well as their physical needs, their social and intellectual development may be severely retarded. Studies of crowded orphanages show that infants may become anxious, then apathetic, when their physical needs are well met but they receive no individual care from one particular person. They may even die.

The orphanage studies have been used to argue that women should stay at home and care for their children. It is clear that an infant or child would suffer if an adequate substitute for a nurturant parent is not provided. And it seems essential that an infant receive the consistent and loving care of one person, especially in the early months. But children who are kept regularly by a loving grandmother, aunt, paid nurse, or father often seem to be as well adjusted as they would be if their mothers had stayed with them. There is also evidence that mothers who enjoy their work also relate positively to their children. Mothers who do not like their work outside of the home tend to see their children as hostile towards themselves and may overburden them with household chores. Similarly, mothers who enjoy homemaking tend to form positive relationships with their children and to view them as cooperative. A mother who feels trapped in the home may take out her frustrations on her children and husband.

Until recently, most of the writing on parenting focused on the mother–child relationship. Research into father–child relationships finds that children generally think of their father as the breadwinner and their mother as the homemaker, perhaps because in most families that has been the traditional way of dividing the work load between husband and wife. They think of their fathers as being stronger and more powerful, fearsome, and punitive than their mothers. And they want their fathers to be nurturant—somewhat easy-going, available, and participating in family life. Sons are more masculine when their fathers are dominant but nurturant. When mothers dominate, sons are less masculine and less likely to want to be like their fathers. A daughter's development is more likely to be influenced by the mother. Deliquent boys often have fathers who are absent, alcoholic, brutal, criminal, inconsistent in disciplining their children, negligent or rejecting of their sons. Boys who are rejected by their fathers or in conflict with them are often poor achievers in school.

Because of long working hours, or work that takes them away from home, men often do not have the opportunity to spend much time with their children. Many times they cannot be present at occasions that are especially meaningful to the children. Children would be greatly benefited if both men and women had working conditions that permitted them to spend significant time with their children. Some institutions may be slowly changing in this respect. The City University of New York now permits a man or woman to take a semester or a year of "parental leave" for child care.

When parents are in conflict with each other, the children usually suffer. Children who come from households lacking harmony have poor social skills and are less popular and less assertive than children whose parents are in harmony. They have poorer self-concepts, they measure lower on intelligence tests, and they are poorer students.

The loss of a parent through death may be less disturbing to a child than loss through separation, divorce, or desertion. Children's reactions are, of course, influenced by the way their parents react to the loss. In the case of separation or divorce the parents can minimize the harm to their children by cooperatively working out visiting privileges, planning together for the children's education, and by not belittling each other to the children.

A child may fare better with a single parent who is divorced than with two parents who quarrel. But single-parent families have their own difficulties. The task of breadwinning often falls entirely on the single parent, causing him or her to be away from home all day. A divorced woman, for example, is then forced to find a mother-substitute for her child. If the child is a boy, she needs to also provide him with male role-models. With new legislation focusing on equal rights between the sexes, more fathers may be granted custody of their children when parents separate, or when unwed parents choose not to form a marital partnership.

Unmarried single parents who bear and keep their own children may find that both they and their children are faced with identity problems. The children need to know with some certainty who both of their parents are. Young unmarried mothers who keep their babies and live at home with their parents sometimes feel more like siblings than parents to their own children. In such cases the grandmother may assume the mothering role. In 1970 Booth Memorial Home in Oakland, California, began a model program in which teenaged mothers and their babies lived at the home, often for as long as four to five years, while the mothers received job training or finished high school. Here the girls were allowed the normal social life of teenagers while they learned, in a supportive setting, the skills needed by parents. They gradually assumed more responsibility for the care of their children as they felt ready. Such programs are well worth assessing in depth.

Grandparents, aunts and uncles, or friends can be of great assistance to the one-parent family. But they are not always available. **Parents Without Partners** is a self-help organization in which single parents meet to share their problems and their experience in handling them. Children of single parents can benefit from programs offered by organizations in the community such as Scouts, the "Y", Big Brothers, and so forth.

Estimates are that one-half of pregnant single women who contact social service agencies decide to keep their babies. One-half of the young women who decide to keep their babies marry within six years. Half of these marry the child's father. With recent changes in adoption laws, single persons are sometimes permitted or encouraged to adopt older or hard-to-place youngsters. Single parents who decide to marry find that it is important for the new mate to like and assume a role of responsibility toward the children.

Generally speaking, the luckiest children are those with two parents who are self-con-

fident, happy in their relationship with each other and with their own way of dividing up the tasks of breadwinning and homemaking, and who are involved in the task of raising their children. Parents in other situations need not despair, however. A sincere interest in one's child can be sufficient to create a warm and nurturant atmosphere under most conditions.

Before you go on . . .

1. Children usually think of their fathers as having the role of _breadwinner_ and their mothers the role of _homemaker_.

2. Sons who have domineering mothers often do not wish to be very much like their fathers. True or false?

3. Sons are more masculine when their fathers are dominant and _nurturant_.

4. It is clear that if a mother works outside the home her children will suffer psychological damage. True or false?

5. _Parents without partners_ is a self-help organization for single parents with families.

6. _50%_ percent of the unmarried pregnant women who contact social service agencies decide to keep their children.

7. It is a legal offense for a parent to batter a child. True or false?

Answers:

1. Breadwinner; homemaker.
2. True.
3. Nurturant.
4. False. If she provides a mother-substitute who gives consistent nurturant care, the child can develop normally. High job satisfaction may also contribute positively to the mother–child situation.
5. Parents Without Partners
6. 50
7. True.

The Stages of Social Development

We gradually form our personalities through interaction with other persons. Alfred Adler, who worked with school children in Vienna and New York, noticed that the composition of the family often affects social development. A first or only child is generally around adults much of the time. He learns to relate to adult interests and achievement. Later-born children enter a family with children. Frequently they attempt to catch up with the skills of the older sibling(s). If parents allow competition to dominate the sibling relationships, rivalry and jealousy can develop. But when parents behave cooperatively and teach children to cooperate and have social interest in others, children will learn to work together and feel good about themselves for doing so. Having older or younger sisters or brothers also influences how we learn to relate to persons outside the family. Growing up in a nuclear family (mother, father, children) or an extended family (nuclear unit plus grandparents, aunts, uncles, or cousins) each provides a different experience in living.

Sigmund Freud pointed out that children develop in stages. His theory stressed the ways we use physical energy first to obtain pleasure through our mouths, later to control our elimination processes, and finally in our sexuality. It remained for some of his followers to incorporate the social aspect of development into Freudian theory.

Harry Stack Sullivan suggested an interpersonal theory of development. In his theory, babies are born dependent on other people to satisfy their needs. Each of us wants to feel secure in our interpersonal relationships. If the parents are tender and attentive to the infant, the baby feels secure. But if they are overly anxious or neglectful of the infant's needs, the baby feels insecure. The child whose parents do not value his or her growing expressiveness, curiosity, and eagerness to know all about the world will repress creative possibilities. Instead, he will try to conform to parental expectations. Parents who insist that the child do things only their way and do not respect unique individuality force the child to become **alienated** from his or her real self. This makes it difficult for the child to fulfill his potential.

Children develop a self-image based on the type of treatment they receive. In Sullivan's terms, the respected and well-nurtured child thinks of the self as "good me"—valuable and appreciated. A neglected or frustrated child regards the self as "bad me," unworthy of attention and importance. With the development of language, these feelings about ourselves become part of our self-concepts. The child tries to shape the emerging self-concept and patterns of behavior toward winning parental approval. But the self is creative and unique. It will put its own imprint on family relations.

As we enter school, new social possibilities arise. Earlier aspects of ourselves—usually repressed—may express themselves. This happens especially in the mid grammar-school years. We may pal around with a same-sexed chum who really appreciates our genuine self and gives us an opportunity to share needs and satisfaction on a personal level. Sullivan sees the chum experience as an important preparation for adolescence. It poses the challenge of successfully integrating three desires: personal security (freedom from anxiety); intimacy (collaboration); and lustful satisfaction (genital activity in pursuit of orgasm).

Sullivan ends his developmental stages at adolescence. But Erik Erikson shows how development continues throughout the life cycle and that growth takes place on the physical, social, and personal levels. In each of the eight stages of life a person faces a crisis and can move in either of two directions. By successfully completing a stage, one develops strength that aids in overcoming future crises.

The infant faces the crisis of surviving. If the infant receives physical nourishment, protection from harmful situations, and emotionally expressive care, it develops a sense of basic trust. Nursing provides the infant with the best physical nourishment and a lot of contact comfort which helps to build trust in life. The neglected or mistreated infant feels unwanted. It may become apathetic, withdrawn, or even die.

The toddler is gaining muscular control in walking, speaking, and controlling bladder and bowel functions. Respecting and assisting the toddler in these new skills gives a feeling of autonomy and the strength of "will"—"I will walk, I will talk, I will have a dry diaper." Teasing or putting down his efforts creates shame and doubt. As preschoolers we learn to get along with others and to take the initiative in doing our own projects. Accomplishment gives a sense of purpose, but failure leaves a feeling of guilt over our inability. The school-age child receives instruction, in a formal school setting or by working with parents, in the skills needed to be productive in society. Achievement generates a sense of industry and the strength of competence, but being unskilled leaves a feeling of inferiority.

The adolescent faces the crisis of "Who am I as a person separate from my family?" Finding a firm, but flexible, identity brings her the strength of fidelity. But remaining confused about one's role in life makes productive decisions impossible. The young adult, capable of fidelity, seeks intimacy in building a mutually trusting and sharing relationship with a beloved for work, procreation, and recreation. The young adult who can be intimate possesses the strength of love and avoids isolation. The middle-aged person becomes concerned about establishing and guiding the next generation. The person with the strength of care becomes **generative**—able to find new creative projects and to inspire younger people to find meaning in life. The person who is not generative stagnates and falls into a rut.

The stages of development are also **interpersonal**. If a younger person is to enjoy the conditions that lead to trust, autonomy, initiative, and industry, he or she must be cared for by an older person with a solid sense of identity, intimacy, and generativity. The growing person needs adequate physical care, needs to feel safe, to experience love and belonging, and to gain self-esteem from the accomplishment of productive projects before self-actualizing is possible—that is, to be what one is capable of becoming. Living with nurturant adults is crucial for the growing person to move towards self-actualization and generativity.

In the final stage of old age we face death. If we can look back on life as full of choices that made the best of our possibilities, we experience a sense of completion, and enjoy the strength of wisdom. But the aging person who recalls life as a series of missed and bungled opportunities may despair because life has not been meaningful.

Before you go on . . .

1. According to Sullivan, we need SECURITY , and we will shape ourselves to others' expectations to obtain it.

2. According to Sullivan, bad experiences early in life permanently cripple the person psychologically. True or false?

3. During middle childhood, having a same-sexed chum can be very valuable in developing a positive self-concept.

4. In infancy the child treated well feels a sense of basic _trust_ and acquires the strength of _hope_ .

5. The growing person seeking a sense of trust, autonomy, initiative, and industry benefits by being around an adult with a firm sense of identity, intimacy, and generativity. True or false?

6. The adolescent faces a crisis of _identity_ , that once found gives the strength of _fidelity_ .

7. The young adult is usually incapable of an intimate love relationship. True or false?

Answers:

1. Security.
2. False. Later positive social experiences can help us to discover undeveloped aspects of ourselves.
3. Chum.
4. Trust; hope.
5. True. For this reason it is important for a growing person to live with nurturant adults.
6. Identity; fidelity.
7. False. Young adults may be capable of intimacy and fidelity and avoid isolation through a caring relationship.

Development of Intelligence and Language

The infant is born with many intellectual and language capabilities. With proper nutrition, stimulation, motivation, and opportunities, these abilities will develop in an orderly sequence, though the ages for each stage will vary somewhat from child to child. We are indebted to the Swiss psychologist, Jean Piaget, for describing the stages of **cognitive** (intellectual) development.

The first of the four stages is the **sensorimotor** period. In this stage the child learns to act on the environment. At first the infant cannot move by itself, but notices sights, sounds, and moves objects by bumping into them. Gradually the infant organizes and coordinates certain sensations. For example, when the mother holds it in a customary feeding position, the baby will turn its head and want to nurse. Around three or four months the infant can put fingers and toes in its mouth. As the infant learns to roll over, sit up, and crawl, any object within reach is grasped and explored.

The simplest objects, such as a yogurt cup and top, can be the most fascinating toys. Brightly colored objects that fit inside each other or rings that fit on a pole attract a baby and allow for a lot of manipulation. After the child realizes that objects are permanent and do not disappear when taken away, the second stage begins. The child will now look for an interesting object even when it is hidden.

Being able to represent things through **symbols** in the mind begins a new era. Two signs of symbolic representation are **deferred imitation** (observing something and imitating the behavior at a later time) and **make-believe** (pretending to do something). Thought during this second, **pre-operational** stage is largely intuitive. Thinking remains egocentric; everything is seen from the child's perspective. For instance, when shown a model of a house, the child will describe every side of it as if it were the one being looked at. The child perceives human characteristics in objects—a stone might cry if stepped on, for example. And the child needs direct, external cues to guide and sustain behavior. Toys that are too intricate do not amuse the child. The growth of intelligence is a process that involves trying to assimilate reality to what one already knows and accomodating perceptions and concepts to new experiences.

The development of symbolic representation makes language possible. Language contains shared symbols that are meaningful within a culture. The old approach to language considered a child's language an imperfect copy of adult speech. But Noam Chomsky, a psycholinguist, has discovered that children in all cultures share many language stages in common. They actually generate their own grammars or patterns of speaking. At birth babies cry, and by three months they can coo. The sounds increase in frequency and variety until the child can babble at six or seven months. A few words are used at around one year. Then babies go through a two-word stage. Using just a couple of basic words represents an effort to construct language according to the child's set of rules. By knowing the situation in which the child is speaking or the tone of voice used, an adult can figure out the child's meaning. By age five the child's speech resembles the adult's. During this time the child may learn the rules of adult grammar and apply them inflexibly—"She goed to the store." Once the child masters the use of language, new combinations of words and sentences can be spoken without having ever been encountered before.

Realizing that things can change shape while the same amount of substance remains is called **conservation.** It characterizes the third stage of **concrete operations.** The concrete operational child can see liquid poured from a tall, thin jar to a short, fat one, and understand that the same amount is present in both. Similarly, six eggs spaced far apart are equal to six eggs placed side by side. And a ten-pound sack of potatoes is equivalent in weight to five two-pound sacks. Thus, the concrete-operational child learns to "conserve" volume, quantity, number, and weight. The concrete-operational child also gradually learns to add and multiply **classes.** Adding classes means knowing that several objects belong in a group. For instance, collies, cocker spaniels, and terriers are dogs. In multiplying classes the child can use two kinds of classification at once, such as organizing objects both by shape and by color.

The fourth stage, **formal operations,** begins when the youngster can engage in abstract thought. Interestingly enough, cognitive, physical, social, and emotional maturity all emerge around the same time during adolescence. Through abstract thought a person can ask such questions as "Who am I?" and start to ask philosophical questions. Formal operational thought enables us to carry on systematic scientific experiments. We can formulate a hypothesis, figure out what consequences we want to happen, and then experiment to find out what conditions produce the desired consequences.

The stages of intellectual development cannot be substantially speeded up through instruction. They occur naturally, when youngsters are given the opportunity to work with various types of materials and concepts. Intelligence is not something simple that a person possesses. Instead, it develops in many ways with stimulation and motivation. Over a period of decades the UCLA psychologist J.P. Guilford has worked with a model of the intellect involving 120 different abilities. Through testing of children and adults, 98 of these have already been demonstrated to exist. Classifying individuals on the basis of simplified I.Q. tests, which do not take into account the complexity and potential for growth of the intellect, can hamper the individual's creativity and fulfillment. Informed parents and teachers who are familiar with the implications of sophisticated studies on intelligence, such as those by Piaget and Guilford, can help their children to stimulate their intellectual development.

Before you go on . . .

1. Guilford's model of the intellect claims that there are _____ different intellectual abilities; _____ of these have been discovered through testing.

2. Young children need attractive, easily manageable toys that are not too intricate to stimulate their intellectual development. True or false?

3. According to Piaget, the second stage of intellectual development begins when the infant realizes that _____

4. What is the process by which children come to know that a substance can change shape with no changes in quantity? _____

5. By age _____ children have pretty well mastered the adults' language.

6. Children's language is an imperfect copy of the adult version. True or false?

7. With adolescence, the child becomes capable of _____ thought.

Answers:

1. 120; 98.

2. True. In infancy, they have no interest in toys that are very complicated.

3. Objects still exist even when they disappear.

4. Conservation.

5. Five.

6. False. Children first construct their own patterns of speech with their own rules and later learn adult language.

7. Abstract.

Discipline and Moral Development

In all areas of development, children move from strong dependence on parents or a parent substitute to relative independence. Parents are the first and most important agents in the socialization of the child. From the beginning, children learn what is important or unimportant, pleasant or unpleasant, good or bad, socially acceptable or unacceptable, from observing their parents' reactions. Their siblings, the extended family, teachers, neighbors, and friends all play a part in forming their values and expectations. But the values of their parents are the foundation upon which children build their own value structures.

Parents who want their small children to grow up to be "good" should discuss with one another the qualities they believe a "good" person should have. Next, they might examine their own behavior as individuals and their interaction as a couple, to determine whether they are modeling the kind of behavior they would like their children to imitate. Their children will learn many values from them by imitation, long before they reach the age when one can reason with them.

The word "discipline" in recent years has taken on a poor conotation. It is usually used to mean "punishment." We would prefer to use an earlier meaning—"training to develop self-control or character." If parents have a clear idea of what behaviors they want their children to learn, they will know what types of intervention on their part can help their children to learn to regulate their behavior according to these guidelines.

What forms of discipline work? Is punishment harmful? What about spankings? Different forms of discipline are probably appropriate for the same children at different ages.

Lawrence Kohlberg has studied the moral development of children. His research shows that when they are very young, children tend to be obedient in order to avoid trouble. "Bad" behaviors are those that are followed by punishment. "Right" and "wrong" are determined by what their parents decide is acceptable and what is unacceptable behavior. They behave themselves in order to avoid punishment, or to please their parents or parent-substitute. In middle childhood children begin to define "right" and "wrong" in terms of what is normative or conventional. They move from wishing to please specific other persons to behaving out of a sense of duty, or of general respect for persons in authority. They develop a sense of the importance of earned self-respect.

Adolescents and young adults are able to regulate their behavior in relation to their own internalized set of values. They are often aware of legal rules, moral principles, and contractual relationships, and they have a sense of personal responsibility. As they move toward maturity their individual consciences and sense of social responsibility become their most important guides. Not everyone, of course, moves through all of these stages.

As in all their development, children whose circumstances do not challenge them to grow may reach adulthood without developing to their full potential. But to the extent they do develop, children seem to move through the same stages in the same order. Of course some children will move through the stages more rapidly or more slowly than others. Knowledge of how children of different ages view "right" and "wrong" gives us some insight into how parents can intervene when their child or adolescent is doing something they consider to be wrong.

Infants, of course, are not to be blamed for turning over glasses of milk, getting stuck under chairs, being cranky, or any other annoying behaviors. They are simply exploring their environment or expressing their needs, and should be congratulated for doing so. Curiosity leads to learning, and no parent would want to squelch a child's eagerness to learn or capacity for self-expression. It is the parents' responsibility to make the environment safe for an infant, or to find ways to please or distract one who is fussy.

Small children must learn, for their own protection and their parents' sanity, what activities are truly unsafe or socially undesirable. Heaters must not be touched when hot, for example, and parents and siblings must not be bitten. Toys must be shared, and so forth. We know that young children both fear and expect punishment for misbehavior and want more than anything else to please the important adults in their lives. So we might spank Susie's hand and say "No, no! Hot!" very sternly every time her hand reaches out to the hot heater. If he bites, we may put Johnnie down with a frown and a comment, "We don't bite!" Or we may praise him when he shares a toy voluntarily with a younger sibling.

Reasoning with small children simply doesn't work. They have neither the language nor the social interest for reasoning to work. "Right" is a rather self-centered matter of the young child satisfying needs or of successfully avoiding punishment. Young children are very sensitive about whether the same rules are applied to all siblings, and whether or not they are consistently applied to themselves. Their observations give them a sense of what is normative and help them move towards the next stage of development.

Children in their middle years may respond to reasoning like "You should carry out the garbage because it is your job" (assuming that everyone in the family has been assigned specific duties). They may feel a deep sense of remorse when asked, "Now, is that how a Brownie (or Cub) Scout can be expected to keep her (his) room?" Children of this age may deeply resent physical punishment, feeling that parents are using their greater size to bully them. On the other hand, they may welcome it as a quick way of "paying for their sins," after which they feel free to start sinning again. They may accept as just the temporary loss of certain privileges—"You can't go out and play until the garbage is carried out."

Children in the middle years learn about personal responsibility by carrying out assigned tasks. They will appreciate it if their feelings are brought out and their opinions consulted in the family decision-making process. In this way they can learn the importance of considering others' points of view. But they will still need their parents' reassurance and approval in making important personal decisions. Opportunities to express their own opinions, together with the security that comes from knowing that they can still lean on mom and dad whenever they need to, gives children the confidence that helps them to move on to mature decision-making.

Physical punishment is now considered inappropriate for teenagers. And the rationale "Because I told you to" may sound to them like a power play. At best, it will be viewed as patronizing. Teenagers are capable (or at least are becoming capable) of independent reasoning. While they are often strongly influenced by the behavior of their peers, they themselves wish to be viewed as individuals, to be dealt with directly and rationally. While they may still accept parental authority in some areas, mom and dad will increasingly be called upon to defend their rationale for any disciplinary action. And in some areas—appropriate behavior on a Saturday night date, for example—mom and dad may find that their influence is no longer total. And that is both inevitable and good. Young men and women in their teenage years should have developed some values of their own. The wise parent will allow freedom for testing them, while standing by to offer friendly support and encouragement when they are needed or sought.

At every stage of development, punishment should be commensurate with the size of the crime and with the child's ability to see the relationship between one and the other. A toddler would certainly not benefit if a parent was angry for days over a glass of spilled milk. A child who is required to work for several weeks to pay for a lost library book may learn to dislike reading. We should also not overlook the value of praise, and we should be specific about our expectations. "I like it when you select your own clothing and are dressed in time for school" gives a child much clearer guidelines than "Why can't you get dressed in the morning?" Finally, it is important to keep in mind that the point of discipline is to teach self-discipline, not self-depreciation. A sense of humor can help parents administer justice with a light touch.

Before you go on . . .

1. The most important agents in the socialization of a child are the _parents_.

2. In all areas of development children move from strong dependence upon their parents to relative independence. True or false?

3. The term "discipline" is too often used to mean "_punishment_."

4. When they are very young children tend to be obedient in order to _win affection_.

5. While spankings are clearly appropriate for young children, they are also very effective with children in the middle years and with teenagers. True or false?

6. By the time they are _adolescents_, children may be able to regulate their own behavior in relation to their own internalized set of values.

7. Children in the middle years often respond positively when parents appeal to their sense of duty. True or false?

Answers:

1. Parents.

2. True. Full independence is not reached until early adulthood.

3. Punishment. A better meaning is "training."

4. Avoid trouble.

5. False. Physical punishment is particularly unsuitable for adolescents.

6. Teenaged.

7. True. They learn the importance of earning self-respect.

Learning Sex Roles

Most of us encounter a great deal of **sex-role learning** as children. What we learn about the types of behavior considered appropriate for each sex has a strong influence on us throughout our lives. Traditional ideas about sex-role learning, or **sex-role stereotypes** (as they are more often called), are rigid ideas of male and female roles in American society. For example, men are supposed to be strong, agressive, active, athletic, and have leadership abilities. Many of these qualities can be summed up under the label of **competency**. Women, on the other hand, are supposed to be warm, soft, likable, gentle, and passive. These qualities can best be expressed under the heading of **emotionality**.

Although the stereotypes are often rewarding, if you are a female with only female attributes, many opportunities and possibilities in life requiring psychological strength and assertion (male attributes) will be closed to you. Similarly, a male with only male attributes would lack the dimensions of warmth and emotionality that are needed for friendship, empathy, and love relationships. We should note that individuals of both sexes do not completely lack the opposite qualities, but when these qualities are present or partially developed, both men and women often experience discomfort and embarrassment at their existence.

When we study the socialization of children, we find that sex-role stereotypes are taught in numerous ways. Remember the nursery rhymes you heard as a child? "Jack be nimble, Jack be quick . . .," but "Little Miss Muffet sat on her tuffet . . . ." This male-active/female-passive concept also appears in childhood fairy tales where a prince (preferably in shining armor) rescues the maiden in distress, marries her, and they live happily ever after. This theme is reflected in "Snow White," "Cinderella," and "Sleeping Beauty," all of which present sex-role stereotyped male and female characters.

There are also television shows that foster male and female stereotypes—"I Love Lucy," "The Flintstones," and "I Dream of Jeannie." Interspersed with these programs are commercials, which more often than not show the children in the viewing audience that adult women are most concerned with the yellow wax buildup on their floors, the shine on their dishes, or the ring around their husband's collar. It is worth noting, too, that the voice-over in the commercials—the vocal part—is often that of a man telling the woman which product will solve her problems (remember, he's competent and she's emotional—at least according to the stereotypes).

When the child is not watching television, toys are the main form of entertainment. Even today, we find the inevitable division of dolls for girls and mechanical toys for boys. But most boys, at some time in their childhood, express an interest in playing with dolls. And many girls would like to try the intricate, complicated toys that boys often receive. Traditionally, these interests have been squelched with accusations of "sissy" or "that's not ladylike" for boys and girls respectively. Some enlightened parents will try to reconcile the child's desires with the awareness that a boy should want to play daddy just as a girl should want to learn how an engine works. But it is likely that these parents will still feel the pressure of traditionalism from members of the past generation (such as grandparents) and from other contemporaries.

After reaching the age of six, the child will attend grammar school most of the day. Here she is exposed to readers and texts that further support the already-developed concepts of masculinity and feminity. Although some publishers are trying to eradicate sexism in textbooks, most of the books in use still reflect the traditional role concepts. It is surprising to note that even award-winning children's books have a predominance of male characters as opposed to female characters, and tend to reflect the idea that "boys invent things" and "girls use what boys invent." Furthermore, these stereotypes appear not only in grade-school readers, but in other texts as well. A recent analysis of sixth grade math texts revealed that verbal math examples with male subjects concerned sports, work, and earning money, while female examples concerned food and fabrics.

From these examples, we can see that sex-role stereotypes are learned in many ways. We might expect that children brought up with rigid stereotypes will suffer painful consequences. In fact, the evidence indicates that for women, such stereotyping is often reflected in low ambition or "fear of success"—a woman's fear of appearing too competent or too smart since this might detract from her femininity. In one study, 65 percent of college women associated "unusual excellence in women" with "loss of femininity and social rejection." This phenomenon, however, was rarely observed in college males.

During middle age, the consequences of living out a stereotyped feminine role may appear as depression in women who chose to make their families the sole focus of their lives. This particular depression syndrome is likely to occur in middle-aged women who lose the role of mother when their children become fully grown. When society considers the roles of wife and mother the most important for women, losing these roles can cause a woman to lose her self-esteem. She feels worthless and useless, emotional states characteristic of depression.

Similarly, a stereotyped male role also causes deficiencies in the adult male's personality. For example, the man who has never learned to express his feelings and has concentrated all of his energies in his work may find that his emotional relationships with his wife, friends, and children are severely limited. He may find that he is a "Sunday Father" or a fixture in the house, even though he is physically present. Worst of all, a man who has been taught not to show fear may also be unable to show love.

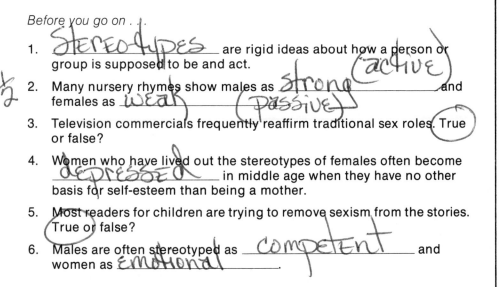

Before you go on . . .

1. __Stereotypes__ are rigid ideas about how a person or group is supposed to be and act.

2. Many nursery rhymes show males as __strong (active)__ and females as __weak (passive)__.

3. Television commercials frequently reaffirm traditional sex roles. True or false? __True__

4. Women who have lived out the stereotypes of females often become __depressed__ in middle age when they have no other basis for self-esteem than being a mother.

5. Most readers for children are trying to remove sexism from the stories. True or false? __False__

6. Males are often stereotyped as __competent__ and women as __emotional__.

7. Because they have learned role stereotypes, women often have lower ambitions or view success as being unfeminine. True or false?

Answers:

1. Stereotypes. Sex-role training often results in sex-role stereotypes.

2. Active; passive.

3. True. Women are shown as emotional and men as rational.

4. Depressed.

5. False. So far, only a few publishers are trying to do this.

6. Competent; emotional.

7. True. Women may fear that being capable will lead to a loss of femininity and social rejection.

Alternatives to Traditional Childcare

41

If you are like most children born in the 1950s or 1960s, you probably were raised in a nuclear family consisting of a mother, father and children. If your family was typical, your father went to work and your mother stayed home to take care of you and your siblings.

But if you choose to have children, the patterns of childrearing will not be as clear as the guidelines your parents followed. You will have many more options and possibilities. Most of the changes in childrearing result from changes in the role of women. For example, many women with children find themselves working either from choice or from economic necessity. In fact, a recent survey indicated that, in 1975, 39 percent of the women with children under the age of six were employed. For the first time in our history, more than half the children of school age now have mothers who work outside the home. But in spite of the obvious need for childcare (or **day care** as it is more commonly called), facilities in the United States have been slow to develop. Some estimates indicate that

child care is available to only about 20 percent of the children who need it. Others indicate that only 2 percent of the children of employed mothers are being cared for in group facilities.

Despite the numbers of women working, the prevailing attitude in American society is that a mother's place is with her children. However, psychological studies indicate that the mother's employment, in itself, is largely unrelated to her child's mental health.

Unfortunately, the concept of "day care" bears a social stigma. It evokes images of facilities designed for lower-class children. One common attitude is that day care centers are merely holding centers for poor children, which offer little educational opportunity. It is interesting that the term "nursery school," in contrast to "day care," is associated with upper-middle-class parents, who are sacrificing income to enrich their child's environment. In fact, there is no guarantee that nursery schools will be any different from day care facilities. The quality of day care centers and nursery schools depends on the quality of the care provided and the attitudes of the parents towards the child, not on the particular label used. In one important study, psychologists observed children who were enrolled in a day care center at three-and-a-half to five months of age and left at 29 months of age. The ratio of caretakers to children was quite high for either a nursery school or day care center. When the day care children were compared with children of the same age, economic, and ethnic background, no differences were found. The researchers concluded that day care seemed to make no difference at all to the children's development.

For those of you who will consider these facilities for your own children, the historical background of day care is important. Far from being a new or radical movement, day care facilities were in widespread use during the Depression and during World War II. By the end of the war, almost 52 million dollars was expended by the federal government and 26 million dollars by the states for day care facilities. But at the end of World War II, public funding for day care was cut, as veterans returned to industry and women left the labor force. It was not until the 1960s and 1970s that the idea of day care picked up momentum again. One of the most important developments in this period has been the reappearance of publicly funded programs to extend day care to children of working-class families. Project Head Start is the most widely known program, but there are many others as well, mostly operating on a smaller, neighborhood scale.

From this information, we may conclude that the United States has a history of child care services, and that these facilities are viable options in childrearing. We should also remember that notions of "home reared children," "day care children," and "nursery school children" are, by themselves, meaningless concepts. For example, a child who stays home with a mother who prefers to work is not getting "better" care just because she is home. And, of course, a day care center or nursery school staffed by noncaring, impersonal people would guarantee a poor childrearing environment. The important point is the quality of the care, and how well the particular facility suits the needs of both parents and child.

Before you go on . . .

1. What percentage of the children of employed mothers are cared for in group facilities? *2%*

2. Extensive research showed that whether a mother stays home or works does not, in itself, determine the child's mental health. True or false?

3. More day care was available in the U.S.A. during the *Depression* and during *W.W. II*.

4. The *Quality* of care makes the difference in childrearing, not the location.

5. Most working women hold jobs from choice, rather than necessity. True or false?

6. The terms *day care centers* and *nursery schools* are sometimes contrasted, but they are not necessarily different in quality.

7. There is no guarantee that nursery schools differ from day care. True or false?

Answers:

1. 2 percent. Child care is available to only about 20 percent of the children who need it.
2. True. By itself, the mother's employment does not determine a child's mental health.
3. Depression; World War II.
4. Quality.
5. False. Women on their own and those supporting families more often work from necessity.
6. Day care; nursery school.
7. True. They are two labels for what is often the same thing.

THE CHILD IN THE FAMILY *Chapter Review*

1. Children more often follow what parents say than what they do. True or false?
2. Children from _____ families are generally better adjusted and closer to their parents. (a) democratic; (b) autocratic; (c) laissez-faire; (d) authoritarian.
3. According to Erikson, the young adult is capable of _fidelity_ and seeks _intimacy_.
4. Physical punishment effectively teaches adolescents discipline. True or false?
5. By _____, Piaget means that a child realizes that the same amount remains, though the shape or arrangement is altered. (a) multiplicative (r) operational; (c) sensorimotor; (d) conservation.
6. Children grow best when their fathers are dominant and their mothers nurturant. True or false?
7. Alfred Adler noticed that the _environment_ [family constellation] often has an influence on how children develop.
8. Infants need to develop a sense of _____ in order to achieve their maximum potential. (a) concern; (b) trust; (c) apathy; (d) solidity.

9. The operational child, who realizes that lions, tigers and leopards are all cats, is able to _add_____ classes.

10. According to Erikson, the adolescent goes through a crisis regarding (a) sex; (b) pimples; (c) identity.

11. The child who can arrange objects both by color and shape can _multiply_____ classes.

12. A number of new mothers experience conflicts about remaining at home or returning to work. True or false?

13. The ability to think _____ comes with formal operations. (a) intuitively; (b) practically; (c) insightfully; (d)abstractly.

14. According to Sullivan, children who are _loved_____ and well nurtured experience the self as _good me_____.

15. Actually caring for a new baby frequently brings unexpected responsibilities. True or false?

16. What we learn as appropriate behavior for males and females are called _stereotypes_____

17. Lawrence Kohlberg speaks of stages of _____ development. (a) social; (b) moral; (c) emotional (d) sexual.

18. Unmarried mothers who keep their babies have an extremely difficult time marrying. True or false?

19. Children often pick up the values parents communicate through their behavior. True or false?

20. Language is not possible without _symbolic rep._____

21. During _____ individuals generally follow the rules that are conventional as agreed upon by the group. (a) middle childhood; (b) preschool; (c) infancy; (d) late adolescence.

22. More day care was available during the Depression and World War II than today. True or false?

23. The _quality_____ rather than the amount and location of child care seems to matter more.

24. Discipline is more effective when it teaches _____, rather than self-depreciation. (a) moral turpitude; (b) ingenuity; (c) self-discipline; (d) psycholinguistics.

25. The child's language is an inferior copy of the adult's. True or false?

26. Insisting that little boys wear blue, or not play with dolls, is an example of _stereotyping_____

27. _____ percent of the children of employed mothers are cared for in group facilities. (a) 16; (b) 64; (c) 2; (d) 2.

28. What is the connection between the development of thought and language? *The development of symbols makes language possible*

29. Describe, briefly, the main stages of moral development. *avoidance of punishment, idea of right & wrong, values of conscience*

30. How can discipline be matched with the level of the child's development? *Teaching self-discipline*

To find the answers, look at page 201.

GENERAL REVIEW *Chapters Four through Seven*

1. According to Erikson, when the toddler gains muscular control in walking, speaking, and controlling bowel and bladder functions, a sense of *autonomy* is gained.

2. The most sexually excitable part of the female anatomy is the (a) vagina; (b) uterus; (c) clitoris; (d) vulva.

3. At adolescence a person generally matures emotionally, socially, sexually, and into formal operational thought. True or false?

4. The male sex cell is called a(n) *sperm* and the female a(n) *egg ovum*.

5. Male and female expectations about sex are fairly similar. True or false?

6. What are antibodies and how can a baby receive them? *Protection from disease through the placenta*

7. (a) Plateau; (b) Excitement; (c) Resolution; (d) Orgasm occurs in both sexes when the genital muscles contract rhythmically forcing blood out of the engorged tissues. *Thin the muscles*

8. What is the purpose of the contractions that occur during childbirth?

9. A male normally has a(n) *X* and a(n) *Y* chromosome, whereas a female has two *X* chromosomes.

10. In males and females, both urine and sexual fluids use the same passageway. True or false?

11. According to J. P. Gilford the human intellect has
    _____ abilities. (a) two; (b) eight; (c) sixty-three;
    (d) one hundred twenty.

12. What four food groups do we need to eat from daily to obtain quality
    nutrition? *grains + cereals, milk+eggs, meats+fish*

13. The mother who works with her body through relaxing and breathing
    techniques will not experience as much discomfort during labor
    contractions. True or false?

14. How did Alfred Adler encourage parents to deal with sibling rivalry? *social interest*

15. What did Harry Stack Sullivan list as the three needs of young
    people? *security, sex satisfaction, + intimacy*

16. According to Piaget, the preoperational child thinks in which
    manner? (a) Sensorimotor; (b) Practical; (c) Additive; (d) Egocentric.

17. The mother and fetus exchange nourishment and waste products
    through the *placenta* _____.

18. A better form of discipline than punishment is training to develop
    self-control or character. True or false?

19. Just as orgasmic dysfunction is the most common female sexual
    complaint, so (a) impotence; (b) vaginismus; (c) premature ejacula-
    tion; (d) dyspareunia is most prevalent among men.

20. Having prior sexual experience gives one automatic knowledge about
    all sexual relationships. True or false?

21. Discuss the role of nutrition in pregnancy and childbirth. *If mother isn't healthy neither will baby*

22. Discuss the purpose of the stages of childbirth. *one develops through 8 stages satisfying your sex partners desires*

23. What does Erikson have to say about personality development?

24. What is meant by pleasuring?

25. What is the most common sexual dysfunction in females and what is
    an appropriate cure? In males?

To find the answers, look at page 203. *orgasm* *premature ejaculation; squeezing*

CHAPTER EIGHT
MARRIAGE THROUGH A LIFETIME

Leading thoughts:

■ The family's ability to cope with stress is influenced by many factors, including unemployment, illness, and the emotional states of its members

■ A stable marriage demands that a couple be able to communicate with one another

■ Modern marriage should be thought of as a helping relationship, in which the couple assist one another to live creatively and to become more fully themselves

■ The time after the youngest child leaves home is often a critical period for the married couple. When the children are gone, the husband and wife may experience serious communication problems

■ With retirement, the family cycle approaches its end. The retired person loses many former roles, and his responsibilities decrease

Coping with Crises 42

A family's ability to cope with stress is influenced by many factors. These include the suddenness of the crises, the family's ability to plan ahead, family income, their social network, their past experience, and the maturity and stability of the people involved. The general problem-solving process may include five steps: being able to see the real issues; openly discussing feelings; looking at all the alternatives; choosing the most suitable option; and dealing with the effects of the decisions made.

A frequent, serious crisis is **unemployment**. When the breadwinner becomes unemployed, the most obvious concern for most families is financial. The worker's feelings may be equally important—fears about self-worth and performance, anxiety about getting future employment, or feelings of jeopardizing the family's security. Fathers and husbands, especially, may begin to feel that unemployment is tied in to masculinity. Many fear loss of authority and esteem from children and overreact, adding to the family's stress. Discussion of the anxiety and resentment may help reduce the stress, so that the family may explore the alternatives more logically.

The couple should consider their supports—how they have handled past financial crises and what planning they have done through savings to cover such emergencies. Almost all workers are covered by Federal Unemployment Insurance. The couple can consider ways to reduce spending. Resorting to credit-card buying may increase long-time pressure rather than decrease it. Even when they have little flexibility in alternatives, honest expression of their fears and anger will help reduce tension for the couple.

Similar anxieties may occur in case of **serious illness**. If one of the spouses becomes seriously ill, financial worries are coupled with fears about the physical well-being of the patient. If insurance coverage runs out, the family may have to apply for welfare. Such a change in status, along with the fear that all financial cushioning will be exhausted, can increase a patient's feelings of anger and dependency. Employment may be difficult to find or continue even when the illness is controlled. Physical changes, such as those which accompany mastectomy, or surgical breast removal in women, may make the person feel less desirable and create fears of rejection.

When serious illness strikes, family members waver between overprotectiveness and feelings of resentment about new responsibilities. There may be extreme changes in routine, to accommodate medical needs. Fears about death or family survival may intensify while a patient is awaiting a serious surgical procedure. In any serious illness, the family and patient must accept the reality of the disease before they can deal with the alternatives open to them. For patients and their families who cannot cope

effectively, social services are available to provide additional support.

When parents face a severe handicap in a child, such as retardation, their first reactions may be denial, followed by grief. They grieve both for the afflicted child they have and for the normal child they had expected. A normal parental wish is that the child should simply die—a natural death, that will free them from having to face the problems of the future. Parents in this situation usually feel two initial compulsions. They want to have another baby immediately; and they want to tell people that the child is retarded—to test others' reactions. As the parents deal with accepting the child, these compulsions subside. But the parents may still worry that they are inadequate. They worry about whether their later children will be normal. They may go anxiously from doctor to doctor hoping for a new cure or a different diagnosis.

Most studies indicate that retarded children do better with their families in the early years. But eventually the couple have to face the question of placing the child in an institution. Parents may also worry about the retarded child's effect on other children in the family. The greater the concrete supports open to the family—day care, homemaker services, and financial aid—the less impact the retardate's physical care will have on the family. Parents' groups, in which feelings can be expressed, and emotional support exchanged, can buffer the psychological stresses of raising a retarded child with respect and dignity.

When a child has a **long-term illness,** the family must accept the fact that they have a chronically and seriously ill child instead of a normal, healthy one. They may need to face the eventual death of their child. As they cope with serious childhood illness, the couple should not hide their feelings from each other. All family members, including the sick child, need to share their feelings of fear and grief. Siblings will see changes in their brother or sister and have questions. If the family cannot grieve, and talk openly, the sick child will be isolated and fearful.

A family in this situation may try to "escape into activity." They may start new projects, such as moving or a pregnancy, to avoid facing the seriousness of the illness. Such reactions add stress at a time when energy should be conserved to maintain as much of the normal home life as possible. The parents may be overprotective of the seriously ill child, particularly if the child is in pain. They may also have to help the child deal with the teasing or staring of young peers. For example, the chemotherapy used in treatment of leukemia often causes severe hair loss and temporary weight gain. A bald-headed first grader is almost certain to be the object of curiosity or ridicule. Teachers should be alerted to any physical changes in their pupils so that they are prepared to deal with them. Parents' groups, run by hospitals or clinics, may help the parents of seriously ill children.

When a child dies after a prolonged illness, the family has had some time to prepare itself. But the crisis is more severe when the death was not expected. **Crib death,** or **sudden infant death syndrome,** usually occurs in children less than one year old. Often a seemingly healthy baby is put to bed at night; in the morning, the parents find a dead infant. The cause of the death is not fully understood, but it may have to do with an immature respiratory system. Special parents' groups, often conducted by parents who have experienced this loss, have been organized to help others who are stricken. Parents often have a mistaken sense of guilt—"If only we had been more observant, more careful. . . ." They blame themselves for the death; they may fear that the same condition will kill any future children. The therapeutic parents' groups try to help couples realize that their guilt and fear are unfounded.

Advancing age may be enough to bring crisis to a marriage. Marital satisfaction and intimacy may decrease in the forties for a number of reasons. While the man may have reached the peak of his career, the woman may be discovering new career opportunities, or may be feeling depression at no longer being a mother. The couple may have to cope with the financial and emotional problems of providing for aging parents, or they may be adjusting to their parents' deaths. As their children plan educations and careers, they may feel proud of their accomplishments, but may be disillusioned and dejected at their failure to live up to their ideals as parents.

During this period activities outside the marriage may take priority over the home. Some people start to have affairs, or divorce and remarry, in order to bolster their feelings of acceptance and self-worth. An affair may create a temporary oasis from boredom, yet it, too, may become routine. Other persons may marry a considerably younger individual. Rates of alcoholism and obesity often rise. The rates of heart attacks and ulcers often increase among workers who rely totally on their jobs to provide feelings of self-worth.

The middle-aged couple may find themselves in the situation of trying to explain their dissatisfaction to each other and finding their partners amazed. If both spouses want to grow, they may choose to revitalize the relationship rather than terminate it. The process may be painful but revealing. It may improve the functioning of the individuals and in the long run it may improve the relationship.

Before you go on . . .

1. A good deal of tension can be relieved in a crisis by _talking over feelings_.

2. When they first learn of a handicap or retardation in a child, parents may experience _denial_, then _grief_.

3. Openness about poor health with the ill child and the siblings makes for better adjustment. True or false?

4. During illness family members may feel both _resentful_ and _overprotective_

5. Overprotectiveness of an impaired child is normal and makes adjustment easier. True or false?

6. Sudden Infant Death Syndrome (crib death) is caused by fatal blood clots. True or false?

7. In what way do some middle-aged couples try to escape marital boredom? _Having an affair_

Answers:

1. Openly discussing feelings.

2. Denial; grief.

3. True. If the family cannot discuss it openly, the sick child will feel alone and isolated.

4. Overprotective; resentful.

5. False. Overprotectiveness may cause problems with siblings or relieve parents' guilt feelings.

6. False. The cause is unknown.

7. They may enter into one or more extramarital affairs.

Communication in Marriage   43

The emerging model of marriage is one in which two persons choose each other as marriage partners for basically personal reasons. Ideally, they share some common values and goals. They have similar or complementary interests. They respect and value each other as persons and want to share their lives with one another.

This kind of marriage, if it is to be successful, demands that a couple be two separate, competent individuals who are able to communicate with each other. When they marry each other, any man and woman are already different from one another in some ways. They are different by sex and have had different experiences. Some of their values and expectations are different. And they have different skills. But some people are afraid of acknowledging their differences. They feel that if they are different from their mate the marriage will be threatened. A wife who feels this way may, for example, cast a ballot identical to her husband's in every election, feeling that she should not "cancel his vote" by voting independently, even though she prefers another candidate. Or a husband may reluctantly attend concert after concert with his wife although he has little interest in music, because he finds it unthinkable that she should go alone or with a friend who also enjoys music. This woman and man have locked themselves into a pattern of noncommunication. They do not communicate their personal interests and values because they believe that marriages cannot endure if a man and wife openly express or cultivate different interests.

Certainly it is hard to imagine a lasting marriage in which the man likes hunting so much that he is away from home ten months of every year on various hunting expeditions, while the wife really likes and expected constant companionship. These persons are so different that if they communicated with each other from the beginning, they would never marry at all. When a couple have enough common interests, values, experiences, and skills, and enough love for each other that they wish to marry, any differences may enhance their relationship. The folk expression "Variety is the spice of life" is perfectly true. We are attracted to others partly because we may see them as somewhat different from ourselves. But as long as they are like us in other ways, we can share our common feelings and experiences.

The college student today is probably acquainted with one or more older couples who curtail their separate interests or activities in order to present a picture of marital unity to the rest of the world. If your own parents did this, you may have first-hand knowledge of how these sacrifices for the sake of apparent harmony may actually harm the marriage. Remarks such as "OK, you win again. My interests are apparently not good enough for your taste" (muttered by a husband as he reluctantly switches the television away from a baseball game to an educational program) show his feeling that he is not valued because his interests are not allowed expression.

We may find it easy to respect a mate for the opinions, interests, and skills we share. It is equally important to show respect for the opinions, interests, and skills we do not share. The husband in the above example is complaining that he, not baseball, is unappreciated.

When a husband and wife have different interests, opinions, or skills, they can creatively incorporate these into their marriage by allowing each other the time or personal freedom to express them. When marriage partners are fully confident of each other's enduring respect, they feel no need to override or cut the other off in conversation between themselves or among friends when it becomes apparent that there are differences of opinion. And both partners need not always attend the same events or cultivate the same skills. Our partners may share our interests or skills but to a lesser degree, or may have a complementary interest. A wife who would never dream of learning to play the violin may dearly love listening while her husband plays. Or we may have some interests which we simply don't share. Even here, respect and freedom of expression make for a more solid marriage as well as for more individual pleasure. He may enjoy reading while she watches television, or she might knit while he watches. The same time can be used to express the individual interests of each.

But what about sharing one's unique interests with persons other than the marriage partner? We have all heard about wives and husbands who are jealous of friends who share the interests of their mates. "You women are always playing bridge. Don't you have anything better to do?" or "You men must be in love with your guns." Comments like these indicate that one spouse feels threatened by friendships in which the other shares an interest with other persons. And heaven forbid that the friendships should be heterosexual! At work, and through social or leisure-time activities, husbands and wives today often come in contact with persons of the opposite sex who share their professional and personal interests. To demand that our mate never have friends of the opposite sex who share his or her interests is unrealistic.

Husbands or wives who fear that any heterosexual friendship is a threat to their marriage betray a lack of confidence in the strength of their relationship with their mate. If they are firmly committed to one another and continue to develop their relationship, as well as their unique interests, they need not feel threatened by outside friendships. Some husbands and wives go so far as to develop other sexual partners outside of the marriage, sometimes with the knowledge and consent of their mate. But sex is by no means a necessary ingredient in extramarital friendships.

When husbands and wives do have unique interests, values, and skills, communication is especially important. Making our partner aware of our unique needs and expectations is an important first step towards meeting them. Communicating about the pleasure we find in special activities or interests can help us to understand and appreciate our partner better.

Must a couple share all of their secrets? They need not. "Telling all" about our past relationships may be a way of testing or tormenting our partner. Or it may be a poor way of handling feelings of guilt, especially if the facts are told and retold.

Husband and wife make the best contribution to the unity of their marriage if both continue to operate as competent and confident individuals, who can communicate about their differences and who are committed to growth and to one another.

Before you go on . . .

1. What are some of the traits a married couple ideally should have? *same values & goals & see each other as indiv*
2. Today most people choose their mates for _*personal*_ reasons.
3. Communication between husband and wife should always center around their common attitudes and interests. True or false?
4. We are attracted to others partly because they are seen as _*a little different than yourself*_
5. Pursuit of individual interests only serves to widen any communication gap between husband and wife. True or false?
6. Many people feel _*jealous*_ and _*threatened*_ by friends who share the interests of their mates.
7. Heterosexual friendships invariably indicate that husband and wife are not contented with each other. True or false?

Answers:

1. They should share some common values and goals, have similar or complementary interests, and respect and value each other as individuals.
2. Personal.
3. False. They should openly share their different interests, attitudes, and opinions.
4. Somewhat different from us.
5. False. Different interests simply provide them with more to communicate about.
6. Jealous; threatened.
7. False. It is perfectly normal for both partners to have friends of the opposite sex.

Marriage as a Helping Relationship

In his work with individuals, married couples, and families, the psychologist Carl Rogers observed that people can either help each other to use their creativity and become more fully themselves, or they can stifle each others' personal fulfillment. Rogers and his colleagues noted that certain ways of behaving towards others help to promote personal growth. He called these helpful ways of acting the **facilitative conditions** for personal growth. Three important facilitative conditions are unconditional positive regard, empathetic understanding, and interpersonal congruence.

Unconditional positive regard is defined as respect for the person as he or she is or can be, without any qualifying restrictions such as "I'll like you if you do it my way." Standards of achievement for growth are necessary, but too often the growing person is not accepted because he or she does not live up to the other person's demands and consequently does not feel valued as a person. **Empathetic understanding** implies viewing life as the other person sees it and feels about it. An American Indian phrase captures this concept: "To walk in another's moccasins." **Interpersonal congruence** indicates being honest, though tactful and sympathetic, in communicating the impression another person is conveying. If we give unconditional positive regard, understand others empathetically, and are interpersonally congruent, we help others to grow to their fullest potential. Ideally, couples and family members share these facilitative conditions with each other, and thus promote personal and family growth.

Unfortunately, some of us are not in touch with our feelings. We do not express our personal selves well, and do not give the facilitative conditions. If we are like this, we may experience frustration and problems in our marital and family lives, and may benefit by consulting a professional helping person—a counselor. Through counseling, we can learn to help ourselves and others grow. Rogers has noted that it is often possible to miss important concerns in the routine of daily life. So many families find that setting aside a time to be together for open and honest conversation is beneficial.

In a society composed of the descendents of pioneers and immigrants, in which individualism is a most admired trait, it is not surprising that going to a counselor or therapist is still considered to be a form of weakness. Our heritage is one of "Keep a stiff upper lip" (no matter how you are feeling inside). Hence, many people continue to suffer in their marriages year after year.

Little attention is paid to the fact that in almost all vocations and learning situations, training is given to the novice. But in one of the hardest tasks of life, being a partner and raising a family, no training is given. It is expected that when we get married and raise a family, we will know just what to do. However, generally, all we really have to go on is the memory of our own experiences in the family where we grew up. Very often we deal with problems just the way our families did, not realizing that there are many, possibly more constructive, ways of handling them. Without counseling intervention, we may continue this pattern and pass it on to our own children.

It is important to understand that going for help is a sign of strength. It means that a person has had the courage to confront his or her dissatisfaction and to seek a constructive alternative. What are some of the signals to look for that indicate there is trouble brewing? Some of these might be: poor communication; feelings of distance from partner; constant fighting or bickering; and general dissatisfaction in the marriage. These feelings are also experienced in constructive relationships. But when they become continuous and pervasive, help should be sought from a competent therapist or counselor.

There are several different approaches which are used in counseling families. For many years, it was felt best to counsel the family members separately. But Alfred Adler, Nathan Ackerman, and Virginia Satir have advocated seeing the couple or family together. Their work is distinguished by its "systems" approach. In a **systems approach**, the therapist views the entire family as a unit composed of parts. If any part misfunctions, the entire system is thrown off.

In every family, when problems arise, there is one person who shows the effects more than the other members. It is usually because of this person that the family comes for help. In the systems approach, the therapist focuses on bringing the entire family in for therapy. The person who outwardly displays the greatest problem is considered the "identified patient." But the emphasis is on showing the family how they need to sustain the problems of the "disturbed" individual in order to maintain the family stability. That is, each of the family members has problems. However, by an unwritten contract, all the family members have given this person permission to act out his or her problems. This acting out covers up the rest of the family's problems.

For example, if a husband and wife have many resentments toward one another which they do not express, their relationship will gradually deteriorate. They may become emotionally estranged from each other. If they see their son getting into trouble in school, they can each become concerned about him. This common concern may then bring them closer (at least about the issue of their son's misbehavior). Moreover, each can vent his or her anger and frustration on the son rather than on each other. (Expressing anger at each other presents a greater threat because it may generate fears about the breakup of the marriage.) Thus the son's misbehavior actually helps to hold the family together. This is an important and necessary role, for which he may get both encouragement and criticism. This reaction tends to create greater ambivalence and confusion in the boy. His problems will continue and probably

grow. If our hypothetical family contains two children, the "good child" may add to the family equilibrium by highlighting the "problem child's" poor behavior.

The therapist attempts to uncover the underlying purpose behind each family's behavior, and shows how each member contributes to the unity of the family. As soon as the therapist begins to intervene, the family balance changes. As the family's stability is threatened, it will resist the change. The therapist's goal is to help the family members find new and more constructive ways of relating to one another, in which no single member has to pay the price for the problems of the entire family. It is interesting to note that as soon as the "problem" child's behavior improves, the other child's behavior often worsens temporarily. This "see-saw" effect occurs because each family member plays a different role. When one role is vacated, another family member will often step into the empty position.

The therapeutic process can greatly increase the couple's or family's self-awareness and can improve their skills in relating. In a sense, family counselors are working themselves out of jobs by teaching people how to help each other to grow within marriages and families. But since many families do not share unconditional positive regard, empathetic understanding, and interpersonal congruence, they are frustrated and blocked in their growth. The sooner they summon the courage to seek counseling, the more easily and quickly positive changes will come. Too many families wait beyond the breaking point. With some professional help, marital and family relationships can become productive and constructive.

Before you go on . . .

1. Carl Rogers discovered that the facilitative conditions of _uncond. pos. regard_ _empathy_, and _interpers. cong._ promote growth in individuals and families.

2. _Systems_ theory views and works with the family as a unit.

3. Setting time aside for family meetings is overly formal for family communication. True or false?

4. Danger signals indicating the need for counseling are _Commun. problem_, feelings of _distance_, constant _fighting_, and general _dissatisfaction_.

5. Empathetic understanding means being honest in communicating one's impression of the other person. True or (false?)

6. According to systems theory, each person plays a _role_ in the family, and the family unit acts to preserve its present setup.

7. Family therapists try to change the _balance_ in unfulfilled families towards more _constructive_ directions.

Answers:

1. Unconditional positive regard; empathetic understanding; interpersonal congruence.

2. Systems.

3. False. For some families such meetings may be the only way to get together for meaningful conversation. All families need to build open and honest communication into their routines.

4. Communication problems; distance; fighting; dissatisfaction.

5. False. Empathetic understanding means seeing and feeling the world through the other person's eyes.

6. Role.

7. Balance; constructive.

When the Children Are Gone

45

The day the youngest child leaves home for good can be a critical point for any couple. This is partly because the parents are almost forced to accept a role change. If their children's development has been typical, they begin careers, go to college, or marry. In short, they strive for independence. This time is sometimes called the "empty nest" period. It may be particularly difficult for a woman whose major focus has been mothering. She may feel unwanted and no longer needed. These emotions may come at the time of menopause, emphasizing the loss of the child-bearing role. Menopause may then be accompanied by feelings of depression and lowered self-worth.

As children become autonomous parents must make a gradual but difficult transition. Instead of treating children as children, they must view their children as adults, responsible for their own decisions. Children still need their parents' emotional support as they begin making well-reasoned decisions of their own. Some parents may enjoy seeing their children as equal adults or as younger friends. But many parents find it very hard to relinquish the sense of final responsibility, particularly if they feel that a son or daughter is making inappropriate decisions.

Such issues may be vividly brought to the forefront by a son or daughter's choice of a mate, or their decision to live with a person rather than to marry. In the former case, the parents must learn to see that their child's primary responsibility is to the new husband or wife. It can be very difficult for parents to give up the position of central importance or authority. But with effort a balance can usually be reached that accommodates the needs of both the new and the original family. In the latter case, it is often difficult for parents to see a child make decisions contrary to their own ethical beliefs or values. Parents may see these choices as rejection, or as failure on their part to instruct

their children properly. But such feelings do not mean that the parents have not brought up their children appropriately. It may simply be that the parents have difficulty in seeing their children as adults who are responsible for their decisions.

Mothers trying to expand their roles after childrearing can still be caught in a form of cultural conflict. This is particularly true of the present generation of women in their forties and fifties. Women in this age range were raised in an era when most women were taught that their major role was that of mother and homemaker. Those responsibilities literally absorbed the entire lifetime of their mothers and grandmothers.

Seventy-five years ago the typical wife had eight or nine children. There was always a child at home during her husband's lifetime, and her life expectancy barely exceeded the maturity of her youngest child. Today women have fewer children. Medical advances have increased a woman's life expectancy. But many modern women forty-five or fifty-five years of age still have been trained only for the roles of wife and mother. And they often outlive this function by 35 years or more. Many do not have adequate job training for employment outside of the home. Her new freedom to become employed may seem a cruel irony for the woman whose training restricts her to a job that generally brings low satisfaction.

Some women, entering the job market at a later age, have skills that they do feel competent about. Through working as aides in day care centers for children or in the elementary schools, some can enlarge or extend the mothering role to a community sense of nurturing. Others want to change their role completely. They are taking advantage of job training programs or attending college classes in areas of their own interests. Other women choose to remain home-oriented, and may transfer their attention to grandchildren that live near them. This arrangement requires a careful balance between caring and respect for their children's decisions about the care and discipline of their offspring.

But being totally home-oriented, particularly after the children have matured, may not provide enough outlet for a woman's creativity or her need to be functional. If she has always "lived for her children" or has constantly "put the children first," her husband may feel that he does not play a significant or vital role in her life. Much of their conversation may have focused on the children. When the children leave, husband and wife may suddenly have little to say to each other. Over the years they may have become strangers in the same house, and may have difficulty re-establishing marital closeness. When this happens the parents may have especial difficulty in relinquishing of their children. The children, in turn, feel unsuccessful and resentful when they are needed to maintain their parents' "happiness." This type of family dependency is probably the exception rather than the rule.

In most families the father's work schedule limits the amount of time he can spend with his children, although they may have a warm, close relationship. When they leave home, he is usually not as directly affected by their absence as his wife may be. In some cases, the departure of their children may actually bring an improvement in the couple's relationship. This is particularly true if the husband often felt neglected because his wife's attention was directed exclusively at childrearing. Now, at his peak earning years, the husband may have more leisure time available than at any time since his marriage. With the children gone, he may also have his wife's undivided attention. For many couples the period after their children leave home can be a time in which they renew their relationship and achieve a new closeness and intimacy.

Some couples view their "empty nest" with undisguised satisfaction. Childrearing is never an easy task, and when it has been successfully accomplished, many couples feel not only pride but also a sense of relief that their responsibility has ended. These couples have usually encouraged independence and maturity in their children, and have made a painless transition to viewing them as adults. Their work finished, they are quite happy to settle back and enjoy a new life style that centers around their own interests and activities.

With improved medical care, better incomes, and with women having fewer children, childrearing may increasingly be viewed as only one of several roles available to a married woman. This could expand the possibilities for a well-rounded marital relationship. In the future, increased leisure at the time of the husband's greatest earning potential may enable older couples to enjoy being with each other.

Before you go on . . .

1. The period just after the last child has left home is sometimes referred to as the _empty nest_ period.

2. A physical change in middle-aged women which underscores the loss of the child-bearing role is _menopause_.

3. Menopause is inevitably accompanied by feelings of depression and worthlessness. True or false?

4. One good way for an untrained woman to expand the mothering role to serve her community is by assisting the trained staff in day care centers or elementary schools. True or false?

5. Modern women have been trained for basically one role, childrearing, a function that they often outlive by _____ *35* _____ years or more.

6. Parents often become _____ *Estranged* _____ when the last child leaves home.

7. If their grown children make what their parents believe to be unwise decisions, the parents have only themselves to blame for not bringing their kids up right. True or false?

Answers:

1. "Empty-nest."

2. Menopause.

3. False. This occurs in women who cannot visualize themselves as being happy or productive in any role other than motherhood.

4. True.

5. 35.

6. Estranged.

7. False. Grown-ups are responsible for their own behavior. Parents who blame themselves may be having difficulty in "letting go" of a parental role appropriate for much younger children.

Aging and Married Life

46

Aging persons change in a number of physical and personal functions, and the changes affect the way they relate in and out of marriage. Retirement is often a major transition for the elderly person. For some, it marks the end of a career that has brought success and prestige. And only a few may continue with a modified role, such as a member of the board or a professor emeritus. But many workers drift into retirement after a lay-off and subsequent inability to find employment. Such persons often become depressed at being a "has-been." Those who retire willingly usually have a certain amount of financial security. Those involuntarily out of work, though, may be heading for a struggling, impoverished old age, often accompanied by physical disability. Looking forward to retirement along with economic security can give a couple pride in their old age. But being unemployable and poor make life more difficult.

Retirement also marks a change in status. The person loses many former roles, his expectations of performance change, and his responsibilities are lessened. Only about 28 percent of workers retire voluntarily because they want more leisure, are needed at home, or are dissatisfied with the job. And while most people anticipate retiring, it always requires some readjustment. Retirement generally keeps people at home more. Many men feel at a loss for something to do. Some couples enjoy homemaking together. Or, they may travel a lot, possibly stopping at various different places for lengthy periods.

If no disease is present, an aging person suffers only a slow decrease in physical ability. Vision, hearing, taste, smell, and even pain sensations decline gradually with age. We reach our full height in our early twenties, but we seem to shrink in old age because our spinal discs have gradually become compressed. Dental problems may also develop. Older people look paler, and their skin seems loose, because fat and muscle tissue have shrunk but the food intake has not been reduced accordingly. Reaction times slow down. About 80 percent of people over 65 die from heart attacks, strokes, cancer, or accidents. Disease slows older people down and restricts their activities. Illness and hospitalization, of course, change a couple's relationship. These may aggravate tensions, and draw the partners away from each other.

Physical changes also affect sexual functioning. In the section on sexual intercourse, we discussed the pattern of the sexual-response cycle as it occurs in younger people, at least up until 40. Sexual responsiveness does not end in middle age, but the pattern may vary as the person ages. A couple can continue to enjoy sex as they age together if they have earlier built an erotic relationship that keeps them interested in each other sexually. Successful sex between aging partners depends mostly on the success of their previous activity together. Sexual activity in old age can calm and soothe anxieties, as well as provide genital and personal satisfaction. When changes start to occur, informed individuals will not panic or think that their sex lives have come to an end.

Studies by Masters and Johnson show that the older man may need a longer time to achieve erection, and the erection may not come automatically but may require stimulation of the penis. The Cowper's gland secretion may not occur, the plateau phase may last longer,

and the feeling of ejaculatory inevitability may not occur or may last longer (5-7 seconds). The erection may disappear immediately after ejaculation, and the refractory period can last several hours. This lessened urgency to ejaculate may be an advantage. The man may be able to stimulate the woman to a greater extent with more thrusts of the penis into the vagina and over the clitoral area.

Several changes also occur in the older woman. The time needed for vaginal lubrication lengthens from twenty seconds to as much as five minutes. The vaginal walls become thinner and lose some of the elasticity that was necessary for expansion during childbirth. The uterus does not elevate as much, and the mons pubis and labia do not contain as much fatty tissue and do not protect the clitoris as well or expand as much. Vaginal and uterine contractions during orgasm are less intense.

Aging men and women show a trend toward changing sex roles. Men become increasingly submissive and women more authoritative. Their temperaments come closer together, as women become more tolerant of their assertive impulses and men of their nurturance. Both sexes approach life less through active mastery than through passive acceptance of reality. Time may hang heavy on their hands, unless they are able to spend it productively and creatively.

Older persons become increasingly aware of death, as friends and relatives pass away and as they themselves begin to slow down. The aging person engages more in self-reflection and introspection. What do life and death mean to me? How valuable has my life been? Old age often brings social isolation—work associates are no longer available and friends are too far away or unable to visit. Aging is accompanied by **disengagement**—a turning inward and a loosening of social ties. A couple at ease with each other can savor their peaceful relationship. But those who have not built an intimate relationship can only endure the boredom of their separate loneliness.

Disease and failing health, of course, can cut into the time and energy available for creativity. But with sound physical and mental health older people can be very productive. The will to live a life full of meaning and oriented toward others can keep the aging person going. For the fortunate, old age brings its own particular satisfactions. The greatest joy may be being married, for married people live longer and suffer less emotional disorder.

A great source of pleasure and comfort for the aging may come from being a grandparent. Having raised children capable of parenting their own families can bring pride to an aging person's heart. Being a grandparent has different meanings. It can signify feeling young through one's grandchildren, carrying on the family lines, or doing things for grandchildren that were not possible during busier years with one's own children.

Now that people are living longer and having smaller families, more time is left after the children leave, so grandparents are assuming different roles. Some grandparents remain formal and leave parenting to the parent, but do special favors for the grandchild. Others assume parental responsibility at the invitation of the parent. Still others act as the storehouse of family wisdom, dispensing advice or teaching skills. A fourth group looks for enjoyment in leisure activities and by minimizing authority roles. And finally, some grandparents lead their own lives and ignore grandchildren except on rare special occasions.

Before you go on . . .

1. One important transition for the aging person is _retirement_.
2. Old age brings an increasing awareness of _death_.
3. People retire because they are forced to by law. True or false?
4. One of the main changes in aging is that sexual responsiveness takes a longer _time_, but with _patience_ and _understanding_ the couple can enjoy sex together.
5. Aging does not abruptly destroy physical abilities unless disease is present. True or false?
6. Becoming a _grandparent_ can bring new sources of joy and comfort to the aging person.
7. Sex roles remain about the same in old age as they were in middle age. True or false?

Answers:

1. Retirement.
2. Death.
3. False. Over a quarter of working people retire voluntarily for their own reasons.
4. Time; patience; understanding.
5. True.
6. Grandparent.
7. False. Men often become more passive and nurturant, while women change toward assertion and authoritativeness.

Coping with Widow(er)hood

Despite rising divorce rates, most marriages are ended by the death of one partner. In the pioneer days, many men outlived their wives, who died from the rigors of bearing and rearing children. But today women usually live longer than men. About 70 percent of women survive until age seventy, but only approximately 51 percent of men do. Since women tend to marry older men, about 80 percent of the widowed are women.

When husband or wife dies, the surviving partner loses the confidante who had been a trusted point of reference and source of concern while roles and responsibilities outside the home were changing. To find life meaningful and to exist satisfactorily, we must have someone in whom we can trust. Those who can find the stable, intimate relationship needed for morale are able to cope with being widowed better than those who are left entirely on their own. Someone—either a child or a friend—is needed, to listen and understand.

Widowed people are only half as likely to remarry as divorced persons, but those who do, do so more speedily. Men are more likely to remarry than women, and they do so more quickly. Old friendships seem to diminish when a spouse dies, either because death takes others or because social ties are loosened. Old friendships are more likely to disappear if the survivor is home-centered, rather than oriented toward the wider community. Many widowed persons remain as head of the household. But some, particularly the old and feeble, must be institutionalized. If the widowed person takes up residence with a family member, an older widowed person usually lives with a daughter. A younger widowed son is more apt to return to his parents than is a daughter.

The widowed person who is trying to build a new life needs some money. Many widowed people who are limited by an inadequate

pension or a small Social Security allotment simply do not have the resources to accomplish much. They face increasing physical disability and loneliness. Limited financial resources contribute to poor nutrition, lack of proper medical care, and narrowing of social opportunities. The particular ways in which most widowed persons die suggest some personal disorientation. These include accidental fire or explosion, accidental falls (for women), suicide (for men), and motor vehicle accidents.

The processes both of dying and of bereavement demonstrate certain characteristic stages. As persons approach death from natural causes or illness, they may pass through five distinct phases. First, they **deny** that death is approaching or that a correct diagnosis was made. Or they may push the awareness of death out of their minds. In the second phase, they become **angry** at being singled out to suffer and pass away. Next, many try to **bargain** for more time to live, politely asking life for the opportunity to accomplish more of their ambitions. In the fourth phase, dying persons usually become **depressed,** as a reaction to their physical disabilities and as preparation for death by grieving over their separation from this life. The fifth stage brings **acceptance**, either partial or total, of death.

Throughout these phases, hope for life or a new cure continues to bolster the dying person. Each phase involves both the dying person and the people around him. If the dying person is going through the anger stage, for instance, those around him may have a hard time coping with the situation. Or the dying person may have come to an acceptance of death, while the family may still not be ready to give him up.

Those who lose a beloved through death also pass through five stages in their grief and mourning: thought and behavior directed toward the deceased; hostility toward the deceased or others; appeals for help and support from others; despair, withdrawal, regression, and disorganization of thought and memory; and reorganization of behavior directed towards a new beloved. Redirection can be particularly dificult for the elderly. Bereaved people need to grieve and mourn. Otherwise their suppressed feelings may prevent them from using their full energies for constructive purposes. Reviewing the process that led up to the death with someone who can be confided in, perhaps a physician or clergyman, can often help the bereaved to accept the reality of the death.

After death, the deceased spouse becomes a remembered person. The memory may be cherished, grieved over, or greeted with relief from years of frustration. The formalities of the funeral often help the bereaved to deal with the death in a culturally meaningful way. Then begins the process of **reorientation**—finding a new direction and meaning for the remaining years of life. Possibly the hardest time is when friends have left after the funeral, and the widowed person faces the loneliness of not being able to converse with the beloved, of solitary meals, and of sleeping alone.

After the passing of a spouse, the widowed person goes through a process of **resocialization**—learning how to deal with life without a spouse in whom she confided and trusted for many years. A younger widow or widower more easily establishes new friendships, finds satisfying sexual expression, and discovers projects in the wider community in which to invest energy and interest. Losing a mate is unpleasant to anticipate, and coping with the loss and loneliness involved may tap our most basic resources. The surviving partner may be left with the sole responsibility for children, a particular burden if there are young children and a constricted budget. But having a family to fall back on, particularly if they are already independent or nearly so, may cushion the time of bereavement, and provide an ongoing interest for the survivor.

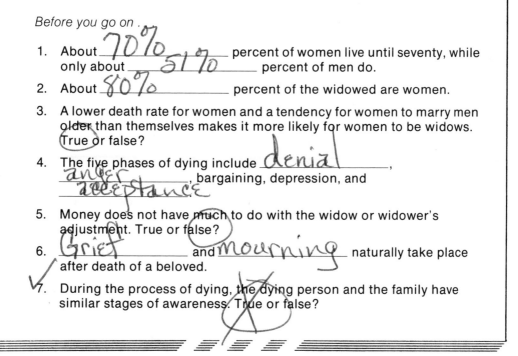

Before you go on . . .

1. About __70%__ __51%__ percent of women live until seventy, while only about __51%__ percent of men do.

2. About __80%__ percent of the widowed are women.

3. A lower death rate for women and a tendency for women to marry men older than themselves makes it more likely for women to be widows. (True) or false?

4. The five phases of dying include __denial__, __anger__, __acceptance__, bargaining, depression, and __acceptance__

5. Money does not have much to do with the widow or widower's adjustment. True or (false)?

6. __Grief__ and __mourning__ naturally take place after death of a beloved.

7. During the process of dying, the dying person and the family have similar stages of awareness. True or false?

Answers:

1. Seventy; fifty-one.
2. Eighty.
3. True.
4. Denial; anger; acceptance.
5. False. Lack of money can contribute to poor nutrition, lack of proper medical care, and a curtailment of social opportunities.
6. Grieving; mourning.
7. False. The dying person and the family are often at different stages of acceptance and may not communicate well about the possibility of death.

MARRIAGE THROUGH A LIFETIME *Chapter Review*

1. Retirement can be easier if the individual assumes new _____ to take the place of the ones lost. (a) references; (b) sports; (c) dividends; (d) roles
2. More couples can look forward to being together after the children leave now because _average life is longer_
3. Really solving a crisis involves facing the problem, communicating one's feelings about it, and finding a suitable solution. True or false?
4. Imagining that one's marriage will go much as one's parents' relationship did can lead the partners to interact more with their _____ than with each other. (a) fantasies; (b) parents; (c) children; (d) finances.
5. Parents of handicapped children frequently need extra financial and emotional _support_.
6. The decade of the _____ often leads people to reevaluate their positions in life and may cause a crisis regarding future directions. (a) 20s; (b) 40s; (c) 60s; (d) 80s.
7. When parents learn of a child's handicap, they may first _deny_ it and then _grieve_ over it.
8. A woman who relies exclusively on her role as mother for fulfillment generally finds herself at a loss for what to do when the children leave. True or false?

9. Middle-aged people frequently pass through a
   _____ crisis. (a) financial; (b) political; (c) spiritual; (d) social.

10. With greater leisure and earning power many couples may be enjoying their post-parenting period more. True or false?

11. About _____28%_____ percent of workers retire voluntarily.

12. Parents of retarded or handicapped children may fear that they are inadequate. True or false?

13. ___X___ imples viewing reality as the other person does. (a) Transcendence; (b) Empathetic understanding; (c) Congruence; (d) Facilitation

14. According to Carl Rogers, _Uncondit. pos. reguard_ means respecting what the other person is and can become.

15. The family member who gets the blame when a family is having troubles is known in therapy as the _____ (a) victim; (b) unfortunate; (c) identified patient; (d) outcast.

16. Late middle age brings an end to sexual capacities. True or false?

17. Bereaved people need to _grieve_ and _mourn_; otherwise their pent-up feelings block constructive activity.

18. Children expect their parents to let go of them at an appropriate age. True or false?

19. With age, the time needed for the male to have an erection and for the female vagina to become lubricated _____
   (a) speeds up; (b) stays the same; (c) lengthens; (d) neutralizes.

20. At death a spouse enters a new status as _remembered person_

21. Counselors are so busy that it is better to wait for a crisis before seeking professional help. True or false?

22. Many parents find difficulty in viewing their children as _adults_.

23. The period after the children leave home is sometimes called the _____ situation. (a) retirement; (b) postnatal; (c) sanguine; (d) empty nest.

24. Sex roles tend to remain fixed during the aging process. True or false?

25. A _systems_ approach to counseling works with the family as a unit.

26. The widowed are _____ as likely to remarry as divorced individuals. (a) half; (b) twice, (c) a quarter; (d) three times.

27. Being widowed leaves the surviving partner in an abandoned frame of mind. True or false?

28. How do the facilitative conditions discovered by Carl Rogers help us to grow as persons? *We choose to grow if we have someone who thinks of us positively*

29. What are some signs of the need for professional help or counseling in marriage? *Fighting & distance*

30. What are the effects of aging on married life? *Retirement gives more time to spend together*

To find the answers, look at page 205.

CHAPTER NINE
DIVORCE AND AFTER

Leading thoughts:

- Divorce rates in the United States are higher than they have ever been, partly because more people now accept divorce as a way to deal with an unsuccessful marriage

- More than three-fourths of all divorced people eventually remarry

- Coping with divorce is, in some ways, similar to coping with the death of a wife or husband

- Very often divorce also forces a person to seek out a new circle of friends and associates

The Facts about Divorce

Divorce rates in America are at an all-time high. They have increased at all educational and income levels, although the percentage of persons ever divorced remains the highest among relatively disadvantaged groups. In 1975, the number of marriages ended by divorce or annulment exceeded the million mark for the first time in history. In the ten years from 1966 to 1976 the divorce rate has constantly increased.

Despite sensationalized reporting in the mass media about the prevalence of divorce, several factors must be considered. First,

should present rates continue, approximately one of every three marriages will end in divorce. However, this figure includes *all* marriages. Subsequent marriages, especially after the second, are more likely to end in divorce than the first. This means that couples contemplating their first marriage have about a one in four chance that the marriage will end in divorce, if the present conditions continue.

One factor usually overlooked in divorce statistics is the increasing life expectancy in our population. As both males and females live longer than in the earlier part of the century, we should expect divorce rates to increase simply because couples live together longer. The age factor can be allowed for, however, and the fact remains that most of the increase in divorce rates is due to changing social conditions.

Despite the increasing number of divorces, there still seems to be a generally high regard for the ideal of being married and living as a family member. But growing numbers of couples are unable to achieve and sustain a satisfactory marriage on the first attempt. About two-thirds of all divorced women and three-fourths of the men sooner or later remarry. In this period when so many people aspire to personal fulfillment and self-awareness, divorce is becoming an increasingly accepted solution to marital dissatisfaction. It is possible that a major problem encountered by couples is one partner's unrealistically demanding expectations about marriage.

Historically, divorce and remarriage rates have displayed similar trends. Each showed low points during the depression years of the 1930s, followed by a gradual climb which reached a peak immediately following World War II. These rates once again declined in the 1950s. But divorce and remarriage rates turned upward around 1960 and continue to increase dramatically. Although the divorce rate currently shows no signs of leveling off, the remarriage rate seems to be declining. There are indications that more divorced persons are waiting longer before remarriage. Such increased waiting periods, if they are used to clarify the person's expectations of a marital relationship, may increase the likelihood of a second marriage's success.

The divorce rates in 1974 were more than three times higher than in 1920. What accounts for the growing number of divorces in American society over the last 50 years? Most current theories attribute these changes in divorce rate to changes in the population, the economic conditions, and fluctuating cultural expectations and values. Divorce is still not generally welcomed nor accepted as the natural outcome for all marriages (except by the more radical theorists). But it no longer has to mean public disgrace and social isolation for the divorced person.

In the United States the institution of marriage seems to be in a state of transition. No longer are the roles of husbands as breadwinners and wives as homemakers clearly defined or agreed upon. With the decreasing emphasis on traditional roles, more options are open to both husband and wife. A married woman who has become economically self-sustaining is in a better position to exercise the option of leaving her marriage if it is unsatisfactory. This can also lessen the economic burdens on a man who is confronted with a potential divorce.

Another view suggests that divorces are mainly the result of early marriages between very young people who are unprepared for the demands of the marital relationship. While very young couples are more likely to suffer marital break-ups, we cannot consider this the entire explanation. In 1974, marriages ending in divorce had lasted an average of about six and a half years. And while at one extreme 41 percent of the men and 52 percent of the women were under 30 years of age when they divorced in 1974, only 28 percent of the men and 21 percent of the women whose marriages broke up that year were 40 years of age or older.

The creation of a satisfactory marriage is difficult and always requires a certain degree of adjustment and compromise. But divorce, even when there is adequate financial as well as social support for each partner, is still emotionally distressing for most persons. In families with young children, divorce can be particularly disruptive. Since 1973 it is estimated that over one million children per year under the age of 18 have undergone the breakup of their homes as a result of divorce. To the maturing child who is searching for identity, the family breakup can be emotionally traumatic. Under certain conditions, however, divorce may be the healthiest response to an intolerable situation that, if continued, could only be more emotionally damaging for all.

Divorce, and to a lesser degree separation, changes the status of the individuals involved. This change has important economic, legal, social and personal consequences. Each of these factors plays a part in the individual's decision either to seek a separation and a subsequent divorce or to remain married.

Before you go on . . .

1. In 1975 there were over ___1 million___ divorces in the United States.

2. Most people who divorce do not remarry. True or (false?)

3. The last peak period in divorce and remarriage rates before the 1970s was ___after WWII___

4. The roles of the husband and wife in marriage are undergoing change for many couples. (True) or false?

5. Most theories of divorce attribute its increase to changes in the population, the economic conditions, and changes in ___values & expectations___

6. One possible problem encountered by marriage partners is that they have inadequately defined marital happiness. (True) or false?

7. (Divorce is only emotionally distressing if a couple has children. True or false?)

Answers:

1. One million.

2. False. Two-thirds of all divorced women and three-fourths of men remarry.

3. Immediately following World War II.

4. True.

5. Cultural expectations and values.

6. True.

7. False. Because divorce means a change in status for the individual, it is usually emotionally distressing regardless of family structure.

Coping With Divorce

49

When we discuss divorce we must consider its legal, financial, and societal implications. But it is on the personal level that divorce makes its greatest impact. Marriage is usually one of the most meaningful and intimate relationships between individuals. There is usually a bond between spouses, whether or not the relationship is a particularly beneficial one. Consequently, most persons who separate mourn the death of their relationship, no matter how unhappy or unfulfilled they felt in the marriage. To both partners, the role of spouse provided their lives with structure, meaning, and often identity. Divorce brings uncertainty, anxiety, and possible loneliness. Marriage permanently alters a person's self-image, daily habits, leisure activities, and relations with friends and family.

It is in this context that we must interpret the comment made by a recently-separated young social worker when speaking of his wife of eight years. "It gets so quiet sometimes, I could scream. Even with all her nagging and yelling, I knew that she cared about me or at least needed me. Now I feel so adrift, so abandoned. Sometimes I think of going back, although I know things won't change." Unless we understand the depth of the attachment that forms within a marriage, particularly in a marriage of some duration, we might easily label this young man as emotionally unbalanced for contemplating a return to what seems to be an abusive and miserable marriage.

What other factors contribute to the strength of this attachment bond between couples? For many individuals, marriage was the method by which they severed the strong parent–child bond. When they married, they assumed adult status. For these people, marriage seems to offer independence with security, the security of another to care for and about them as their parents had previously done. In time, individuals may grow apart and no longer find fulfillment within the confines of their particular marriage. But many still maintain the ideal of marriage with its promised security, independence, and caring. Thus, dissolution of a marriage threatens that ideal. The divorced person often thinks "I'm a failure. I couldn't make it work. Will I ever find someone to care for and who cares for me?"

Separation and divorce are usually not periods of unremitting distress. Even during the relatively early stages of separation, the individual may experience periods of relief and even happiness as it is learned that the periods of distress can be survived. As one encounters and overcomes the everyday problems of living alone, the female re-establishes confidence in herself and her abilities. In fact, separation can initiate a period of self-discovery and growth that may lead to the later establishment of a more mature and enhancing relationship. This self-knowledge may come too late to save the existing marriage. In fact, it may assure the termination of an unsatisfactory one. But it also can help to establish a more realistic basis for the next marriage. This is particularly important when we consider that most divorced individuals remarry.

For some, divorce becomes the greatest tragedy that ever happened or will happen in their lives. They mourn the loss of their marriage for a lifetime, much like the widow who wears black for thirty years after her husband's death. This person is the man or woman who constantly refers to his or her "lost" mate. The former marital partner may be referred to in totally damning terms, as the source of all past unhappiness. "If he hadn't left me, I would have never taken up with that creep." "I never get to go anywhere now that Jim's gone." But it is not unusual, however, for the former partner to take on an idealized character. In these instances, the old saying "Absence makes the heart grow fonder" seems to be true. The physical distance between the divorced person and the former partner and the memory of pleasanter times act as a psychological buffer against the pain of the separation and the dissatisfaction with the current life style. But such attitudes as these hinder the recovery and growth of the individual. Although these individuals may remarry, their new marriage is jeopardized from its beginning. No one wants to be compared to another, particularly not a former spouse.

Another approach, equally maladaptive as a long-term response, is to seek to escape from one's fears and anxieties by living through others. This response is more often seen among women than men, for many women have been conditioned from birth to believe that fulfillment lies in service to others. The children of divorce then become the tie to the former identity which once provided meaning. Such an attitude toward one's children can only destroy the relationship. The children will, as a natural result of growing up, eventually leave, thus duplicating the experience with the former spouse.

We can use objects as well as people to alleviate pain and avoid confronting the emotional trauma in our lives. Men may escape into their work, becoming obsessed with it because it seems to provide the only remaining stability in their lives. Since so much of masculine identity in this society is related to the work role, men often suffer less identity confusion than women when their marriages are disrupted. Temporary escape may also be found in the bed of another (or several others) who demands little more than an adequate sexual performance. With the growing relaxation of the sexual double standard more women now engage in this type of escape. But such behavior is still largely regarded as unacceptable for a woman. Needless to say, this manner of escape can be physically and psychologically dangerous for the emotionally vulnerable person. The divorced man is often envied by the divorced homemaker for his

job and his freedom to carouse, unfettered by home or children. But such escapes only allow him to hide his fears and anxieties rather than confronting, accepting, or eliminating them.

The emotional dissolution of the marriage bond is usually a gradual process. The difficulty of severing this attachment is even acknowledged by the law. Several states enforce a waiting period before the finalization of a divorce decree, allowing the persons involved to cool down and take a more objective view.

This does not mean that they can or will reconcile. But if they decide to continue with the divorce, their decision will involve greater awareness of the pressures that will accompany this major change in their lives.

Before you go on . . .

1. Divorce makes its greatest impact on the ___personal___ level.

2. What effects does the role of spouse have on the individual? ___structure meaning identity___

3. Most couples planning to divorce feel that they are well rid of each other. True or ___false___?

4. Many people try to escape the emotional trauma of divorce by ___having an affair___

5. The divorced man will probably become obsessed with his new freedom. True or ___false___?

6. Why do many states require a waiting period before divorce becomes final? ___Give people time to think & not act irrationally___

7. Women may try to escape from their fears and anxieties by ___living for their children or others___

Answers:

1. Personal.

2. It may bring structure, meaning, and identity to their lives.

3. False. They often undergo a temporary nostalgic period during which they form an idealized picture of each other.

4. Having sexual affairs.

5. False. He is more likely to become obsessed with his work.

6. The waiting period allows the couple to think things over objectively before making a final decision.

7. Living for others.

Moving Toward Divorce: A Case History

Sylvia and Bob have been married for four years. They have no children. Sylvia is 26 years of age and a teacher. Bob is 29 years old and recently completed law school. Both are from lower middle class backgrounds. They met in college and knew each other for three years before they decided to marry. All their friends thought that they were the "perfect couple," and during most of their marriage they would have agreed with this assessment. Their future looked very promising. Their finances were modest, since they depended solely on Sylvia's salary. But with Bob's graduation they expected an increase in their financial resources. However, Bob has had trouble finding a job in his chosen field. Bob and Sylvia are now separated and in the process of filing for divorce.

■ The Breakup

Both will now admit that their marriage had problems from the beginning, difficulties that they hoped would in time disappear. Bob thought Sylvia was too dependent on him, asking his opinion and enlisting his aid in every aspect of their lives. Sylvia felt that Bob had grown more silent and moody throughout the marriage. His reserve, which she had once admired, seemed to act as a wall between them. When Bob asked for a separation, Sylvia was surprised and hurt, even though he had been staying away from home more than usual. This added to their increasing number of disagreements.

It was nearly four months before Bob and Sylvia actually separated. During this time both of them made overtures at reconciliation. At times it seemed that they might be able to renew their marriage. But their communication continued to deteriorate and the quarreling became more bitter. They were at the point of physical confrontation when they decided that separation

was the only recourse open to them. Sylvia still hoped that the marriage could be saved. Bob just wanted to be free from the constant demands that marriage seemed to require. In the following section we will examine their lives as separated persons.

■ Sylvia Alone

When Bob and Sylvia separated, they both left the home that they had shared together. They decided it was wiser, financially and emotionally, for both of them to move. Sylvia had lived alone for about a year before she married Bob, but did not look forward to resuming the life of a single person. She feared being alone and possibly lonely. What should she do about their families and friends? What should she tell them about the breakup, or should she mention it at all? Sylvia felt apprehensive every time she thought of the pity that the announcement of her separation might bring. Of course she would have to tell her family, but she would wait as long as possible before saying anything specific to her friends. Anyway, she and Bob would be getting back together shortly. These were just a few of the thoughts that troubled her.

Sylvia delayed in retaining legal counsel during this stage. Somehow, she felt that this step would confirm the dissolution of her marriage. Anyway, they had very little property. They were both sane and sensible people, and they could surely settle the details of their separation between themselves. At least, this is what she thought until the actual move began. Then they found themselves bickering over every item they owned. Sylvia was so outraged that she was sure she would never want to see Bob again.

But even after they had taken up separate residences, they seemed to be engaged in a growing number of conversations and meetings, after an initial lull in communication. Many of these contacts were initiated by Sylvia, but a number came from Bob. So many things had to be discussed. Who was to pay the health insurance? Would Bob be able to make it to Sylvia's brother's graduation? Did Sylvia have his sweater? Such issues as these formed the basis of their early contacts. Sylvia began anticipating these communications with Bob. Often she even manufactured reasons for them, although she was angry with herself for wanting to see him. After all, hadn't he left her? After these conversations Sylvia was often depressed and angry. She wondered if she had done everything she could to save her marriage. After the first few months, during which Sylvia occupied herself with fixing up her new apartment, a lethargy descended upon her. She didn't seem to have the energy or the will to do anything but go to work and come home to spend the evening watching television.

■ Bob Alone

Although Bob had initiated the separation, he was not as happy with his decision as he originally thought he would be. He did go out often, particularly in the beginning, usually visiting old friends who had known him before his marriage or taking in the local singles' clubs. But he found that he was lonely. He began to have many short-term sexual liaisons with women he encountered. These affairs were often enjoyable, and even exciting. But if any woman seemed to be seeking even a minimal emotional commitment Bob withdrew immediately. After all, hadn't he just left the wife he still cared about in order to avoid being stifled? He wanted to be on his own, without emotional or financial burdens and obligations to shoulder.

The exhilaration and freedom Bob felt at the start of the separation began to wane after the first months. He grew more ambivalent in his feelings for Sylvia. Sylvia, by her dependency on him, had made it impossible for him to develop himself. But often he would remember their life together as a warm and caring one. With Sylvia there was at least certainty. This thought was both comforting and frightening during Bob's anxious moments. It was on these occasions that he would contact Sylvia. How was she

making out? Did she need anything? "Remember," Bob would tell her, "I'll always care for you. Just call me when you need me." Sometimes Bob thinks of going back to Sylvia; maybe she has been changed by the separation. She seems more independent now, more like the "old Sylvia" he married. He wonders if she is seeing some other man.

■ The Mourning Process

We can draw a comparison between the way people react to death and the way they react when their marriages are breaking up. Both these situations involve loss. With divorce, the person loses a spouse who was important. This loss is usually distressing no matter how unhappy the marriage was. People about to die pass through five psychological stages. The usual progression of these stages is from denial of death through rage, bargaining, depression, and finally acceptance. An almost identical pattern of response can be found in divorcing couples. Bargaining, in this context, is usually the promises each spouse makes to change if the other will continue in the marriage.

In the case history above we can find a few examples of just such patterns. The denial response was particularly evident in Sylvia's refusal to tell her friends of her breakup with Bob or to contact an attorney. During the four months preceding their separation Sylvia and Bob still tried to be the "perfect couple." Both obviously felt anger, not only directed at each other but extended outward to encompass others. Sylvia "knew" that her friends would feel superior, so she chose to reject them first. Bob, in his determination not to be trapped and therefore hurt by anyone, rejects all emotional contact with other women. Both Bob and Sylvia, by their constant contact and inquiry into each others' lives, seek to maintain a semblance of the marital bond. This, of course, hinders their development of independent lives. Many separated and divorced couples re-establish sexual relations during the separation, to maintain this tie with their former life.

Before you go on . . .

1. In many cases, the causes that lead to divorce were present ~~from the beginning~~

2. Once separated, a couple are likely to ignore each other and go their separate ways. True or false?

3. ~~lonliness~~ _____ is the greatest emotional hazard faced by the newly-separated person.

4. After separation, both partners often have ~~ambivalent~~ _____ feelings about each other.

5. By the time divorce takes place, each person has usually broken all emotional ties to the other. True or false?

6. How can we compare a person's reaction to approaching death and the reaction to the breakup of a marriage? ~~denial bargaining anger depression acceptance~~

7. When separated persons try to maintain contact with each other they are hindered in ~~becoming independent~~

Answers:

1. At the start of the marriage.
2. False. Often they choose to remain in contact with each other.
3. Loneliness.
4. Ambivalent.

5. False. The attachment bond often continues long after the divorce is final.
6. Both involve the psychological stages of denial, anger, bargaining, depression, and acceptance.
7. Developing independent lives.

Building a New Life 51

Divorce is generally considered to indicate that a marriage has failed. And people often mistakenly believe that a divorcing couple are not really capable of successful intimate relationships. One of the first problems divorced persons confront is the stereotype of the divorcee as a failure. Persons who divorced unwillingly and feel they were pushed out of the marriage may readily agree with this image. Those who divorced willingly and without bitterness may combat it. Many people who divorce do have personal and interpersonal problems. But many do not. They may simply have made a poor choice of a marital partner. Or, a couple may have been compatible at first but have grown apart over a period of years. Divorce is generally less destructive to the self-image of partners whose decision to divorce is mutual and when little hostility is involved.

The network of family and social relationships usually changes radically when a couple divorce. If the duration of the marriage was short and there were no children, contact with the mate's family may virtually end. In a longer marriage, especially if there were children, lines of communication may be maintained with the closer relatives (between children and their grandparents, for example) or with relatives who have become personal friends. The newly divorced may wish to avoid family members who are either blaming or overly sympathetic, while they sort out their own reactions to their new status.

One of the more difficult initial readjustments the recently-divorced person must make is the loss of friends the couple shared. Former friends may feel embarrassed to align themselves with either of the former mates in preference to the other. They may feel that dissolution of an apparently stable marriage puts the stability of their own marriage in question. So the recently separated may be rejected by friends who wish to avoid the anxiety created by the breakup of their marriage. The popularized image of the "gay divorcee," out to trap a new mate, may also alienate the newly separated or divorced woman from her former friends. The divorced man is often perceived as less of a threat to the marital partners. But he may become the extra man at the party and the object of matchmaking attempts by his married friends. For all of these reasons, divorced persons often find that over a period of months they are seeing less and less of many of their old friends and must establish a new network of friendships.

For professional women and men, their work may be the one thread of continuity between their former and their present status. Sometimes it is the one thing that "keeps them going." Especially if a person feels successful at his or her work, pouring oneself into it can be a healthy antidote to the anxiety and self-doubt that always accompany the breakup of a marriage. But if work is primarily necessary for "keeping bread on the table," these emotions may threaten to come spilling out at work. The person may fear losing the position and the meager amount of security and stability it provides.

Women who are not job-skilled often suffer most. This is particularly true if the former husband was a moderately good provider and if the woman is granted custody of the children. (Many more women than men are granted custody of the children by the courts. This pattern is changing somewhat with new legislative emphasis on equal rights for men and women.) Alimony payments are less than a full salary. Usually they are inadequate to support the divorced woman, and are increasingly burdensome to the former husband who must also pay for his own room, board, and entertainment. If he remarries, his income must be stretched to support the new wife and any children she may bring to the marriage.

It is not surprising that alimony payments often become intermittent or stop altogether as time passes. Some persons feel that requiring men to make alimony payments is unfair, since women are not required to do so. Others feel that women who have kept house, worked, and raised the children for a man and have forgone job training to do this have "earned" the man's support. They are quick to point out that a man who earns an adequate salary can hire a housekeeper, have his laundry done, and eat out. But the woman without job skills or income cannot hire someone to keep the house or tend the children while she goes back to school or works at a low-paying job. These points may all be true of many middle-class couples. But if both are professionals, they may be equally equipped to finance their own futures. Or, if the couple are poor neither may have adequate job skills, and the husband may be unable to make alimony payments. Divorced parents who have custody of the children and who do not have an adequate income are eligible for Aid to Dependent Children.

The loss of a sexual partner creates another area in which divorced persons have to make adjustments. Under the traditional double standard, it is considered normal for men to find an outlet for their sexual desires. But divorced women are often regarded as sexually promiscuous if they seek sexual gratification. However, women are increasingly being granted equal freedom with men in this area. The desire for a continuing sexual partner and the desire for companionship may be factors that lead many divorced persons to remarry. Statistically, those with children are more likely to remarry than those who do not. This may be because they wish to provide male and female role models for the children or to divide the labor involved in raising a family.

Persons who have once been married are probably more capable than those who have not of selecting an appropriate mate for themselves. If they learned from their first marriage what their marital needs and expectations are, there is every reason to believe that their second marriage will be better than the first. But people who have no understanding of how their own personality or life-style affected their first mate, and who ascribe the failure of the marriage to "fate," are more than likely to find new mates who resemble the old, and to relive their marital mistakes. Such persons may be helped to gain insight into their marital problems and to learn successful ways of relating to their mates by a well-trained and sympathetic marriage counselor.

Before you go on . . .

1. Divorce often brings a radical change in the person's network of
   family & social relationships

2. Divorced persons are more likely to remarry if they have no children. True or false?

3. A recently divorced woman is often considered
   sexually promisc.

4. _Alimony_ is the financial payment often required of divorced men.

5. A person whose first marriage fails will probably fail in any future marriage. True or false?

6. One of the most difficult adjustments for the newly divorced person is
   loss of shared friends

7. A divorced person's _work_ may provide continuity while he adjusts to his new status.

Answers:

1. Family and social relationships.

2. False. Those with children are more likely to remarry.

3. Sexually promiscuous.

4. Alimony.

5. False. The divorced person is very likely to succeed in a second marriage.

6. The loss of friends the couple shared.

7. Work.

DIVORCE AND AFTER *Chapter Review*

1. Divorce occurs more frequently among better educated people. True or false?

2. How did divorce rates in 1974 compare with divorce rates in 1920? (a) They were the same; (b) They were twice as high; (c) They were three times as high; (d) They were lower.

3. Divorce is a public disgrace and leads to social isolation. True or false?

4. With an increasing emphasis on working among women, divorce is more of an option for a woman because *financial independence*.

5. Since 1973 about how many children per year experience the breakup of their homes through divorce? (a) 300,000; (b) 400,000; (c) 1 million; (d) 2 million.

6. The larger number of marriages among very young people accounts for the rise in divorce rates. True or false?

7. Divorce and remarriage rates always parallel each other. True or false?

8. Many divorced people feel a loss because they developed what for the spouse? (a) An open communication; (b) Hostility; (c) Aversion; (d) An attachment.

9. In 1975 the divorce rate for the first time exceeded *1 million*.

10. Divorced persons, especially women, may seek to escape from fears and anxieties by living through *others*.

11. The divorced person often feels like a (a) success; (b) failure; (c) dunce; (d) genius.

12. Some divorced persons seek escape through *work* or *sex*.

13. Most people do not look forward to and do not accept divorce as the natural outcome of marriage. True or false?

14. A person may end an unsatisfactory marriage and be able to build a better relationship because of increased (a) age; (b) self-knowledge; (c) social graces; (d) number of children.

15. Alimony payments are generally viewed as *inadequate* by the woman and *burden* by the man.

16. People are often disappointed for not finding (a) independence; (b) security; (c) caring; (d) all of the above in their marriage.

17. Several states require a waiting period before a divorce in the expectation that some couples may reconcile. True or false?

18. Divorced individuals with custody of children and an inadequate income are eligible for *ADC* _____.

19. Alimony payments provide as much support as a wife receives during marriage. True or false?

20. What percent of divorced persons remarry? ~~80~~ 70%

21. Regarding divorce as the greatest tragedy, or idealizing a former relationship as better than it was, (a) hastens recovery; (b) makes no difference; (c) slows recovery; (d) is not common.

22. Divorce happens all at once with the divorce decree. True or false?

23. The loss of certain _friends_____ that the divorced couple shared may be one of the most difficult adjustments.

24. Contact with former in-laws often depends on (a) geographical proximity; (b) finances; (c) the presence of children; (d) the law.

25. With divorce any previous attachment quickly ends. True or false?

26. The image of the "gay divorcee" and anxiety about one's own relationship may serve to _distance_____ one from former friends.

27. For professional people, _____ may be the only thing that keeps them going. (a) friends; (b) status; (c) finances; (d) work.

28. How can we compare the process of divorce to that of dying? *the 5 stages*

29. Do rising divorce rates show that marriage is becoming outmoded? *Not necessarily but people get out of unhappy marriages*

30. How do people generally react to divorce? *loniness & grief*

To find the answers, look at page 207.

CHAPTER TEN

MARRIAGE AND ALTERNATIVES

Leading thoughts:

- Despite the social and economic handicaps, more and more people are deciding to remain single or unmarried

- Living together has become increasingly popular as an alternative to traditional marriage

- Couples who choose to live together do not necessarily plan to marry each other

- The commune as a lifestyle dates back at least to pre-Christian times

The Single Life 52

Bureau of the Census statistics show that a little more than 25 percent of all persons over eighteen were without marriage partners in any year from 1970 to 1973. More females than males were without marriage partners, as were more non-whites than whites. Schulz and Rogers report that around 27 percent of all persons over eighteen are without marriage partners in any given year. In 1973, there were about 22 million persons over the age of eighteen who were not married. Of course, some of them intended to marry soon. People who have never married make up about eight to ten percent of

our population. We have no accurate way to measure how many of these would like to marry but for one reason or another do not. Our discussion here will focus on single persons without children who have no intention of marrying or remarrying.

We call the single life an "alternative" lifestyle because most people do marry. At one time our society looked askance at single people, and marriage was viewed as the only viable lifestyle. At best, single people were considered less capable or less mature than married people. At worst, they were suspected of deviating from the heterosexual norm. In a society that extolled the virtues of marriage, single women were stereotyped as "old maids" who had not "made it" in the marriage market. Single men were somewhat more attractively cast in the role of "eligible bachelor," but they were often thought of as "not quite respectable."

Even today, our institutions seem to be prejudiced in favor of marriage, and against those who remain single. Singles must contribute a greater proportion of their salary for income taxes, while married couples and families can take advantage of various tax breaks. Until recently, only couples could adopt children in most states. Some people who fear the new stereotype of the "swinging single" hesitate to rent housing to unmarried persons, expecting loud parties, late hours, and a continuous stream of visitors of the opposite sex. Until the 1960s, few housing units were tailored to the needs of an individual living alone, and the few that are now available are mainly in urban areas. Much of the social life of any community revolves around the interests of couples and families.

But despite these economic and social handicaps, many people are now consciously choosing to remain single. This is especially true in urban areas, where their special needs are more easily met. Choosing to remain single has a number of positive aspects. Single people have more mobility than the average married person. They can change jobs or travel without the problems of moving a whole family. They are freer to set their own schedules, without having to compromise or to be considerate of a mate who may have different priorities or needs. (Although singles who share housing with a friend may have to make some of the same kinds of personal adjustment that married couples do.) Single people may have more freedom to form heterosexual friendships, as well as to make friends of their own sex. There is very little pressure on them to have children. They may find it easier to find time for themselves, and they probably have more privacy.

On the negative side, single persons may be more prone to loneliness, unless they have a great number of friends or an exceptionally companionable housemate. But we cannot ex-

pect our friends to be around whenever we feel the need for companionship; husbands and wives are usually available to each other. At holidays, single persons may feel particularly left out, since these are often a time for family celebrations. The singles have no other person to consistently share their hopes and dreams, their ups and downs. Sometimes it is difficult for them to meet other singles, especially in small towns where most social life revolves around couples and families. Barhopping in the cities is usually oriented toward finding sexual partners. It has not proved to be a good way to make long-term friendships.

Life is more expensive for single people. What they must pay for room and board would sometimes feed and house a couple as well. And they need more outside entertainment since, as one woman remarked, "The nice thing about marriage is that a lot of your entertainment is right at home." Singles may also feel the lack of a regular sex life. But in spite of these drawbacks, more persons seem to be choosing the single life these days.

We can think of singles as a minority in a society where the majority are married. Like a number of other minority groups, many of their needs are not well met. But there have been some changes for the better. In California and New York (where large numbers of singles live) housing units have appeared in the past decade that cater to the special needs of singles. Their attractions sometimes include regularly scheduled social activities. Some people dislike their dormitory atmosphere, but they appeal to others. There are many social clubs where singles can meet and make friends with other singles. Places and events (restaurants and cruises, for example) that used to require "couples only" may now permit singles or even solicit "singles only." And social attitudes are slowly changing. As women achieve status in their own right by succeeding in various professional fields, they may feel less pressure towards marriage for reasons of financial security or status. As social attitudes change, and as we develop ways of meeting the special needs of those who choose to remain single, it is likely that more people will feel free to make that choice.

A minority of single persons do not marry because they prefer intimate relationships with other persons of the same sex. Public sentiment about homosexuality seems to be changing, if only very slowly. The American Psychiatric Association no longer considers homosexuality to be pathological. The slight relaxation of public opinion has encouraged a number of persons to identify themselves as homosexual, and to join with others in defending their life style.

Before you go on . . .

1. About ___25%___ percent of those eighteen or older are without marriage partners in any one year.

2. Single people pay a lower income tax than married couples. True or *false?*

3. People who have never married make up approximately ___8–10%___ percent of the population.

4. Fewer people are choosing to remain single today than ever before. True or *false?*

5. Single women used to be stereotyped as "___old maids___" and single men as "___bachelors___."

6. Increasingly, more entertainment and other social events are open to singles as well as couples. *True* or false?

7. Is the single life usually easier in the city than in small-town America? *city*

Answers:

1. Twenty-five.

2. False. Singles pay a larger tax on their income than married couples.

3. Between 8 and 10 percent.

4. False. More persons are now choosing to remain single.

5. Old maids; eligible bachelors.

6. True.

7. Yes. Housing, recreation, and greater social acceptance are attracting increasing numbers of singles to urban centers.

Living Together  53

When we speak of "living together," we are talking about a man and a woman sharing a common residence without being married. Living together became popular as a life style during the 1960s, when it emerged as a new form of social relationship. Previously couples who lived together were mostly Bohemians (unconventional artist types), poorer people who were unable to make long-term economic commitments, and couples who simply were not interested in social formalities. Fourteen states consider some of these unions "common-law marriages." During the frontier days when preachers and justices of the peace were not available, marriages by consent of the couple alone were perfectly legal. Today, however, they involve legal questions about the legitimacy of the children and the right of inheritance.

But today most couples who are living together are not planning on marriage. Nor do many consider their present arrangement a "trial marriage"—a test to see if they are compatible enough to commit themselves to a permanent relationship. Living together occurs mostly among the young, though some oldsters who do not want to lose their individual pensions are now cohabiting without marrying.

Why have some young people decided to live together? Personal and social reasons both enter into this decision. Many young adults want the intimacy of sharing a continual, close heterosexual relationship. At the same time, they are not sure whether they are ready for a permanent commitment or whether they really want to spend the rest of their lives with this particular person. Many of those who live together intend to marry eventually, but not necessarily the present partner.

During the 1960s socially conscious young people pointed out that many of the older generation were saying one thing while they were doing another. For example, the laws supposedly offered freedom and justice, yet minorities were denied their civil rights. American citizens purportedly enjoy the good life, yet poverty is still widespread in our society. The United States proclaims itself interested in peace, yet it exports more arms than any other country, and women have still not legally achieved full equal rights with men. The youth movement questioned the credibility of institutions that resulted in so much repression. It also encouraged individuals to develop new ways of living that allow more personal expression, spontaneity, and fulfillment.

Couples who live together tend to be liberal in their political and religious attitudes. They view a marriage certificate as just a piece of paper, unless it stands for a meaningful interpersonal sharing between the partners. Conforming to the institution of marriage, without growing and finding fulfillment together, seems like hypocrisy to most of them. One young man commented, "They say we are kidding ourselves about our relationship because we have not married; I say they are kidding themselves about marriage because they do not have a relationship."

Those who criticize living together consider sex to be the all-important point. They do not raise an eyebrow about same-sex persons rooming together. But to couples who live together, sex is not necessarily the main reason for their decision. Some couples rule sex out of their relationship entirely. Others may engage in it only occasionally. Economic, social, and emotional reasons seem to predominate. Many couples find it less expensive, more comfortable, and more enjoyable to live with someone of the complementary sex. And for those who do have a sexual relationship, sex is probably more pleasurable and satisfying in familiar, private surroundings, which give them a sense of security and closeness.

Living together gives a couple the opportunity to experiment with flexible living arrangements. They can learn to know and interact with each other more intimately in the ups and downs of daily routine, to assess their individual capacities for building a meaningful heterosexual relationship. They can search for new ways to define their sex roles and to share the homemaking responsibilities, without feeling locked into an institution that seemingly dictates set patterns. Through living together, a man and woman become much better acquainted than they can during the artificial situation of formal dating. Rising divorce rates only underscore the need to know one's partner very well before marrying.

Couples who live together do not regard themselves as revolutionaries. Nearly three-quarters expect to marry eventually, usually when they decide to have children. Breaking up a living-together relationship seems easier than breaking off an engagement, both because personal plans are generally more transitory and because social expectations have not been built as high. Since living together does not imply permanency, breaking up the relationship does not necessarily mean failure. It only means that the couple have decided that they are not compatible enough, or that they are not fulfilling each other's needs sufficiently to continue sharing a residence. Those who live together do not usually assume legal obligations, nor do they have legal safeguards if they separate. In the most satisfying of these relationships, both individuals continue to build up their own personalities. Even if they do marry, their relationship will be enriched by their self-development. Some couples, after deciding to marry, may live together to economize on expenses, or to begin sharing a life together. Later, the ceremony itself will be a meaningful symbol of their sharing.

Living together, in some cases, may express disillusionment and discouragement with social institutions, and uncertainty about personal identity and the future. In others, it may symbolize the earnest seriousness of young people willing to commit themselves wholeheartedly only when they are sure about the genuineness and depth of a lasting relationship. Margaret Mead believes that young people are not rejecting marriage, but rather an obsolete form of marriage. She believes that couples will discover greater happiness in creative relationships.

Not all parents who learn that their child has entered a living-together relationship will react favorably. Parents have a right to their feelings. Honest and sympathetic communication may help to bridge the gap between parents and children. Many parents do eventually accept their child's personal decision as responsible, and will respect his or her partner.

Before you go on . . .

1. What do we mean by "living together"? Sharing house without marriage

2. In a trial marriage, the couple live together to determine whether they are really suitable for each other.

3. Living together does not have the legal obligations of marriage, but it has the legal safeguards. True or **false**?

4. Couples who live together tend to be liberal in their political and religious attitudes.

5. Social, emotional, and financial reasons tend to predominate over sex in living together. **True** or false?

6. Margaret Mead sees youth as turned off not on marriage, but on ~~obsolete form of marriage~~ that does not allow for creative relationships.

7. Breaking up a living-together arrangement means the couple has failed. True or false?

Answers:

1. A man and a woman sharing a common residence without being married.

2. Trial marriage.

3. False. Living together is not recognized by the law.

4. Liberal.

5. True. Couples usually have such practical reasons.

6. An obsolete form of marriage.

7. False. They may have found out they simply are not compatible or able to fulfill each other's needs.

Communes

Some people, dissatisfied with traditional family or single life, have joined communes. A **commune** is made up of several individuals not bound by blood or legal ties, who share living quarters and some responsibility for their lives together. Many types of communes exist. The history of communes extends back to pre-Christian times. The Essenes, of which John the Baptist may have been a member, were a religious commune. The early Christians often lived communally, sharing possessions among the group. Inspired by a desire to construct a more satisfying utopian way of life, more than sixty communes existed in the United States around the middle of the last century.

Communes can be set up in many ways, according to their purposes and members. They may arise casually because several individuals

want to economize on expenses and believe they can get along together. At the other extreme, a group of people may begin a commune with an ideal of how to live, and may set out to structure their common existence accordingly. Communes provide an alternative style of living for their members. They are frequently looked upon unfavorably by the wider society.

The patterns of living within communes vary widely. They all represent some form of an economic arrangement. In some communes everybody has a job to do. In others, several members contribute their salaries for the support of all the members. The more successful communes discover how to be self-sustaining through productivity. The majority, though, eventually disintegrate, because the members lack useful skills or shirk their responsibilities to contribute to the common good.

A number of communes have been founded with the idea of promoting social change. But since only about a quarter of a million people have lived in communes in our country during this century, their influence has not been sweeping. Membership may be open to anybody, or members may be selected according to set criteria. Often members are expected to focus their daily lives on a particular cause, line of action, or religious orientation. Most of the better-organized communes use the democratic system of allowing everybody to express an opinion and deciding on a course of action through group consensus. The more structured communes divide the work responsibilities equitably. In more laissez-faire groups, each member "does his own thing." Where members are dedicated and productive, this arrangement works out. But often a member will use individualism as an excuse to live off of others' efforts.

Communes place less emphasis on partnership than does living together. Some individuals do pair off together because they are already married or find each other attractive. Some communes involve group marriage, where everyone is considered married to all cross-sex partners. However, this is not the dominant pattern. Some members of communes seek heterosexual companionship outside the group, especially when the sex ratio is imbalanced. Communal members who pair off in a sexual alliance probably share greater compatibility than they would in the dating situation, because they have experienced each other in many different ways and are still attracted to each other.

There are broad classifications of individuals who join a commune: those who drift together, and those who intentionally form a community. Some young people who feel alienated from family and society find social encouragement within the mini-society of a commune. In this substitute family, they desire ready tolerance rather than traditional demand for achievement. Experiencing acceptance by the commune allows individuals to experiment with new social roles, discover a personal identity,

and learn adult responsibilities. Unfortunately, many shirk communal responsibilities and only aggravate their rootlessness.

Looking at some intentional communes may help us understand them better. The Oneida community that existed in upstate New York from 1849 to 1880 tried to follow a "perfectionistic version" of Christianity, affirming that every person can become perfect. The greatest number of people in this commune at one time was 288. Making Oneida financially solvent involved ten years of difficult labor. The two distinctive features of Oneida included "complex marriage" and mutual criticism. Every adult was considered married to every cross-sex person. Monogamous exclusivity, romance, and passion were repudiated as selfish and possessive. This commune disintegrated partially because it was unable to socialize the younger generation to its way of life.

The Bruderhof commune, first established in Germany in the 1920s, has three settlements of about 750 members in the United States. Families retain a nuclear form with their own living quarters, while collective child-rearing takes place in a community school. This commune also has branches in England, Paraguay, and Uruguay.

The kibbutzim of Israel constitute the best-known and most successful communes. They have transformed arid desert into fertile farmland. The kibbutzim actively participate in the defense of Israel. Children are cared for communally, though they visit their parents' quarters. Interestingly, children of different parents often develop unusual "brother-sister relationships" as a result of growing up together in the same child-raising center. As adults they do not marry each other, but seek husbands or wives from another communal group. The kibbutzim are experiencing some difficulty in maintaining sex-role equality because they did not plan for it. However, equality often developed automatically, as a result of the need for hard labor by both sexes. Today some 93,000 individuals live in about 255 settlements.

Despite the wide variation in types and purposes, all communes must solve several problems if they continue to exist. Economic support is crucial. Questions concerning childbearing and child-rearing must be addressed. Will the community assume the socialization function, or leave it to the biological parents? Sexual relationships and the accompanying feelings of jealousy and exclusiveness present potential problems. Thought must also be given to the political functions. How will decisions affecting members be made? Who determines the division of labor? What is the leadership structure? Finally, those communes which have existed for a long time period have had some means of integrating values, encouraging members to work toward common goals, and an *ideology* for solving problems. In Oneida, the belief in perfectionism provided value integration. Twin Oaks, a commune in Virginia, is based upon the science of behaviorism advocated in B. F. Skinner's novel, *Walden Two*. There, members literally thumb through the novel seeking guidance in everyday living.

Many of these problems in communal living apply to the nuclear family also. While there may be dramatic differences between a given family and a specific commune, the idea of communal living differs from nuclear family living in only three substantial ways. First, there are more persons in the commune and thus increased interaction. Secondly, children have a greater number of role models, both male and female, to learn from. Third, communal living implies a greater sharing of economic responsibility than is found in the family. These differences mean that the commune has some of the characteristics of the extended family system. Many believe that the commune continues to be an alternative to the nuclear family largely because personal needs such as recognition, security, and a sense of belonging are met more adequately in an extended family system.

Before you go on . . .

1. In a commune, how many people share living quarters and responsibilities? 3 or more

2. Communes are easily classifiable into four types. True or **false?**

3. The most successful communes are probably the _Kibbutz_ in Israel.

4. Christianity has always been opposed to communes. True or **false?**

5. Many communes use a _democratic_ system for decision-making.

6. About sixty communes existed in the United States in the middle of the nineteenth century. **True** or false?

7. Communes may be referred to as _intentional communities_ if they are formed for the purpose of promoting some cause.

Answers:

1. Three or more.

2. False. There are so many types of communes that categorization is difficult.

3. Kibbutzim.

4. False. The early Christians often lived in communes, and several Christian groups through the centuries have established communes.

5. Democratic.

6. True.

7. Intentional communities.

Marriage–Today and Tomorrow

While marriage and family mean relationships between and among persons, the family is also a social institution, We began the book by considering the various ways family life could be structured, and some of the functions which families perform for society. The remainder of the book focused on how partnerships form, how they develop in marriage, and in some cases, how they terminate. This final section will summarize some of the ways the family in the United States has changed and what these changes mean for the future.

During the past one hundred years, the family institution in the United States has had responsibility in five important areas: (1) sex regulation—during much of the period marriage constituted the only legal or moral means for the expression of sexual behavior; (2) reproduction; (3) socialization of children; (4) gratification of affectional needs and (5) protection—physical health, mental well-being, and economic maintenance.

Family function can be altered either by the passage of new laws or by changing customs and behavior. Usually, changes in social attitudes precede changes in the law. To the extent that nonmarital sex is legally

sanctioned, we could conclude that the traditional role of the family in this area is eroding. Prostitution is now legal in one state— Nevada—and a few states have voided laws that prohibited homosexual behavior between consenting adults in private. However, most laws regulating extramarital sex (adultery) and the fornication laws prohibiting premarital sex are still in force. On the whole, legislation has not radically altered the family's role as a moral arbiter in society.

In behavioral change, there is much mass media discussion of a sex revolution. But careful surveys show only moderate increases in premarital and extramarital sex. The large changes are toward more permissive **attitudes**. Perhaps the most accurate assessment is that the family is slowly evolving toward a less important role in sex regulation, but that no major revolution has occured.

The reproductive function has changed little. One hundred years ago the population was replenished mainly by the children born to married couples. This remains true today.

The family's role in socialization of children has markedly declined. Formal education, peer groups, and the mass media have become important cultural transmitters. Formerly, the farmer and housewife roles could be taught by fathers and mothers. In our industrial society, children must move outside the family for instruction in performance of complex roles.

In the past our self-needs for personal recognition, security, and belonging were met partially by the family. However, in rural and small-town America an individual belonged to a community, or in cities, to an ethnic neighborhood. Everyone knew everyone else personally in these settings, thereby gaining a sense of well-being and identity. Urbanization has eliminated these sources of need satisfaction. The family is now the primary and sometimes the only long-term agency for companionship and intimate association. We move away from our friends and neighbors frequently—one fifth of the families in the United States move each year. In gratifying affectional needs, the family now has increased responsibility because of the decline of other primary group agencies.

At one time families assumed financial responsibility for physically and mentally disabled and elderly members. The growth of the welfare state has resulted in the transfer of much of this responsibility to the government or to corporation pension plans.

The overall picture is one of declining family responsibility in modern society. An accompanying change in family structure has also occurred. Family size has decreased from an average of about six to slightly over two children in the past one hundred years. Family makeup has changed from a quasi-extended to a nuclear family. Divorce rates have increased. Authority patterns have changed from patriarchal toward equalitarian. More mothers are working outside the home.

The changes in both family function and structure occurred because of the industrial revolution and its effects. The effects continue and often, the trends of the past can be used to forecast the future. What will the family be like in the forseeable future?

As attitudes toward sex without marriage continue to be more tolerant, the incidence of sexual behavior outside marriage will probably increase. Two factors could cause a revision in the family's reproductive function. Population growth pressure could increase so that intervention by other agencies may be necessary. Or, technological innovations such as the artificial womb may make reproduction in non-family settings feasible. Both possiblities seem remote for the immediate future.

Parents will probably have to accept less responsibility for teaching their children as day care centers, schools, and the mass media increase further in importance. As behavioral science broadens our base of knowledge about human development, parents may have to relinquish most teaching functions to experts or, alternatively, to acquire the requisite knowledge to guide another human being to adulthood. In a highly rational society, love may eventually not be enough.

In the twentieth century we became more aware of our psychological makeup. Some individuals have turned to communes or encounter groups because the small, rather isolated nuclear family was unable to meet their needs for intimate association with other persons. We can expect continued experimentation with alternative life styles, such as clusters of families living separately yet sharing many responsibilities. But for most people, none of the alternatives has yet proven able to meet the diverse physical and self needs better than the nuclear family.

Legislative proposals periodically under consideration include a negative income tax and a guaranteed annual income. The fact that we seriously discuss proposals indicates we view government as a legitimate economic protection agency, and that family responsibility for members' financial well being will continue to decline. Health care and recreation will also be focused more outside the family, if present trends continue.

Movement toward greater sex-role equality is a trend which seems irreversible. Traditional expectations for husband and wife roles will be less important, and relationships will depend more upon interpersonal commitments. In time, more alternatives outside marriage and less conflict over changing roles may decrease the probability of divorce for those who choose to marry.

The death of the family has now been

seriously discussed for thirty years. The time of death is always forecast as a few years away or a decade, or perhaps a quarter century at the latest. But we are not a suicidal society, and until the vital contributions of the family are responsibly assumed by other agencies, the death of the family seems less than imminent. But there is little doubt that the family of today will change in our lifetime. We have the obligation to weigh these changes carefully, and to decide what effects they will have on the human condition,

Before you go on . . .

1. In most states, prostitution is now legal. True or false?

2. Surveys show that _attitudes_ about premarital and extramarital sex have become more permissive than behavior.

3. In the United States today, how many children are there in the average family? _2.2_

4. Families today are less responsible for the socialization of their children than those of several generations age. True or false?

5. The one area where the family institution has gained function is in gratifying _affectional_ needs.

6. Which two major legislative proposals could further remove family responsibility for the economic well-being of members, if they become law? _neg. income tax guarenteed income_

7. The divorce rate will inevitably increase as a result of greater sex-role equality. True or false?

Answers

1. False. Prostitution is now legal only in Nevada.

2. Attitudes. There have been only moderate increases in premarital and extramarital sex activities.

3. The average is slightly more than two per family.

4. True. Schools, peers and the mass media now socialize children to a greater extent than before. Churches and synagogues assume more responsibility for teaching religious values.

5. Affectional, or companionship.

6. Negative income tax and guaranteed annual income.

7. False. With greater equality there may be fewer divorces among those who make the decision to marry.

MARRIAGE AND ALTERNATIVES *Chapter Review*

1. Singles experience all of the following except (a) tax breaks; (b) less pressure to have children; (c) more freedom in scheduling life; (d) greater privacy.

2. Single people have suffered from difficulties regarding (a) higher taxes; (b) inability to adopt children; (c) inadequate housing; (d) all of the above.

3. Previously women were more looked down upon for not marrying than were men. True or false?

4. About half of everyone over 18 years is married. True or false?

5. The over-eighteen part of the United States population which has never been married is: (a) 1–2 percent; (b) 3–4 percent; (c) 5–7 percent; (d) 8–10 percent.

6. Single people tend to remain in urban areas. True or false?

7. Children from common-law marriages may face difficulties regarding _legitimacy_ and _inheritance_.

8. Most singles experience more _lonliness_ than do married couples, unless they live with a congenial companion.

9. In the past, if a person remained single he or she might be thought (a) less mature; (b) less capable; (c) homosexual; (d) all of these.

10. In order to find sexual partners, many singles resort to (a) family celebrations; (b) barhopping; (c) small towns; (d) all of the above.

11. Single people usually live more cheaply than couples. True or false?

12. Most couples who are living together expect to get married. True or false?

13. _Sexual_ reasons usually seem less important to couples in deciding to live together than do economic, social, and emotional ones.

14. Which of these can be described as representing a commune? (a) Kibbutzim; (b) Walden Pond; (c) Oneida; (d) Bruderhof; (e) All of the above; (f) a, c, and d only.

15. Most communes involve group marriages. True or false?

16. During the 1950s, there was a sharp increase in the number of unmarried couples living together. True or false?

17. When a state officially recognizes that two people live together the relationship is called (a) certified; (b) common-law marriage; (c) Bohemian; (d) economic.

18. When an unmarried couple live in the same house to see if they can get along on a permanent basis, their relationship may be called a "_trial_____ marriage."

19. In the past ten years, housing built specially for singles has appeared mainly in the states of _N.Y_____ and _Calif._____.

20. Two factors that affect a woman's desire to marry are financial security and status. True or false?

21. Living together can provide couples with opportunities for exploring how to relate intimately without the possible trauma involved in breaking an engagement. True or false?

22. The kibbutzim have had difficulties in maintaining _sex-role_____ equality because it was not consciously planned for.

23. The American Psychiatric Association no longer considers homosexual acts necessarily deviant, but an alternative life style for consenting adults. True or false?

24. Most singles are homosexual. True or false?

25. The movement toward communal living is increasing rapidly. True or false?

26. Couples do NOT live together for (a) heterosexual contact; (b) general social approval; (c) economic reasons; (d) interpersonal intimacy.

27. Communes are always planned ahead of time. True or false?

28. Explain how two modern-day alternatives to conventional marriage have their roots in other centuries.

29. Singles, living-together couples, and communes have some things in common. Explain.

30. Suggest how the personal values of people who have chosen alternatives to marriage may be related to the way they see social institutions.

To find the answers, look at page 209.

GENERAL REVIEW *Chapters Eight through Ten*

1. Not fulfilling earlier expectations or moving beyond one's parents' social status are examples of how (a) emotions; (b) ideals; (c) circumstances; (d) hopes can change a marriage.

2. Only married couples can adopt children. True or false?

3. What are the five stages of dying? *anger, denial, bargain depression, acceptance*

4. The Oneida silverware company began its existence as a(n) *commune*.

5. According to Carl Rogers what three facilitative conditions does a person need in order to grow? *uncondit, pos regard empathic under*

6. A group of people living together for some financial or ideological reason is called a(n) (a) social system; (b) commune; (c) institution; (d) community.

7. A dying person usually receives appropriate emotional support from his family. True or false?

8. If they adapt to their changing *physical capabilities*, the aging couple may retain their capacity for sexual enjoyment indefinitely.

9. Communes have existed since pre-Christian times. True or false?

10. The aging person becomes increasingly aware of the inevitability of *death*.

11. Couples are more likely to live together for *emotional* rather than *physical* reasons.

12. As a result of more tolerant social attitudes and norms, more unmarried mothers are remaining at home but placing their babies up for adoption. True or false?

13. During unemployment the worker's *feelings* as well as financial consideration are important.

14. What are two frequent reactions to having a retarded or handicapped child? *denial grief*

15. Which status can give one greater freedom to set one's own schedule and to travel? (a) Married; (b) Engaged; (c) Single; (d) Pregnant.

16. What has contributed to rising divorce rates during the last fifty years? *Econ conditions*

17. A divorce can be traumatic to a developing child's identity. True or false?

18. The divorced person is more likely to continue to relate to in-laws if there are (a) financial ties; (b) social expectations; (c) children involved; (d) political considerations.

19. Why are divorced people with children more likely to remarry? *Finances*

20. Divorce means failure. True or false?

21. Describe in a few sentences the typical reaction to losing a beloved.

22. What are some alternative life styles to traditional marriage?

23. What is meant by marriage as a helping relationship?

24. What are some of the problems of the divorced?

25. Is divorce difficult to cope with? Explain your answer.

To find the answers, look at page 211.

SUGGESTED READINGS

Chapter 1: The Meaning of Marriage

Billingsley, Andrew. *Black Families in White America.* Englewood Cliffs, N.J.: Prentice-Hall, 1968.
Dr. Billingsley brings historical, economic. and sociological data together to give us a comprehensive view of black families. He uses family case histories to illustrate how the black family functions within the wider social system.

Blitsen, Dorothy R. *The World of the Family.* New York: Random House, 1963.
Blitsen explores the major human family structures—the nuclear, extended and corporate families—and discusses cultural and social influences on the family in a number of countries. The phases and functions of each family type are dealt with.

Bowen, Elenore Smith. *Return to Laughter.* Garden City, New York: Doubleday and Company, 1954.
This anthropological novel describes a polygynous African culture with sensitivity, humor and insight. The Africans feel as protective about their form of marriage as we do about monogamy in this society.

Hostetler, John A. *Amish Society.* Baltimore: Johns Hopkins Press, 1968.
A description of one of our most famous subcultures by a former member of the group who is also an anthropologist. The book contains two chapters (7 and 8) about marriage and family customs in folk society.

Kenyatta, Jomo. *Facing Mt. Kenya.* New York: Vintage Books, 1962.
In his younger days as an anthropology student in Great Britain, the President of Kenya, Jomo Kenyatta, described family life among his people. the Gikuyu. His first-hand account (first published in 1938) gives a valuable perspective on the stability and functioning of family life among a nonindustrialized people.

Mead, Margaret. *Sex and Temperament in Three Primitive Societies.* New York: Dell Publishing Co., 1963.
Margaret Mead shows through her studies of three cultures that the ways girls and boys are raised, and the ways men and women relate, can vary dramatically from group to group. Her descriptions of three New Guinea societies make fascinating and enjoyable reading.

O'Neill, Nena, and George O'Neill. *Open Marriage.* New York: Avon Books, 1972.
Contrasts the traditional "closed" marriage with a new set of marital expectations. The authors advocate change of our marriage institution to allow for greater individuality.

Rogers, Carl R. *On Becoming a Person.* Boston: Houghton Mifflin, 1961.
Several chapters discuss how to find fulfillment by growing as a person, with emotions, thoughts, and behavior integrated in a positive way. Rogers shares his personal experience in human growth and in helping others to grow. Two important chapters deal with growth as a student and applying these principles to the family.

Chapter 2: Building a Relationship

■ Bardwick, Judith M. (ed.). *Readings on the Psychology of Women.* New York: Harper & Row, 1972.
Bardwick has collected a series of articles from many authors with insights on woman's life today. Topics include sex differences between females and males, roles for women, the woman's liberation movement, women in relation to their bodies, and women and mental health.

■ Bird, Joseph, and Lois Bird. *The Freedom of Sexual Love.* New York: Image Books, 1967.
Co-authored by a married couple, this book sensitively explores the differences in the way females and males approach a sexual relationship. They discuss sexual anatomy, love-making, and many ways of cooperating in building a mutually satisfying sexual relationship.

■ Frankl, Viktor E. *The Doctor and the Soul.* New York: Bantam Books, 1965.
In his chapter on love, Frankl points out that genuine love really encounters the depths of the other person and not just the superficial characteristics. Authentic love moves beyond appearances. infatuation, and possession and allows both persons to find their highest fulfillment through nurturing each other.

■ Fromm. Erich. *The Art of Loving.* New York: Bantam Books, 1956.
Fromm discusses the many meanings of love and how true human fulfillment can be discovered through practicing the art of loving. This is a very popular book with young persons interested in finding and growing in meaningful love.

■ Greer, Germaine. *The Female Eunuch.* New York: McGraw-Hill, 1971.
This is a well-written analysis and advocacy of women's plight and rights in modern society.

■ McMurtry, Larry. *The Last Picture Show.* New York: Dell Publishing Company, 1966.
A contemporary novelist's comment on adolescence in a small Texas town. The reader can gain an understanding of how dating patterns and attitudes about premarital sex have changed since the 1950s.

■ Pierson, Elaine C. *Sex is Never an Emergency* (3rd ed.). Philadelphia: J. B. Lippincott, Company, 1973.
A brief, compact guide to sound information on contraception, pregnancy, abortion, venereal disease and sex.

■ Simons, Joseph, and Jeanne Reidy. *The Risk of Loving.* New York: Herder & Herder, 1968.
Through many down-to-earth examples, the authors

point out the disappointments and possibilities of human love. They describe how to develop the emotions of love by not being buried in the past or being overanxious about the future.

■ Sorenson, Robert C. *Adolescent Sexuality in Contemporary America.* New York: World Publishing, 1972. Reports research and implications for premarital sexual behavior, for ages 13-19.

■ Stuart, Irving R., and Laurence E. Abt (eds.) *Interracial Marriage: Expectations and Realities.* New York: Grossman Publishers, 1973. A collection of readings which survey the interracial marriage situation in the United States.

Chapter 3: Adjusting to Marriage

■ Bach, George R., and Peter Wyden. *The Intimate Enemy: How to Fight Fair in Love and Marriage.* New York: William Morrow and Co., 1969. The authors contend that some fighting is inevitable in marriage and that fighting can be used creatively to improve the relationship. Their book describes the ground rules for fighting fairly.

■ Komarovsky, Mirra. *Blue-Collar Marriage.* New York: Random House, 1967. Parts of the book deal specifically with in-law and kinship relations; the book on the whole is an excellent portrait of marriage among the blue-collar segment of society.

■ Landis, Judson T., and Mary G. Landis. *Building a Successful Marriage.* Englewood Cliffs, N.J.: Prentice-Hall, 1973. The authors describe their research into happy and unhappy marriages and discuss the factors that contribute to satisfaction or dissatisfaction in marriage. The book surveys most topics affecting marriage and family life.

■ Nelson, Roger H. *Personal Money Management.* Reading, Mass.: Addison-Wesley, 1973. Couples can read this book and gain insight into basic money management techniques without undergoing years of trial and error.

■ Schulz, David A.. and Stanley F. Rodgers. *Marriage, the Family, and Personal Fulfillment.* Englewood Cliffs, N.J.: Prentice-Hall, 1975. In this general text on marriage the authors focus on personal meaning and commitment in the development of marriage "partnerships." The text gives both information and insight.

■ Steinmetz. Suzanne K., and Murray A. Strauss. *Violence and the Family.* New York: Dodd, Mead and Company, 1972. A solid collection of articles analyzing the extreme end of the conflict continuum. For many families the term fighting has physical, rather than verbal, meaning.

■ Wilson. Barbara. *Complete Book of Engagement and Wedding Etiquette.* New York: Hawthorne Books, 1970.

The term complete is reasonably accurate. Practically all questions about norms for engagement and weddings can be answered by consulting this source.

Chapters 4 and 5: Reproduction and Sexuality

■ Belliveau, Fred, and Lin Richter. *Understanding Human Sexual Inadequacy.* Boston: Little, Brown, 1970. Two professional writers convey the essential logic and practical techniques involved in Masters and Johnsons' pioneering work on sexual dysfunction. Their treatment is far preferable to attempting to read the turgid original.

■ Berne, Eric. *Sex in Human Loving.* New York: Simon & Schuster, 1970. With humor and wisdom, Dr. Berne describes ways that adults avoid and seek sexual intimacy. He discusses the implications of human sexuality for physical and emotional well-being.

■ Bradley, Robert A. *Husband-Coached Childbirth.* New York: Harper and Row, 1965. Several insights can be gained from this book: the role of the father, natural childbirth, and many techniques for reducing the tension involved in childbirth.

■ Cuber, John F., and Peggy B. Haroff, *Sex and the Significant Americans.* Baltimore: Penguin Books, 1965. The subject matter is more broadly on marriage than the title indicates. This remains one of the few studies available on sexual mores among the affluent.

■ Davis, Adelle. *Let's Have Healthy Children.* New York: Signet Books, 1972. A thorough and informative discussion of the effects of both a healthful and an inadequate diet during pregnancy and the crucial early years of development. She cites specific cases of the role of nutrition in health and development and makes specific recommendations about eating habits.

■ Dick-Read, Grantly. *Childbirth Without Fear.* New York: Harper & Row, 1959. A British physician describes the method of natural childbirth which he developed.

■ Ewy, Donna, and Roger Ewy. *Preparation for Childbirth.* New York: Signet Books, 1970. In this illustrated and easy-to-understand manual, a husband-and-wife team outline exercises which help couples, and the woman particularly, to prepare for natural childbirth using the Lamaze method. It includes diagrams of the birth process.

■ Flanagan, Geraldine L. *The First Nine Months of Life.* New York: Simon and Schuster, 1962. This is a short book but beautifully illustrated. Actual pictures allow the reader to follow fetal development visually.

■ Francoeur, Robert T. *Eve's New Rib: Twenty Faces of Sex, Marriage and Family.* New York: Harcourt Brace Jovanovich, 1972.

The readings consider contraception and reproduction in terms of the impact various practices will have on society.

■ K., Mr. and Mrs. *The Couple.* New York: Coward, McCann, & Geoghegan, Inc., 1970.
The authors share their experiences as a couple at the Masters and Johnson clinic for treatment of sexual dysfunction. They discuss in detail their problems with sex, what happened in their two weeks at the clinic, and the results of their treatment.

■ Katchadourian, Herant A., and Donald T. Lunde, *Fundamentals of Human Sexuality* (2nd ed.). New York: Holt, Rinehart and Winston, Inc. 1975.
One of the most thorough surveys on sex available for the general public. Sections on biology, behavior and culture are included. The culture section treats the erotic in art, literature, film, etc.

■ La Leche League. *The Womanly Art of Breastfeeding.* The La Leche League of Franklin Park, Inc., 333 Rose St., Franklin Park, Ill., 1958.
This manual, produced by the La Leche League for nursing mothers, instructs new mothers in how to breastfeed their infants and how to cope with typical problems which are related to nursing.

■ Lamaze, Fernand. *Painless Childbirth.* New York: Pocket Books, 1972.
Dr. Lamaze, a French physician, describes how mothers who have received the proper training may deliver their babies painlessly using the method he developed.

■ Masters, William H., and Virginia Johnson. *Human Sexual Inadequacy.* Boston: Little, Brown and Co., 1970.
Through their description of sexual anatomy, physical processes, and case histories of couples suffering from sexual dysfunction. Masters and Johnson share the findings of their fifteen years of research into sexual functioning. They offer insights on achieving satisfying sexual relations, overcoming sexual problems, and enjoying sexual expression in the later years.

■ Masters, William H.. and Virginia E. Johnson, *The Pleasure Bond.* New York: Bantam Books, 1975.
A question-answer format is used to explore the ideas of the famous research team. Very readable, unlike the other Masters and Johnson books.

Chapter 6: Family Planning

■ Anderson, David C. *Children of Special Value: Interracial Adoption in America.* New York: St. Martin's Press, 1971.
Four extensive case histories of adoption are presented. Collectively they provide insight into the problems and special relationships of adopted children and their parents.

■ Calderone, Mary. *Manual of Family Planning and Contraceptive Practice.* Baltimore: Williams and Wilkins, 1970.

The book contains valuable information for the sophisticated reader. Chapters 2 through 4 discuss how professionals approach family planning.

■ Callahan, Sidney. *Parenting.* Garden City, N.Y.: Doubleday, 1973.
The author discusses the rights and responsibilities of both parents and children. She draws on her own experience and borrows from the ideas of Erikson, Piaget, and Ginott in describing traditional and non-traditional models of parenting.

■ Faber, Adele, and Elain Mazlish. *Liberated Parents and Liberated Children.* New York: Grosset & Dunlap, 1974.
Both authors are mothers who worked with Dr. Haim Ginott in workshops for parents. Through many examples they describe Dr. Ginott's suggestions for building a cooperative family.

■ Francoeur, Robert T. *So You Want to Adopt a Baby.* Public Affairs Pamphlets, 381 Park Avenue S., New York, N.Y. 10016.
This practical guide is a good place to begin reading about adoption. It is updated periodically.

■ *What Are the Facts about Genetic Disease?* Washington, D.C.: U.S. Government Printing Office, 1976.
This interesting booklet discusses various hereditary diseases, their origins, characteristics, and effects, as well as the research in progress to combat each one.

Chapter 7: The Child in the Family

■ Ansbacher, Heinz L., and Rowena R. Ansbacher (eds.). *The Individual Psychology of Alfred Adler.* New York: Harper Torchbooks, 1956.
The Ansbachers have put together Adler's most pertinent remarks on human development, problem children, and the cooperative approach to life, and they have added informative commentaries. Both the principles of maladjustment and ways to overcome it are explored.

■ Aries, Philippe. *Centuries of Childhood.* New York: Alfred A. Knopf, 1962.
A scholarly investigation into how our conceptions of children have changed over several centuries. Shows clearly how current thinking about children differs substantially from that of the past.

■ Elkind, David. *Children and Adolescents: Interpretive Essays on Jean Piaget* (2nd ed.). New York: Oxford University Press, 1974.
Those who have difficulty reading Piaget in the original can gain a thorough understanding of the great thinker's ideas from this volume.

■ Erikson, Erik H. *Childhood and Society* (2nd ed.). New York: W. W. Norton and Company, 1963.
The classic explanation of childhood from a Freudian revisionist who has become one of our foremost thinkers. Chapter Seven outlines the famous "eight ages of man."

■ Fraiberg, Selma H. *The Magic Years*. New York: Charles Scribner's Sons, 1950.
The author combines humor and sensitivity with great insight in this manual for helping parents to understand and deal with their children in the early years.

■ Keller, Helen. *The Story of My Life*. New York: Airmont Publishing Company, 1965.
The stages of development are illustrated in this book as in no other. Miss Keller's socialization, overcoming several physical handicaps, has fascinated generations of students.

■ Lynn, David B.*The Father: His Role in Child Development*. Belmont, California: Brooks/Cole Publishing Company, 1974.
David Lynn provides us with a comprehensive summary of the father's role in many cultures. He summarizes the latest findings on father-child relationships, father-mother relationships, and the father's influence on areas of development such as sex-role behavior, mental health, moral development, aggression, and delinquency.

■ Piaget, Jean. *The Moral Development of the Child*. New York: The Free Press, 1965.
A world-renowned child psychologist describes the development of moral judgment in children. He gives examples from actual dialogues with children.

■ Rosenberg, Morris. *Society and the Adolescent Self-Image*. Princeton: Princeton University Press, 1965.
Sociological study reporting results of a large scale survey into the various things that influence how high-school students see themselves and what factors determine their self esteem.

■ Sullivan, Harry Stack. *The Interpersonal Theory of Psychiatry*. New York: W. W. Norton & Company Inc., 1953.
Sullivan discusses his approach to human development, which emphasizes the social and interpersonal influences on our growth. He broadens Freud's approach, but not as completely as Erik Erikson.

Chapter 8: Marriage Through a Lifetime

■ Berne, Eric. *Games People Play*. New York: Grove Press, 1964.
A noted psychiatrist describes typical neurotic ways of relating, which many couples will recognize in their own relationships. The book is written for the lay person, is easily readable, humorous, and very helpful.

■ Kimmel, Douglas C. *Adulthood and Aging*. New York: John Wiley & Sons, Inc., 1974.
Kimmel has written an up-to-date account of youth, middle age, and aging in contemporary society. Actual interviews with people at different stages in life clearly illustrate the course of human development.

■ Kübler-Ross, Elisabeth. *On Death and Dying*. New York: Macmillan Publishing Co., Inc., 1969.
Through her work with many dying patients, Dr.

Kübler-Ross has discovered the stages that dying people go through and how they want to be treated. She has developed ways to train people to be helpful to dying persons by interacting sensitively and honestly with them.

■ Neugarten, Bernice L. (ed.). *Middle Age and Aging*. Chicago: The University of Chicago Press, 1973.
Neugarten has collected a variety of readings on the psychology of the life cycle, family relations, work, leisure, retirement, aging in other societies, dying and death.

■ Putney, Snell, and Gail Putney. *The Adjusted American*. New York: Harper and Row, 1965.
A consideration of some of the misdirected ways people use relationships to fulfill needs. The chapters on marriage, sex, intimacy, and love are in-depth explorations of interpersonal relationships.

■ Satir, Virginia. *Peoplemaking*. Palo Alto, California: Science and Behavior Books, 1972.
This well-known family therapist outlines effective ways to help families break unproductive patterns of relating and to discover through discussion and the use of insight-oriented games how to build a family life style that is open to communication.

Chapter 9: Divorce and After

■ Baer, Jean. *The Second Wife*. New York: Doubleday, 1972.
The book explores several facets of subsequent marriage, including husband-wife relationships, the role of stepmother, and relations with first wives.

■ Bohannan, Paul. *Divorce and After*. Garden City, New York: Doubleday & Company, Inc., 1970.
The author deals with divorce as a process involving several stages: the emotional deterioration of the relationship, legal and economic aspects, arranging for the welfare of any children involved, changing friends, and regaining autonomy as an individual.

■ Epstein, Joseph. *Divorces in America: Marriage in an Age of Possibility*. New York: Dutton, 1974.
A well-written attempt to communicate how it *feels* to undergo a marriage breakup, divorce, and readjustment. The book is essentially autobiography, written by an editor.

■ Goode, William J. *After Divorce*. New York: The Free Press, 1956.
Goode reports research on problems encountered after divorce and on the positive aspects of ending a nonproductive relationship.

■ Krantzler, Mel. *Creative Divorce*. New York: New American Library, 1973.
This best-seller argues that divorce can be a growth process if approached constructively.

■ Lyman, Howard B. *Single Again*. New York: McKay, 1971.
Concerns problems of adjustment and coping after

the loss of a spouse, either through death or through divorce.

■ Steizor, Bernard. *When Parents Divorce*. New York: Random House, 1969.
Some of the specific legal information has changed but the orientation toward legal problems is still thought provoking. The personal impact of divorce on children is thoroughly discussed.

Chapter 10: Marriage and Alternatives

■ Baldwin, James. *If Beale Street Could Talk*. New York: Signet, 1974.
A novelist's sensitive account of a couple who live together without marriage. One message is that community and family support have an important effect on the relationship.

■ Bettelheim, Bruno. *Children of the Dream*. New York: Macmillan, 1969.
One of the best studies of patterns of life in the Israeli *kibbutz*. The author uses a Freudian framework in his discussion of childrearing.

■ Bowman, Henry A. *Marriage for Moderns* (7th ed.). New York: McGraw-Hill Book Company, 1974.
The third chapter of this general text on marriage discusses marriage and alternative lifestyles. The full text covers many of the topics covered in this book.

■ Melville, Keith. *Communes in the Counter Culture: Origins, Theories, Styles of Life*. New York: William Morrow and Company, 1972.
Written in the informal counter-culture style of the 1960s, this book has interested college students ever since its first publication.

■ Muncy, Raymond L. *Sex and Marriage in Utopian Communities*. Baltimore: Penguin Books, Inc., 1973.
A scholarly survey of communes in 19th century America. Rather than presenting case studies, practices from different communes are used to illustrate general principles.

■ Rogers, Carl. *Becoming Partners: Marriage and its Alternatives*. New York: Delacorte Press, 1972.
Through interviews with a number of couples, Rogers examines the process of change and growth in a variety of contemporary relationships. He finds that being in touch with one's feelings, openness toward the partner, and communication are essential for a fulfilling relationship.

■ Scanzoni, Letha, and John Scanzoni. *Men, Women and Change*. New York: McGraw-Hill Book Company, 1976.
Chapter 5, alternatives to marriage, contains the most thorough discussion available on cohabitation as a phenomenon in contemporary society.

■ Skinner, B. F. *Walden Two*. New York: Macmillan Co., 1962.
Skinner presents a fictional account of a utopian commune that is both alluring in the benefits it offers and frightening in the control that its members surrender.

GLOSSARY/INDEX

If you miss a question, go back and restudy the topic. Module number(s) are in parentheses.

Chapter 1: The Meaning of Marriage

1. c (**1**, 2)
2. Scandinavia (**2**)
3. False. Different cultures teach their children to act according to many different standards, as Margaret Mead's work has shown us. (**1**, 2)
4. a (**3**)
5. divorce; annulment (**2**)
6. True. Men may take on responsibilities formerly handled by women, and women may assume responsibilities in areas traditionally reserved for men. (**3**)
7. Marriage (**2**)
8. b (**1**)
9. False. Among the Tchambuli the women are considered more highly sexed, and they are the ones to choose a mate. (**1**)
10. d (**2**)
11. True (**1**)
12. d (**2**)
13. False. A father's honor was established by his ability to marry off his daughters. (**1**)
14. True. These factors made it difficult for the black family to stay together. (**1**)
15. c (**2**)
16. norms (**2**)
17. False. An increasing number of people seek a friend in a marriage partner; this is more possible when couples want and work on this arrangement. (**3**)
18. aware; communicate (2, **3**)
19. 25 (**2**)
20. False. A good marriage involves continually working on the relationship and growing together. (2, **3**)
21. 90 (**2**)
22. a (2, **3**)
23. True (**2**)
24. relationship; roles (**3**)
25. b (**2**)
26. False. Around 1900 about one in ten marriages ended in divorce while today more than one in four do. (**2**)
27. Communication (**3**)

ANSWERS

If you miss a question, go back and restudy the topic. Module number(s) are in parentheses.

28. The behaviors that are considered appropriate for each sex are taught by adults to children. Children may learn that the same kinds of behaviors are expected of both sexes, for example, gentleness or aggressiveness. Or one sex may be taught to be assertive and the other one dependent. What is considered proper varies from culture to culture. **(1**, 2)

29. A social institution is a pattern of expectations and behaviors that most members of a society participate in. Marriage involves a legal relationship defined in the marriage contract and approved by society. During marriage the partners have socially agreed upon roles and responsibilities. **(2)**

30. For a couple who try to cooperate with each other and who work together on their relationship, marriage can be enjoyable. If the partners are antagonistic or badly mismatched, the marriage leads to unhappiness and becomes burdensome. But when married persons share themselves with a partner who is understanding, supportive, and willing to develop a harmonious family life style that leaves room for individual and mutual growth, marriage is fulfilling. (2, **3)**

If you miss a question, go back and restudy the topic. Module number(s) are in parentheses.

Chapter 2: Building a Relationship

1. a, b, c, or d **(4)**
2. twenty **(5)**
3. True **(7)**
4. b **(7)**
5. True. The older person usually has more dating experience, self-knowledge and maturity, and better vocational preparation. **(6)**
6. True **(4)**
7. cooperate **(6)**
8. d **(7)**
9. False. Since 1966 Catholics may request special permission from their bishop to be married in a civil ceremony by a justice of the peace, or in a religious ceremony in another church or synagogue by a minister or rabbi. **(7)**
10. mixed **(7)**
11. c **(4)**
12. True **(7)**
13. False. They want the occupation of homemaking to have more status and greater security. **(8)**
14. twenty-five **(8)**
15. double **(4)**
16. e **(8)**
17. syphilis; gonorrhea **(10)**
18. older **(7)**
19. a **(8)**
20. True **(5)**
21. upper **(4)**
22. False. The lack of privacy, security in the relationship, and practice with one's partner all may make premarital sex less satisfying especially for the woman. **(9, 10)**
23. b **(7)**
24. c **(8)**
25. True. She may marry or remain single. She may undergo a legal abortion or elect to bear and keep the child or place it for adoption. **(5)**
26. d **(10)**
27. a **(4)**
28. The dating couple need not be introduced by a family member. There is no chaperone and no obligation to one another after the date ends. The couple plan their date. Some degree of sexual intimacy can be expected. **(4)**

ANSWERS

If you miss a question, go back and restudy the topic. Module number(s) are in parentheses.

29. The person who marries to get away from home has not had the experience of living independently or of relating to a number of persons, and may through inexperience marry someone very much like the parents he or she wishes to escape. **(5)**

30. If the prospective bride and groom come to the marriage feeling secure and independent in themselves, if they respect and trust each other, if they share some interests and values—and if they are open with each other and communicate about their disagreements as well as their agreements—their marriage has a good chance of enduring. **(6, 7)**

If you miss a question, go back and restudy the topic. Module number(s) are in parentheses.

Chapter 3: Adjusting to Marriage

1. d (14)
2. d (11)
3. True. A person who feels unlovable will be insecure about his or her partner's feelings and, hence, often possessive and jealous. (14)
4. True (11)
5. c (15)
6. c (16)
7. d (17)
8. spending (16)
9. False. Their annual interest rate is usually between 10 and 12 percent. (17)
10. b (16)
11. c (14)
12. style of life (13)
13. b (17)
14. False. People with an unrealistic, Pollyanna attitude protect themselves and others from any uncomfortable feelings by denying their existence. They are incapable of having authentic interpersonal relationships. (14)
15. False. It is formed at an early age and usually remains unchanged throughout life. (13)
16. treasurer (16)
17. poverty (16)
18. True (15)
19. nuclear; extended (15)
20. internal conflict (14)
21. social interest (13)
22. d (11)
23. False. The car loses a lot of its cash value through depreciation in the first two years and ordinarily does not need major repairs for five years. (17)
24. civil (11)
25. True (17)
26. economic (12)
27. True (12)
28. The primary purpose of a honeymoon is for the newlyweds to have some time together when they can relax and begin developing their own marriage lifestyle. A honeymoon also affirms the newly married couple as a new social unit in the community. (11)

ANSWERS

*If you miss a question, go back and restudy
the topic. Module number(s) are in parentheses.*

29. Labor-saving devices, convenience foods, **(12)**
    public education, and childcare facilities,
    together with rising standards of living, have
    all encouraged more married women to
    work.

30. Husbands and wives come to marriage with (13,
    different frames of reference and different   **14**)
    personality traits. These, plus specific situa-
    tional factors and internal sources of irrita-
    tion, are often the cause of marital conflict.

If you miss a question, go back and restudy the topic. Module number(s) are in parentheses.

General Review: Chapters One through Three

1. It helps them to learn behavior appropriate in relating to the opposite sex, to learn more about themselves, and to develop inter-personal skills. **(4)**

2. False. Black husbands tend to accept this more easily than do whites. **(8)**

3. death, divorce, annulment, and desertion **(2)**

4. holes **(1, 2)**

5. feminism **(8)**

6. b **(1, 2, 15)**

7. institution, process **(3, 3)**

8. True **(7)**

9. True **(1)**

10. True **(7)**

11. b **(17)**

12. family life style **(13)**

13. False. In 1971, 60 percent of all women who worked were married. **(8)**

14. They mask the true source of conflict. **(14)**

15. To establish the new (married) status of the couple in the community. **(11)**

16. Frequently couples unable to cooperate in general find their sex lives disrupted, and difficulties in sex often signal other problems in the marriage. **(14)**

17. b **(17)**

18. cooperation, commitment, communication, copulation, competence interpersonally, and caring **(3)**

19. the dole system, the family treasurer **(16)**

20. False. They often feel powerless and believe they are being taken advantage of. Their aggressiveness is a defense mechanism. **(13, 14)**

21. The purpose of casual dating is to get acquainted. Steady dating implies that the couple expect to date each other frequently. Going steady means that the couple expect to date each other exclusively. Being engaged-to-be-engaged is a trial engagement. Engagement is a commitment to marriage. **(4)**

22. They are compatible with family life. A woman can often schedule her working hours to coincide with her children's school schedule. The work to be done at home is minimal. **(8)**

23. The man who as a single person may have sought many women for his sexual gratifica-

ANSWERS

If you miss a question, go back and restudy the topic. Module number(s) are in parentheses.

tion must now channel his attention toward encouraging and satisfying his wife's desires as a source of his own pleasure. The woman who may have been shy or reluctant to participate freely in sexual exchanges is now expected to enjoy expressing her sexual desires and pleasing her husband as a sexual partner.

24. A couple who elope or marry secretly are **(11)** likely to have made an unconsidered, spur-of-the-moment decision to marry. If they choose to keep the marriage secret, they may be under great pressure from their families. Furthermore, they do not have the advantage of social approval to help them through the early days of adjusting to marriage. Since there is no social recognition of their new status, they may feel "not really married."

25. The couple are more sure of their relation- **(15)** ship after a number of years. Older couples have had more time to find workable solutions to their in-law problems, or time may have solved some problems through the death or illness of an offending relative. Some marriages in which in-laws were perceived as severe problems may have failed after a year or so.

If you miss a question, go back and restudy the topic. Module number(s) are in parentheses.

Chapter 4: Reproduction

1. b **(20)**
2. scrotum **(18)**
3. False. A teaspoonful of semen contains 200 to 500 million sperms. **(18)**
4. a **(21)**
5. False. Spermatozoa need a constant temperature, and the testicles move closer to or farther away from body warmth as the need arises. **(18)**
6. True. The female's clitoris is the most sensitive part of the body. **(19)**
7. lubricated with mucous secretion. **(19)**
8. d **(18)**
9. b **(18, 19)**
10. they began from a single fertilized ovum **(20)**
11. c **(20)**
12. fourth **(21)**
13. a **(19)**
14. False. A high hormone level around ovulation can make a woman a little more elated and a low hormone level around menstruation may slightly depress her. **(19)**
15. True **(20, 22)**
16. social **(21)**
17. last three **(21, 22)**
18. False. The woman who is prepared and knows what to expect can usually stay in control by relaxing and working with her body. **(23)**
19. True **(19)**
20. c **(21, 22)**
21. Carbohydrates, protein, vitamins, and fats. **(22)**
22. True **(21)**
23. d **(21)**
24. seventh **(21)**
25. true **(22)**
26. b **(23)**
27. urine; blood **(20)**
28. The advantages of nursing are both emotional and physical. Both mother and baby enjoy the emotional closeness of body contact involved in nursing. In mothers' milk the baby receives a constant supply of antibodies that serve as protection against disease. If the mother is well-nourished and

ANSWERS

*If you miss a question, go back and restudy
the topic. Module number(s) are in parentheses.*

relaxed, the baby will get milk that is more
suited for it in terms of nutrition than either
cow's milk or formula.

29. Pregnancy begins with the union of male with (20,
    female. Childbirth also brings an opportunity **23**)
    for a couple to share a meaningful event. If
    the couple is trained to work with a medical
    team, the father can help his wife to stay
    relaxed and work with her body during labor.
    Many couples who share the experience of
    childbirth find their total relationship more
    fulfilling and feel closer and more loving
    towards their children.

30. A baby begins with a sperm fertilizing an (20, **21**)
    ovum. The zygote becomes embedded in
    the uterus where it grows approximately for
    nine months. The cells multiply rapidly. The
    main organs develop during the first six
    months. Babies cannot survive outside of the
    womb until the seventh month, but even then
    they need special care, both physical and
    social.

*If you miss a question, go back and restudy
the topic. Module number(s) are in parentheses.*

Chapter 5: Sexuality

1. True. A child learns about sex from his **(24)**
   parents and their attitudes will affect future
   sexual behavior.

2. False. This is common stereotype of the **(25**, 29)
   male.

3. a **(24**, 28, 29)

4. reflex; cerebral **(25)**

5. clitoris **(25)**

6. False. The clitoris is more sensitive to **(25)**
   stimulation.

7. perineum **(25)**

8. d **(25)**

9. False. Breasts are more sensitive. **(25)**

10. petting; foreplay **(25)**

11. d **(25)**

12. vasocongestion **(26)**

13. orgasm; resolution **(26)**

14. c **(18)**

15. False. Refractory period. **(26)**

16. True. Both are needed for natural and **(25**, 28, 29)
    spontaneous sexual arousal to occur.

17. False. There is no medical reason for this **(26)**
    belief, although certain religions and cultures
    forbid intercourse during menstruation.

18. more frequently. **(26**, 28)

19. d **(27)**

20. premature ejaculation **(28)**

21. a **(29)**

22. True. This system may be unconscious, **(24)**
    however.

23. d **(28)**

24. False. A man with secondary impotence has **(28)**
    had at least one erection in the past.

25. b **(24**, 25)

26. dyspareunia **(28**, 29)

27. False. This severe contraction of vaginal **(29)**
    muscles is an expression of emotional ten-
    sion.

28. Females and males have many features of **(26)**
    the sexual response in common. Both pass
    through excitement, plateau, orgasm, and

If you miss a question, go back and restudy the topic. Module number(s) are in parentheses.

resolution phases, and they show similar physiological changes. However, the two sexes often differ in their expectations about sex.

29. A male can have an erection in a few seconds, while a female generally takes longer to become aroused. Problems arising from this difference are overcome when each partner makes efforts to learn what stimulation most pleases the other. Their adjusted behavior results in a mutually pleasurable sex relationship. **(25)**

30. The inability to develop a sincere and meaningful relationship with another person leads to feelings of frustration. An attitude of frustration, in turn, can become an inability to establish a sexual relationship. **(24, 28, 29)**

*If you miss a question, go back and restudy
the topic. Module number(s) are in parentheses.*

Chapter 6: Family Planning

1. False. Most couples have personal and social **(30)** reasons.

2. genetic **(30)**

3. False. He may be able to reassure the **(31)** couple that a physical problem in their family background is not hereditary.

4. a **(30)**

5. genetic problems, careers, ecological concerns **(30)**

6. contraception **(32)**

7. pregnancy **(32)**

8. False. Both partners will assume responsibility if they are mature and thoughtful. **(32)**

9. True. All other methods involve some risk of failure. **(32)**

10. contraceptive pill; intrauterine device. **(32)**

11. False. Menstruation continues regularly, even if it was irregular before use of the pill. **(32)**

12. False. The pill may cause unpleasant side effects and even serious illness in some cases. **(32)**

13. c **(32)**

14. fallopian tubes **(32)**

15. False. Emotional stress, alcoholism, and drugs also play a part in lowering fertility. **(33)**

16. c **(33)**

17. low sperm count **(33)**

18. False. Male infertility is just as often the cause. **(33)**

19. ovulation **(33)**

20. False. Artificial insemination can use the husband's semen, concentrated from several ejaculations. **(33)**

21. True, but many cases can be medically corrected. **(33)**

22. three; five **(34)**

23. True. This is important in deciding who will make a good parent. **(34)**

24. d **(34)**

25. True. He should be told when he begins to ask where babies come from. **(34)**

26. False. Agencies usually require an age under 35 for the mother and 38-40 for the father. **(34)**

*If you miss a question, go back and restudy
the topic. Module number(s) are in parentheses.*

27. overprotection; discipline **(34)**

28. Zero population growth would mean that **(30)** families could have two or at most three children. Family planning simply means that couples may decide how many children they want. Birth control must be used for both of these approaches to population planning.

29. The Roman Catholic Church and Orthodox **(32)** Judaism oppose artificial birth control, but Reform and Conservative Jews and most Protestant denominations approve of it. Surveys show that the majority of college students of all religions favor availability of birth control information.

30. Abortion is a termination of pregnancy. Other **(32)** methods of family planning depend on the prevention of pregnancy. There is more risk to health from abortion than from the use of ordinary birth control devices.

*If you miss a question, go back and restudy
the topic. Module number(s) are in parentheses.*

Chapter 7: The Child in the Family

1. False. Children most often imitate their parents as models. **(39)**
2. a **(36)**
3. fidelity; intimacy **(37)**
4. False. Adolescents profit more from reasoning about discipline and being respected as individals. **(39)**
5. d **(38)**
6. False. Children need nurturance from both parents. (36, **37**)
7. family constellation **(37)**
8. b **(37)**
9. add **(38)**
10. c **(37)**
11. multiply **(38)**
12. True (35, **41**)
13. d **(38)**
14. "good me" **37)**
15. True **(35)**
16. sex roles **(40)**
17. b **(39)**
18. False. One-half of unmarried mothers keeping their babies marry within six years, half of them to the fathers of their children. **(36)**
19. True **(39)**
20. symbolic representation **(38)**
21. a **(39)**
22. True **(41)**
23. quality **(41)**
24. c **(39)**
25. False. Each child constructs his or her own grammar and later learns the adult form. **(38)**
26. sex-role stereotyping **(40)**
27. d
28. Thought and language development both follow a sequence of steps. The development of symbolic representation makes language possible. Both thought and language develop as time passes. **(38)**
29. Moral development appears to proceed through several stages. The very young child obeys simply to avoid punishment. In middle **(39)**

*If you miss a question, go back and restudy
the topic. Module number(s) are in parentheses.*

childhood the concept of right and wrong is
based on norms or conventions. Adolescents develop an internalized set of values.
As they mature they are guided by conscience and a sense of social responsibility.

30. Discipline means training to develop self-   **(39)**
control or character. With very young chil-
dren a system of praise or reprimand
probably works best. Children in their middle
years often respond to reasoning and resent
physical punishment. Teenagers will expect
their parents to defend their rationale for
disciplinary action. Punishment, at all ages,
should be proportionate to the crime and to
the child's ability to understand what infrac-
tions have occurred.

*If you miss a question, go back and restudy
the topic. Module number(s) are in parentheses.*

General Review: Chapters Four through Seven

1. autonomy (**37**)
2. c (**25**, 26)
3. True (**38**)
4. sperm, ovum (**18**, **19**)
5. False. Frequently females and males have different expectations about sex. A couple must communicate their expectations and resolve any conflicts. (**24**)
6. Antibodies are substances that protect the body against disease and can be obtained from the mother through the placenta and in her milk. (**22**)
7. d (**26**)
8. The contractions during childbirth first thin out the muscles of the cervix so the baby can leave the uterus and then force the baby down the vagina. (**23**)
9. X, Y; X (**21**)
10. False. Men both pass urine and ejaculate semen through the urethra, but in women the urethra is separate from the vagina. (**19**)
11. d (**38**)
12. The four basic food groups are (1) grains and cereals; (2) meat, fish, or eggs; (3) milk and dairy products; and (4) fats. (**22**)
13. True. She will be better able to relax and to use her muscles to help expel the baby. (**23**)
14. He urged parents to teach their children to cooperate and have "social interest." (**37**)
15. We seek personal security, intimacy, and satisfaction of our sexual desires. (**37**)
16. d (**38**)
17. placenta (**20**)
18. True. Instead of learning what *not* to do, the individual learns what should be done. (**39**)
19. c (**28**)
20. False. Every couple is somewhat different and needs to learn to relate to each other as unique individuals. (**24**)
21. Unless a mother is adequately nourished with proteins, vitamins, minerals, and other essential foods before and during pregnancy, her baby will not reach its full potential. The baby that is well-nourished before and after delivery will be more intelligent, have a stronger body, and be less prone to diseases. Childbirth can be made easier with solid nutrition since the mother will have more stamina and her muscles will be more elastic and more easily stretchable. (**22**)

*If you miss a question, go back and restudy
the topic. Module number(s) are in parentheses.*

22. The purpose of the stages of childbirth is first **(23)** to open up the cervix so the baby can leave the uterus, and second to force the baby down the vagina or birth canal. The cervix expands as the abdomen contracts. The woman can stay in control of the contractions by keeping the rest of her body relaxed. She can work with the contractions at the end by pushing down with her diaphragm to help the baby out.

23. Erik Erikson describes the life cycle as **(37)** consisting of eight stages. At each stage we encounter a crisis—for example, at birth we want to survive securely. As a result of the crisis we can move either forwards or backwards—the infant develops a sense of trust with good care, or if neglected, develops a sense of mistrust. Each stage successfully passed brings a strength helpful in later stages.

24. Pleasuring means learning what makes **(25)** one's sexual partner feel good and doing it. Pleasuring each other brings a couple sexual enjoyment. It involves generously cooperating with another and being able to receive sensual stimulation.

25. The most common sexual problem among **(29)** females is orgasmic dysfunction, not having an orgasm during sexual intercourse. A woman can become orgasmic by allowing herself to be maximally pleasured and feeling enough attachment to her partner to surrender herself to him. Among males the most common sexual problem is premature ejaculation, ejaculating before the female partner has experienced satisfaction. He can control this by learning to tolerate more stimulation of the penis and trying to please his partner.

*If you miss a question, go back and restudy
the topic. Module number(s) are in parentheses.*

Chapter 8: Marriage through a Lifetime

1.	d	**(46)**
2.	the average life span is longer.	**(45)**
3.	True	(**43**, 44)
4.	a	**(44)**
5.	supports	**(42)**
6.	b	(**46**, 47)
7.	deny; grieve	**(42)**
8.	True	**(45)**
9.	c	(45, **46**)
10.	True	**(45)**
11.	28	**(46)**
12.	True	**(42)**
13.	b	**(44)**
14.	Unconditional positive regard	**(44)**
15.	c	**(44)**
16.	False. Couples can enjoy sexual relations, if they maintain good health and interest in each other, at least into their 70s.	**(46)**
17.	grieve; mourn	**(47)**
18.	True	**(45)**
19.	c	**(46)**
20.	a remembered person.	**(47)**
21.	False. Seeking help when trouble begins saves a lot of grief and makes positive changes easier.	**(44)**
22.	responsible adults	**(45)**
23.	d	**(45)**
24.	False. Often aging men become more nurturant and women more assertive.	**(46)**
25.	systems	**(44)**
26.	a	**(47)**
27.	False. The death of a spouse can bring relief from an unhappy marriage; and family, especially children, can cushion one's loss.	**(47)**
28.	Carl Rogers discusses ways of behaving that help other people to grow as persons. We grow when we feel that someone thinks of us positively and really understands what we are trying to express; we feel accepted and may choose to grow.	**(44)**
29.	When a couple or family fight with each other often and are unable to get along, they may need professional help; it is better to seek	**(44)**

*If you miss a question, go back and restudy
the topic. Module number(s) are in parentheses.*

help early when the problem starts than
when the damage is done. Poor communication, feelings of distance, and constant fights
are common danger signs.

30. Aging brings retirement, so the partners   **(46**, 47)
have more time together. The physical
processes slow down, and memory may
lapse. Sexual functioning changes, but
partners can still have great enjoyment. A
seriously ill partner may need intensive care
from the other. Eventually, death separates
the partners.

*If you miss a question, go back and restudy
the topic. Module number(s) are in parentheses.*

Chapter 9: Divorce and After

1. False. Divorce rates are higher among people with less education and income. **(48)**

2. c **(48)**

3. False. This used to be the case, but not so much anymore. **(48)**

4. she can more easily be economically self-sustaining **(48**, 50)

5. c **(48)**

6. False. They greatly contribute, but do not explain the whole trend. **(48)**

7. False. They generally have, but recently divorcees have waited longer before re-marrying. **(48**, 50)

8. d **(49)**

9. one million **(48)**

10. others **(49**, 51)

11. b **(49)**

12. work; sex **(49)**

13. True **(48)**

14. b **(48**, 51)

15. inadequate; burdensome **(51)**

16. d **(49)**

17. True **(49)**

18. Aid to Dependent Children. **(51)**

19. False. They rarely compensate completely. **(51)**

20. 70 **(48)**

21. c (49, 50, **51)**

22. False. It is a gradual process—both psychologically, as the couple separates, and legally, in many states where a waiting period is required. **(49)**

23. friends **(51)**

24. c (**49**, 51)

25. False. Though the married relationship was unhappy, divorced persons frequently feel a loss. (**49**, 50)

26. distance **(51)**

27. d **(49)**

28. Divorce can be compared to dying because in both cases people experience a loss. The divorced and widowed both do some grieving for a lost friend or relationship. In order to recover from the separation, both need to redirect their attention to a new beloved. (**50**, 51)

*If you miss a question, go back and restudy
the topic. Module number(s) are in parentheses.*

29. Higher divorce rates may not mean that **(48)**
marriage is no longer a workable institution,
but that couples are unwilling to tolerate
rather unfulfilling relationships. Couples usually decide that the present relationship is
not fulfilling their personal needs and ideals
of marriage. They may use the self-
knowledge obtained from this experience to
form a better relationship in the future.

30. Many divorced people suffer from the loss of **(49,**
a spouse, even though the relationship may **50)**
have brought unhappiness and grief. Marriage provided an identity, some intimacy
and sharing, and an interpersonal meaning
to life. Loneliness may bring anxiety and
uncertainty, and sometimes divorce leaves
one parent with the sole responsibility for
dependent children.

*If you miss a question, go back and restudy
the topic. Module number(s) are in parentheses.*

Chapter 10: Marriage and Alternatives

1. a   **(52)**
2. d   **(52)**
3. True. Single women were usually considered "old maids."   **(52)**
4. False. The figure is about three-quarters.   **(52)**
5. d   **(52)**
6. True. They find more cultural and friendship opportunities in the cities.   **(52)**
7. legitimacy, inheritance.   **(53)**
8. loneliness   **(52)**
9. d   **(52)**
10. b   **(52)**
11. False. They usually have relatively higher expenses.   **(52)**
12. True. Almost three-quarters of them plan to be married when they have children.   **(53)**
13. sexual   **(53)**
14. f   **(54)**
15. False. A few communes involve group marriage, but most do not.   **(54)**
16. False. The increase came in the 1960s.   **(53)**
17. b   **(53)**
18. trial   **(53)**
19. New York; California   **(52)**
20. True. Professional women feel less pressure to find a husband.   **(52)**
21. True. Couples may live together to enjoy intimacy without intending to marry.   **(53)**
22. sex-role   **(54)**
23. True.   **(52)**
24. False. Most are heterosexual.   **(52)**
25. False. The numbers have dropped greatly since the nineteenth century.   **(54)**
26. b   **(53)**
27. False. They sometimes form when people drift together.   **(54)**
28. Living together as a personal decision between man and woman, without the permission of Church or State, was normal on the American frontier, where judges and preachers were scarce; in the 1800s many communes, such as Oneida and the Bruderhof, were established in the United States.   **(53, 54)**

*If you miss a question, go back and restudy
the topic. Module number(s) are in parentheses.*

29. People in these groups all live outside the **(52,** mainstream of society although they have **53,** quite varied patterns of living. Some singles barhop, while others join social clubs; some **54)** couples living together have sex very often, while others do not; some communes have established communal marriage, and in others monogamy is the rule.

30. During the 1960s the civil rights movements **(53)** and criticisms of America's national image led to doubt about many social traditions. Many young people began to question institutions which they had taken for granted. Some rejected the institution of marriage as they found it, either modifying it or replacing it with new arrangements.

*If you miss a question, go back and restudy
the topic. Module number(s) are in parentheses.*

GENERAL REVIEW: Chapters Eight through Ten

1. c   **(42)**

2. False. A number of states now allow single persons to adopt children.   **(34, 52)**

3. Denial, anger, bargaining, depression and acceptance.   **(47)**

4. commune   **(54)**

5. Empathetic understanding, unconditional positive regard, and interpersonal congruence.   **(44)**

6. b   **(54)**

7. False. Often the dying person may feel one way (e.g., angry or acceptant) and his family another way.   **(47)**

8. physical capabilities   **(46)**

9. True   **(54)**

10. death   **(46**, 47)

11. emotional; sexual   **(53)**

12. False. More unmarried mothers are both remaining in their own communities and keeping their babies.   **(34**, 52)

13. feelings   **(42)**

14. To want to have another baby; to test other people's reactions   **(42)**

15. c   **(52)**

16. Economic conditions and changes in cultural values and expectations.   **(48)**

17. True. A child may wonder whether the parents really love him/her or whether he/she is guilty of breaking up the marriage.   **(48**, 49)

18. c   **(51)**

19. To provide male and female role models and to divide the labor of childraising.   **(48, 51)**

20. False. The couple may be leaving a disastrous relationship, or they may have grown apart.   **(49**, 51)

21. The typical reaction to losing a beloved is to grieve and mourn one's loss. A memory is not as supportive or loving as a person. For a time one may be angry or hostile at being abandoned. Later on one seeks help from others and may withdraw from contact for a period. Finally, the bereaved redirects his or her energies to a new beloved or to a project.   **(50)**

22. One alternative to traditional marriage is for a man and woman to live together without marrying. Other people might choose to live   **(52, 53, 54)**

*If you miss a question, go back and restudy
the topic. Module number(s) are in parentheses.*

in a commune where responsibilities and
obligations are shared with a number of
people, either for financial convenience or
because of some common purpose. Some
people now choose to stay single for personal reasons, such as pursuing a career or
wanting to travel at one's own pace.

23. Marriage can be a helping relationship when   (43,
the couple helps each other to grow and   **44**)
become more fulfilled. Partners who listen to
each other, try to understand, have mutual
respect, and encourage each other to grow
both as individuals and as a couple will find
their relationship helpful and happy.

24. Often divorced people find that they still   (**49**, **51**)
have an attachment to the other person and
mourn their lost relationhsip. They frequently
miss the familiar and the routine pattern of
living together. They may hop from bed to
bed with sexual partners. Some people
become lost in work or in other people's
lives. Many find difficulty in redirecting their
lives to constructive purposes.

25. A divorce can lead to a loss of identity,   (**49**, **51**)
status, and the support that the previous
relationship provided. It is hard to face the
fact that one does not belong to a familiar
relationship anymore. Rearranging one's life
and being on one's own, especially with
dependent children, proves difficult. And the
divorced person may hesitate to redirect
hopes and ambitions towards another person who may only hurt and disappoint
him/her again.